MW00716871

Nuer-American Passages

New World Diasporas

UNIVERSITY PRESS OF FLORIDA

Florida A&M University, Tallahassee
Florida Atlantic University, Boca Raton
Florida Gulf Coast University, Ft. Myers
Florida International University, Miami
Florida State University, Tallahassee
University of Central Florida, Orlando
University of Florida, Gainesville
University of North Florida, Jacksonville
University of South Florida, Tampa
University of West Florida, Pensacola

New World Diasporas
Edited by Kevin A. Yelvington

This series seeks to stimulate critical perspectives on diaspora processes in the New World. Representations of "race" and ethnicity, the origins and consequences of nationalism, migratory streams and the advent of transnationalism, the dialectics of "homelands" and diasporas, trade networks, gender relations in immigrant communities, the politics of displacement and exile, and the utilization of the past to serve the present are among the phenomena addressed by original, provocative research in disciplines such as anthropology, history, political science, and sociology.

International Editorial Board
Herman L. Bennett, Rutgers University
Gayle K. Brunelle, California State University at Fullerton
Jorge Duany, Universidad de Puerto Rico
Sherri Grasmuck, Temple University
Daniel Mato, Universidad Central de Venezuela
Kyeyoung Park, University of California at Los Angeles
Richard Price, College of William and Mary
Sally Price, College of William and Mary
Vicki L. Ruiz, Arizona State University
John F. Stack Jr., Florida International University
Mia Tuan, University of Oregon
Peter Wade, University of Manchester

More Than Black: Afro-Cubans in Tampa, by Susan D. Greenbaum (2002)

Carnival and the Formation of a Caribbean Transnation, by Philip W. Scher (2003)

Dominican Migration: Transnational Perspectives, edited by Ernesto Sagás and Sintia Molina (2004)

Salvadoran Migration to Southern California: Redefining El Hermano Lejano, by Beth Baker-Cristales (2004)

The Chrysanthemum and the Song: Music, Memory, and Identity in the South American Japanese Diaspora, by Dale A. Olsen (2004)

Andean Diaspora: The Tiwanaku Colonies and the Origins of South American Empire, by Paul S. Goldstein (2005)

Migration and Vodou, by Karen E. Richman (2005)

True-Born Maroons, by Kenneth Bilby (2006)

The Tears of Hispaniola: Haitian and Dominican Diaspora Memory, by Lucía M. Suárez (2006)

Dominican-Americans and the Politics of Empowerment, by Ana Aparicio (2006)

Nuer-American Passages: Globalizing Sudanese Migration, by Dianna J. Shandy (2007)

Nuer-American Passages

Globalizing Sudanese Migration

Dianna J. Shandy

University Press of Florida
Gainesville/Tallahassee/Tampa/Boca Raton
Pensacola/Orlando/Miami/Jacksonville/Ft. Myers

Copyright 2007 by Dianna J. Shandy
Printed in the United States of America on recycled, acid-free paper
All rights reserved

12   11   10   09   08   07   6   5   4   3   2   1

Library of Congress Cataloging-in-Publication Data
Shandy, Dianna J.
Nuer-American passages : globalizing Sudanese migration / Dianna J. Shandy.
p. cm.—(New world diasporas)
Includes bibliographical references and index.
ISBN-13: 978-0-8130-3047-0 (alk. paper)
1. Nuer (African people)—Migrations. 2. Nuer (African people)—United States—Ethnic
identity. 3. Nuer (African people)—United States—Social life and customs. 4. Cattle
herding—Economic aspects—Sudan. 5. Sudan—Economic conditions. 6. Sudan—
Emigration and immigration—United States. 7. United States—Social life and customs.
8. United States—Ethnic relations. 9. United States—Race relations. I. Title.
DT155.2.N85S43   2006
304.8'730624—dc22
     2006030452

The University Press of Florida is the scholarly publishing agency for the State University System of Florida, comprising Florida A&M University, Florida Atlantic University,
Florida Gulf Coast University, Florida International University, Florida State University,
University of Central Florida, University of Florida, University of North Florida, University of South Florida, and University of West Florida.

University Press of Florida
15 Northwest 15th Street
Gainesville, FL 32611-2079
http://www.upf.com

For David, Rhetta, and Oran

Contents

Tables

Maps

Note on Nuer Names

The orthography of Nuer and other Sudanese names or words in this study diverges from the approaches used by Johnson (1994) and Hutchinson (1996). The purpose is not to challenge the accepted norms but rather to reflect the actual usage in the Nuer diaspora. Stephen Jay Gould (1998) notes that immigrants to Ellis Island frequently underwent name changes due to poor orthography or penmanship on the part of the official filling out the form. The experience of the Nuer in America is similar. Many Nuer-speaking Sudanese speak but cannot write the Nuer language. Immigration officials and Sudanese refugees have together generated a tremendous degree of diversity in the spelling of Nuer names in the United States. In systems of Nuer orthography employed by scholars such as Hutchinson and Evans-Pritchard, the letter *c* sounds like *ch*. Therefore, the Nuer name Cuol, made famous by Evans-Pritchard (1940a, 12–13) in recounting his circular conversation trying to elicit the man's lineage, is spelled Chuol (or Chol) by Nuer living in the United States. Throughout the text, except when referring to place-names in Sudan, I adopt current practices of Sudanese living in the United States.

To preserve the anonymity of the individuals whose experiences are reflected in this study I have used pseudonyms and disguised other identifying variables as appropriate.

Prologue

On February 12, 1998, a plane crashed in Sudan, killing key figures engaged in brokering a promising peace accord to end the civil war that had raged there since 1983. Eerily prescient of more recent, headline-grabbing events in which southern Sudanese rebel leader John Garang perished in a helicopter crash only weeks after being sworn in as vice president of Sudan in July 2005, this earlier disaster reverberated throughout the Nuer diaspora. A Nuer physician was among the casualties in 1998. After this crash, members of the Nuer diaspora who lived in the United States organized a memorial service in Nashville, Tennessee, where some of the victim's family members lived. Nuer from across the United States rallied in support, and perhaps several hundred made the journey to Nashville to pay their respects.

I joined a group of Nuer people traveling to Nashville for the memorial service. We traveled, not in the customary car or minivan, but in a forty-foot recreation vehicle, obtained by an American woman who at the time was involved heavily in her own U.S. church and the quest for peace in Sudan. Although the war in Sudan is much more complex, as evidenced by the subsequent eruption of the Darfur crisis in western Sudan, she and some, at least initially, saw the conflict as a religious war pitting northern Arab Muslims against southern black Christians such as the Nuer.

In my quest to understand Nuer adaptation to life in the United States, their evolving relationship with those who remain in Africa, and the advancing peace process in Sudan, as will be described in the pages that follow, I keep returning to this road trip as a defining moment in my research with this diaspora population.

One of the most dramatic experiences during this journey for me as a young graduate student in the mid-1990s was the opportunity to observe the intersection between the Nuer as refugees in modern American society and their ethnographic past. When my Nuer traveling companions filed into the RV at midnight—after the second shift at the factories, nursing homes, and security desks in public housing complexes that so often comprise their occupations—I was surprised to see one of them carrying a dog-eared copy, with its unmistakable gold cover, of the classic text *The Nuer* (1940) by famed British social anthropologist Sir Edward E. Evans-Pritchard. Other Nuer men, who climbed aboard with jaunty greetings of *"maale"* and *"jinathin,"* sported their own Nuer texts, including Evans-Pritchard's *Nuer Religion*

(1956), historian Douglas Johnson's *Nuer Prophets* (1994), and anthropologist Sharon Hutchinson's *Nuer Dilemmas* (1996).

The speed with which some of my traveling companions flipped the pages as we drove down the highway called into question the symbolic versus the utilitarian value placed on these books. Many of the Nuer men and women with whom I worked had very little formal education before they arrived in the United States. However, during this trip and in subsequent interviews, my questions about Nuer social organization, beliefs, and values were sometimes met with gentle chiding to revisit the anthropological literature: "Have you read that book with the red cover about Nuer families?" referring to Evans-Pritchard's *Kinship and Marriage among the Nuer* (1951).

Foner (2003, 51) points out that in the United States it is increasingly more common for anthropologists to work with "'classic' subjects of anthropological study," like the Nuer. In the mid-1990s, however, the arrival of the Nuer in the United States was a novel phenomenon, and this study charts their initial entrée into U.S. society, while providing a longitudinal perspective as their experience unfolds over time.

Acknowledgments

While I alone am responsible for any shortcomings of this work, any credit for its success must be shared among many. This book came into being through the generosity and hospitality of the many refugees and humanitarian workers in the United States and Africa who were willing to share their experiences with me. I am profoundly grateful to all those (who remain nameless to protect their confidentiality) who shared of their lives, their losses, and their triumphs. I hope that this book in some small way contributes to the efforts of those Nuer in the diaspora and in Sudan who want their children to understand the struggles they endured so that the family might keep its name in the world. Throughout this project, I was humbled and awed by their sacrifices, their resiliency, and their hope for the future.

I appreciate the input of the many individuals who helped shape this work at various stages of its development: Rogaia Abusharaf, George C. Bond, Charlanne Burke, Lambros Comitas, Katherine Fennelly, Sally Findley, Elzbieta Gozdziak, Arjun Guneratne, Julia Hess, Ginger Hope, Sharon Hutchinson, Charles Keely, David W. McCurdy, Jason Owens, Sonia Patten, Corinna Roy, Lesley Sharp, David Turton, Hervé Varenne, Jack Weatherford, Marcia Wright, and the late Tania Forte. In addition, the book was improved greatly through the comments of the anonymous reviewers.

Mathematica Policy Research in Washington, D.C., awarded me a generous summer fellowship to initiate work on chapter 7. Macalester College provided support at many levels, including a Wallace Faculty Travel and Research Grant that allowed me to participate in the International Summer School in Forced Migration at Oxford, which helped me frame some of the issues in the book. The Lilly Foundation provided support for the development of a course on Refugees and Humanitarian Response, which has informed the direction the book took.

My students at Macalester College over the years have engaged me in rich discussions that fed back into this work. Jessica Gilbert provided invaluable assistance with formatting, and Birgit and Ian Muehlenhaus did a fine job with the maps.

Karine Moe, Melissa Wright, Rob Alfano, MaryLou Byrne, Peggy and Winter Lane, Gary, Joy, and Greg Shandy, Pat and Louis Power, Delaney Kreger-Stickles, and Amy Wilkolak all provided diffuse yet critical support at various stages of this project. To my husband, David Power, and my children, Rhetta and Oran, I am most grateful for their many kindnesses, patience, and support.

Nuer-American Passages

Popular images of African forced migrants, particularly refugees fleeing conflict situations, often depict people leaving "Stone Age" societies en route to Western countries and fail to recognize the ways Africans use social networks, technology, and information flows in their quest for better lives for themselves and their families. These flawed representations, which fail to credit African populations with linkages between what they have known as home and the diaspora, overlook important realities in how these ties shape the lives of people in both settings.

This multisited study draws predominantly on research conducted in various locales throughout the United States and, to a lesser degree, in Ethiopia to describe what happens when a population of mostly rural African cattle herders from Sudan becomes caught up in a web of global geostrategic political maneuvering, is vaulted into U.S. society, and attempts to chart a course for a future that encompasses both life in America and in Africa. The Nuer people, whose lives are depicted here, are a unique case in the documentation of globalizing processes, because they represent one of anthropology's most celebrated peoples, as chronicled by the famed late British social anthropologist Sir Edward E. Evans-Pritchard. This is a study of the complex social networks that develop for Nuer refugees as they travel through multiple sites of displacement.

In the 1990s, half a century after Evans-Pritchard's work introduced the Nuer people into the global scholarly consciousness, they began to arrive in the United States as refugees. Dispersed beyond the usual metropolitan gateways, such as New York, Miami, or Los Angeles, this population of approximately twenty-five thousand African refugees is among the newest immigrants in locations such as Sioux Falls, South Dakota; Nashville, Tennessee; and Saint Paul, Minnesota.

In documenting Nuer as a twenty-first-century refugee population, this study moves beyond description of a specific temporal-spatial moment to situate Nuer people within a broader social and historical framework of migration. This approach attempts to convey the complexity and fluidity of Nuer refugee migration. It describes and analyzes the ways that Nuer people's lives weave together and expose local, national, and global processes as they are inducted into the refugee system, bureaucratically processed, deposited in and incorporated into the United States, and, ultimately, embark on return trips of varying duration to Africa.

This analysis contributes to methodological and theoretical debates about the anthropological unit of analysis, about concepts of home, about the nature of structure and agency, and about the relationship between culture and territory. For those concerned with refugees and other migrants, this book provides more empirical evidence that the categories used by refugee organizations are misleading because they fail to capture the "lived experience" of most migrants and refugees. For an African area studies audience, it blurs the boundaries of the scope of inquiry in which the African context can be understood fully only when linkages with those in the diaspora are taken into consideration by showing how the actions of diaspora Nuer transfigure social relations in Africa (see Koser 2003).

In some respects, Nuer people's experiences resemble that of the waves of immigrants to the United States that have preceded them. Yet Nuer are differentiated from other migratory populations to the United States in other critical ways. Within the literature on contemporary African migration to the United States, for instance, Nuer are distinct from the Sierra Leoneans that JoAnn D'Alisera (2004) or the Senegalese that Paul Stoller (2002) portray in that the Nuer described in this study lacked a preestablished ethnic community upon arrival. Unlike the northern Sudanese that Rogaia Abusharaf (2002) depicts, the Nuer migrants discussed here lacked the social and material capital and prior experience with international migration necessary to make them eligible for immigration to the United States through student, labor, or tourist visa designations. Therefore, the category of refugee is essential to explaining their arrival in the United States.

By examining Nuer within a refugee migration framework, this book updates the anthropological record by describing the deliberate ways in which Nuer refugees cope with their changing world and explores "connections between political instability and social life" (Greenhouse 2002, 1). As such, it probes the tension between Nuer refugees as victims of larger structural events beyond their control and their adaptive strategies in negotiating complex and shifting circumstances. The processes by which refugees are made into what anthropologist Liisa Malkki (1995, 296) describes as "objects of a special philanthropic mode of power" emphasize their dependency, needs, and vulnerability. The tendency to highlight refugees' presumed helplessness augments the power of those offering assistance while diminishing the ways in which refugees are social actors. In this way, the book engages questions pertinent to the rapidly expanding fields of humanitarian assistance and peace and conflict studies (see Anderson 1999; Bob 2005; Helton 2002; Krulfeld and MacDonald 1998; Minear 2002; Terry 2002).

This book contributes to the growing body of literature that strives to surpass previous conceptualizations of the rather artificially drawn division between political refugees and economic migrants by arguing that the ubiquitous aphorism, derived from legal distinctions, in which "immigrants are pulled out of their country of origin while refugees are pushed," is insufficient as a means of framing social science analytic categories (Zolberg, Suhrke, and Aguayo 1989). This book demonstrates the ways in which this model fails to capture the complexity of lived experiences and challenges the paradigm, derived from a psychological understanding of forced migration, that the refugee experience produces what is commonly understood as "refugee behavior."

By recognizing that the social field for understanding Nuer refugees' lives spans African and U.S. contexts, this study is positioned to perceive refugees' roles as social actors and active agents in producing culture and shaping their own futures. It shows how, as anthropologist Carol Greenhouse (2002, 2) puts it, "under circumstances of extreme instability and doubt, society itself can become a genre of performance, narrative, remembrance, critique and hope" by depicting how Nuer people carried on social life through courtship, marriage, the birth of children, and planning for the future in the midst of what can be characterized as extreme social change. Moreover, through its exploration of the phenomenon of refugee remittances from those in the diaspora to those who remain in Africa, this study locates the unidirectional flow of cash within the transnational circulation of people, goods, information, and reciprocal social obligations and demonstrates how this money is used to create new configurations of social power.

Defining Refugees

Contemporary understandings of refugee populations represent an amalgam of legal distinctions, psychologically derived models of refugee behavior, and lived experience that spills messily out of both explanatory paradigms, leaving outsiders to the refugee process confounded when refugees act in ways that fail to conform to expectations generated by these models. Therefore this study seeks to problematize dominant modes of defining refugees by illustrating how the conflation of legal distinctions with behavioral models that attempt to universalize "the refugee experience" can work at cross-purposes with ethnographic attempts to understand refugees' experiences from the point of view of those who are displaced.

LEGAL DISTINCTIONS

It is a truism that international migrants, regardless of the circumstances precipitating their movement, cross borders. Similarly, all refugees are migrants, but not all migrants are refugees. Accordingly, these different classifications provide migrants with different constraints, opportunities, and access to resources. For migrants the stakes are often very high, sometimes even life and death, for how legal distinctions are applied to their experiences.

This situation is rendered even more complex, as refugee definitions, produced in dramatically different temporal and spatial contexts, vary notably. This slippage in the categorization of "refugeeness" is significant in understanding the articulation between the Nuer forced migrants described in this study and the institutional structures that govern their access to resettlement in the United States.

While most refugee definitions derive from the 1951 United Nations Convention Relating to the Status of Refugees and the 1967 Protocol Relating to the Status of Refugees, important differences can be seen in how refugees are defined in the United States and in Africa. The UN convention defines a refugee as

> any person who is outside any country of such person's nationality or, in the case of a person having no nationality, is outside any country in which such person has habitually resided, and who is unable or unwilling to return to, and is unable or unwilling to avail himself or herself of the protection of, that country because of persecution or a well-founded fear of persecution on account of race, religion, nationality, membership in a particular social group, or political opinion and is unable or, because of such fear, is unwilling to avail himself of the protection of the government of the country of his nationality (quoted in Zolberg, Suhrke, and Aguayo 1989, 4).

Significant differences exist among the definitions adopted in various settings. For instance, the U.S. definition is narrower in scope, as articulated in the U.S. government's Refugee Act of 1980.[1] When referring to refugees within Africa, however, definitions adopted in 1969 by the Organization of African Unity (OAU; now called the African Union) apply, which have been generated within an African context and are somewhat broader in scope to allow for the experience of colonialism and the ensuing struggles for pendence.[2]

Common to these definitions, however, is persecution on the basis of race, religion, ethnicity, membership in a particular social group, or beliefs within the country of origin and the crossing of an international border. Yet this classification does little to recognize the most recent category of refugees in Africa, what Schultheis (1989a, 1) calls "hunger migrants," resulting from civil conflict, which disrupts the basic modes of existence, including agricultural cycles, herds, and water supplies. Similarly, statutory definitions of refugees posit the crossing of an international border as the sine qua non of their migratory status, and it is the act of crossing that border, in conjunction with recognition by the host country, that renders them eligible for certain kinds of international humanitarian assistance. Therefore people who are uprooted in their country of origin are not, according to the convention's definition, refugees, but internally displaced people, or IDPs. Legal scholar James Hathaway succinctly summarizes the challenges to the convention's definition:[3]

> that it fails to recognize the claims of persons whose predicaments do not resemble those of the post–Second World War ideological émigrés; that it is insufficiently attentive to dilemmas that result from the failure of states, rather than from more active forms of persecution; that it unfairly ignores the needs of involuntary migrants who cannot link their fear to one of the five enumerated grounds of civil or political status; and that its alienage criterion inappropriately excludes the claims of the internally displaced. (1997, 79)

Yet Hathaway ultimately concludes that while the convention's definition of *refugee* is not ideal, in the context of contemporary political realities it remains of significant value.

These debates regarding how we define and categorize forced migrants are not limited to sending regions. The distinction between economic migrants and asylum seekers, or those who seek protection after entering another country's borders, is far less polarizing in the United States than it is in places like contemporary Europe (see Pirouet 2001; Garner 2004). Anthropologist Jamie Saris (2004, i), in his foreword to Mark Maguire's book on Vietnamese in Ireland, observes that most political debates have focused on getting the categories to fit rather than a sustained reflection on the categories themselves. Similarly, my study, in documenting the ways in which the lives of Nuer refugees are more complex than categories used to classify them imply, seeks to problematize the means and criteria by which their suffering is "evaluated."

PSYCHOLOGICALLY DERIVED MODELS

The orientation of the psychologically derived theoretical model of refugee behavior is illustrated in the following quote by refugee specialist Barry Stein:

> Superficially, when viewing refugees one is struck by diversity, a large number of refugee groups from distinct cultures forced to flee due to a wide variety of historical circumstances. However, scientifically, it is possible to develop a perspective that sees certain consistencies in the refugee experience and refugee behavior. The basic premise with which this chapter approaches refugee research is that there is a refugee experience and this experience produces what we can call refugee behavior. (1986, 5; Stein also cites David 1969; Kunz 1973; Liu, Lamanna, and Murata 1979)

In this approach, the social, historical, and cultural elements of the refugee's background are secondary to the experience of forced migration. Malkki soundly critiques this model of the "universalization of the figure of 'the refugee'" (1995, 8) and the related depiction of refugees "as a social-psychological type" (Stein 1981b, 64, in Malkki 1995, 8).

Refugees do not simply depart; they flee. When they are resettled in a third country they are said to begin to rebuild meaning, suggesting a void in which there was no meaning. *Meaning* in this sense, therefore, alludes to notions of citizenship, territory, or homeland. This paradigm, in which the forced migration experience is paramount, portrays refugees as uprooted, denuded, and deprived not only of their territory but also of their culture. Culture seems to take on a material or physical connotation, as if it were something one could leave behind like dishes, cattle, or children. Indeed, the question I am most frequently asked by anyone familiar with the work of Evans-Pritchard, about my research is, what do the Nuer do without cattle? In contrast, as this study will show, the recounting of experiences by Nuer and other Sudanese refugees emphasize the continuation and elaboration of social and spiritual life after leaving Sudan, rather than the "loss" of culture.

This work, therefore, feeds into the expanding body of literature in which scholars assert that refugee populations need to be seen in relation to their sociohistorical context (see Indra 2000; Jacobsen 2005; Malkki 1995). Within this framework, there is expanded space in which to appreciate the ways in which refugees are active agents in shaping their own lives. While indicators suggest that this insight is now a virtual cliché or truism ii temporary refugee studies, if not the discipline of anthropology in general, there is ample evidence that this model continues to shape and condition expectations in the "real world," where these refugees' lives unfold. Even though the quote from Stein referenced earlier originally was written more than twenty years ago, it came to my attention in excerpted form in a recent packet of training materials on refugee health for medical practitioners.

The Globalization of Migration, Refugees, and the Transnational Social Field

Migration is a lens through which we can examine certain processes, systems, and relationships that contribute to the phenomenon called globalization. Castles and Miller (2003, 7) state that this "globalization of migration" can be observed in the increasing number of countries significantly affected by migratory movements, and in a concomitant broadening in scope of both the diversity of areas of origin for migrants, as well as the spectrum of economic, cultural, and social backgrounds. In this way, Nuer refugees are emblematic of post–Cold War shifts in the globalization of migration, particularly in the domain of refugee resettlement. Until 1990 refugee resettlement cases in the United States came from only a handful of countries. As global alliances shifted, U.S. refugee policy could most aptly be described as idiosyncratic triage; assistance to refugees became more a symbolic gesture rather than a part of an international solution to a crisis. The number of refugee resettlement slots has remained relatively constant but must now be divided among many more groups.

Within this framework, this study explores the global flow of people across national borders from an anthropological perspective—or one that examines how these processes are experienced locally. Highlighted in this discussion are issues of refugee categories, identity construction, nation-state membership, migrant networks, and the humanitarian support system that facilitates these flows.

APPROACHES TO MIGRATION

Geographic mobility has been an important adaptive strategy in Africa "to maintain ecological balance, to seek a more secure environment, and to achieve better conditions of living" (Schultheis 1989b, 3). Indeed, gathering and hunting, an adaptive strategy characterized by mobility, has been dominant in the survival of humankind for roughly 90 percent of human history. Evans-Pritchard's work (1940a, 1951b, 1956) has situated the Nuer as one of the most celebrated migratory populations. When not disrupted by war, Nuer life in Sudan was punctuated by a transhumant pastoral rhythm dictated by the dry and rainy seasons. The dry season lasts from late September to early April. During this period, Nuer moved to lower ground to access water and graze their cattle. During the rainy season, the low-lying areas resemble a swampy lagoon. This soaking contributes to abundant grass, which prepares the area for the next season's grazing. Daily life among rural Sudanese Nuer as described by Evans-Pritchard (1940a) was dominated by cattle concerns. In addition to cattle, Nuer in Sudan also herd small animals such as goats and sheep (Duany 1992, 38) and grow maize, millet, and vegetables to supplement their milk-and-meat diet. In more recent years, the dry and rainy seasons also have dictated the rhythm of war: the dry season allows heavy artillery to traverse the clay plains, which are impassable during the rainy season.

Therefore, while migration is nothing new, the context in which it occurs has changed substantially. Increasingly, links related to a worldwide capitalist economy, political systems, and military order are facilitated through the proliferation of increased global information systems. In a similar vein, while immigrants have always retained some ties with the homes they leave behind, in the twenty-first century the possibilities are greatly expanded. Communication and transportation are now much cheaper and speedier and are accessible to a broader swath of the population, and African refugees, despite popular media representations that suggest otherwise, are well aware of these technologies.

These shifts articulate with local processes in myriad ways. Indeed, as Aristide Zolberg, Astri Suhrke, and Sergio Aguayo (1989) argue, refugee flows can be understood only in light of regional and global contexts. Despite its surface seeming unpredictability, refugee migration can indeed be traced to broad historical processes (Colson 1987, 4; Zolberg, Suhrke, and Aguayo 1989). History is likewise an important consideration in this study, not only in terms of recent events precipitating the departure of refugees from Sudan, but also earlier decades, or even centuries, as Jok Madut Jok (2001) argues, when the seeds of contemporary crises were sown. Historical considerations that inform the current situation in Sudan, particularly with respect to the intersection of education, religion, and politics, play a substantial role in this study (see chapter 2).

Given the limiting set of circumstances imposed by war in Sudan, this book describes the deliberate ways in which Nuer refugees coped with their changing world. Taking steps to become an officially recognized refugee is one action, or adaptive strategy, among a very limited array of options. This action, which involves crossing an international border, as opposed to migrating within Sudan, brings its own perils and possibilities. Emphasizing the strategies Nuer used to seek and sustain an existence in the United States does not diminish the dire circumstances that precipitated their departure from Sudan. Rather, focusing not on what the Nuer have lost but on what they have retained and on the actions they took to secure their own and others' survival testifies to their very capacity to overcome tremendous hardship (see also Hutchinson 1996, 20). This approach, which highlights the actions these migrants undertook, may accord more closely with the ways in which many Nuer forced migrants see themselves and wish to be seen by others. One Nuer man described being dispatched by his father from the refugee camp where the family was perishing, with the goal of seeking out resettlement in the United States to keep the family's name alive, should the rest of the family not make it. And not only does resettlement hold promise for the survival of the family in the United States, it also helps secure the survival of those left behind through money that now flows from resettled refugees in the United States to those remaining in Africa.

THE TRANSNATIONAL SOCIAL FIELD

With more than fifteen million refugees in the world, and a ten-year annual average of 87,000 refugee resettlements to the United States, the Sudanese refugees who live in the United States represent a tiny fraction of Sudanese who have been uprooted by the conflict in Sudan. Approximately 25,000, or less than 4 percent, of the estimated 700,000 Sudanese forced migrants have been resettled in the United States. The filtering mechanism, which I call the refugee apparatus, governs access to resettlement in the United States and exerts considerable influence in shaping and defining the demographics of that group. Moreover, it sets its own standards for the values ordering society and defines and legitimates some basic human relationships, such as certain kinship and affinal ties, while discounting others. This process therefore has important implications for the emergent social structure of Nuer refugees in the United States.

In order to understand the social organization and modes of incorporation of Nuer refugees in the United States, it is necessary to have a rudimentary grasp of the process of induction into the arena of third-country resettlement. In contrast to the war-induced relative power vacuum of southern Sudan, the progress of a refugee through the selection and resettlement apparatus is rigidly orchestrated and governed by specific policies originating in a complex web of national and international jurisdictions. At

res, the rules and policies that circumscribe refugees' choices
evail. Within any vortex of attempted social control, however,
re are interstices that allow more room for choice, action, and
ity than the policies' designers anticipated. It is within these
.........es that strategies of Nuer refugees begin to take shape.

The previously discussed portrayal of refugees as passive victims has important implications for the handling of refugee resettlement in the United States. The institutions involved in resettlement are prepared to assist refugees for a limited time after arrival, but only if the refugees submit to certain terms that include remaining where they are geographically "placed." James C. Scott summarizes the challenges mobile populations pose for sedentary societies: "Efforts to permanently settle these mobile peoples (sedentarization) seemed to be a perennial state project—perennial, in part, because it so seldom succeeded" (1998, 1).

Current conceptualizations of "refugee behavior" in the United States have arisen predominantly from observations of the experiences of Southeast Asians, who represent 1.2 million of the approximately two million refugees resettled in the United States since the 1970s. In contrast, as Woldemikael (1997) points out in his work on Ethiopians in the United States, little is known about how other cultural groups, particularly Africans, experience resettlement. This study demonstrates, through an analysis of secondary migration after arrival in the United States, the ways in which the experiences of Southeast Asians are generalized to create a framework in which new waves of refugee groups are assessed.

The trajectory of migration originating in Africa and continuing after arrival in the United States provides a transnational analytic framework—or the concept of "social fields that cross geographic, cultural and political borders"—in which to understand historical and current contexts for the experiences of Nuer refugees in the United States and the relations they maintain with those who remain in Africa (Basch, Glick Schiller, and Szanton Blanc 1994, 7; see also Greenhouse 2002, 19–22).

By recognizing that the social field for understanding Nuer refugees' lives spans both African and U.S. contexts, this study is positioned to perceive refugees' roles as social actors and active agents in producing culture and shaping their own futures. The understanding of social transformation within refugee groups has been hampered by the assumption that social life is held in abeyance during the period between departure from the country of origin and resettlement in the country of placement. This analytic framework of lost culture or meaning has undergirded the theoretical construction of refugees as unidimensional objects, rather than actors, in their own lives. Yet some of the refugees described in this study, who are now in their twenties or thirties, were born in refugee camps. There they underwent scarification initiation ceremonies marking their transition into adulthood; they were baptized in Christian churches, got married, and transferred bridewealth cattle. They buried their parents, gave birth, cared for their children, and actively sought to maximize their chances for a better future, all within the spatial confines of a refugee camp. The experiences of Nuer refugees suggest that uprooting and deterritorialization, while introducing severe suffering and change, did not suspend the flow of social life.

Clearly, refugee camp experiences vary widely. The degree of hardship, level of security, access to benefits, and the extent to which camp conditions differ from those beyond the confines of the camp exist as a constellation of variables. The experiences of Nuer refugees, however, suggest that the refugee camp is not necessarily a site of cultural depletion or erasure. On the contrary, it can function as a site of creative cultural production (see Greenhouse 2002; Malkki 1995; Schechter 2004). In other words, the construction of social networks in these settings appears to function as a strategic practice to meet contingencies in the face of rapid change.

Discussions of refugee issues tend to downplay third-country resettlement, because it is the rarest of the three durable solutions recommended by the United Nations High Commissioner for Refugees (UNHCR) and is seen to affect such a small minority of refugees. Third-country resettlement, however, has material and cultural impacts on refugees in Africa far beyond the small numbers that actually board a plane and set off for a new land. The case of Nuer refugees therefore illustrates the vibrant and vital transnational linkages among refugees in the United States and their homeland—bonds that go beyond mere longing, extending to temporary return migration, especially among young men for the purpose of marriage, to East Africa.

Sudanese refugees' actions begin to take shape within these transnational social fields as adaptive strategies. This challenges ideological constructions of refugees as helpless, uprooted victims whose experience is defined merely by the reactive aspects of their actions. Refugee flight in reaction to catastrophe accords well with a tendency to interpret African action as focused on short-term outcomes rather than long-term strategies. The emphasis on African refugee flight evokes African philosopher V. Y. Mudimbe's (1988) objection to the ideological construction of Africans as individuals and groups prone to decisions based on emotion or reaction rather than on rationality, objectivity, or long-term planning.

Refugees' departure from their country of origin—even if it requires careful advanced planning, involves the movement of cattle herds, and consists of a slow and circuitous journey across multiple countries—seems etched forever in the literature as "flight." To add temporal depth to the study of newly arrived refugees, this book incorporates Nuer refugees' experiences before and after arrival. Thus it treats arrival in the United States as one step in a much longer journey.

This book highlights the actions of individuals in the process of transnational migration across international borders that include those within Africa as well as between African countries and the United States. In stressing the actions of individuals, it is not my intent to argue that these actions are disengaged from the needs, desires, or aims of larger social groupings (Kapferer 1972). Rather, in many cases described here, individuals undertake actions on behalf of others. The sociocultural context informs the perceived array of options. For forced migrants, this array of options is often circumscribed politically, economically, and geographically. The use of the term *strategy* does not necessarily imply that the actor has a firmly conceived map of outcomes. Rather, it connotes action in tandem with a set of socioculturally derived values, beliefs, and goals. Furthermore, actions undertaken by individuals can be seen as functions of larger social groupings (Kapferer 1972). This dynamic is illustrated in the case studies that follow.

Anthropology and the Nuer

When Evans-Pritchard wrote his famous trilogy: *The Nuer: A Description of the Modes of Livelihood and Political Institutions of a Nilotic People* (1940a), *Kinship and Marriage among the Nuer* (1951b), and *Nuer Religion* (1956), he could scarcely have imagined the RV journey described earlier as a venue for the consumption of his scholarly efforts among a population that he portrays as extremely remote. In the decades since Evans-Pritchard conducted his research in southern Sudan, the Nuer people who live there have undergone many changes. Nearly fifty years of intermittent civil war have disrupted the most fundamental aspects of life. Yet, more often than not, anthropological discourse locks the Nuer in time in a dramatic example of what Arjun Appadurai (1988b, 36) calls "metonymic freezing." The Nuer are used as a foil by scholars in academic debates within and beyond the disciplinary boundaries of anthropology (see also Moore 1994, 123). The Nuer, through the writings of Evans-Pritchard and his admirers and detractors, have played an important role in the construction of the discipline of anthropology. In fact, a review of the literature reveals a virtual cottage industry of Nuer ethnography, deployed in remarkably diverse settings.[4]

It is difficult to specify precisely what contributed to the making of Evans-Pritchard's work on the Nuer into such an enduring classic. For some anthropologists, invoking Evans-Pritchard is synonymous with good fieldwork (Gupta and Ferguson 1997, 1). Katherine Dettwyler (1994, 74), for instance, thought she had encountered the "spirit of Evans-Pritchard [riding] on the wind" after a particularly triumphant fieldwork experience. Mary Douglas (1980, 10) locates Evans-Pritchard's enduring appeal in his common sense approach, which eschewed "grand theoretical schemes." In her posthumous biography of Evans-Pritchard, Douglas credits him with a "theory of social accountability" (2). Jack Goody (1995) notes Evans-Pritchard's role in guiding teaching and research in Africa in postwar Oxford until 1950. Sharon Hutchinson (1996, 21) also views Evans-Pritchard's contributions in a favorable light when she refers to his "intellectual virtuosity." Yet she and others critique Evans-Pritchard for, among other things, his emphasis on Nuer life as portrayed through the eyes of men (see Hutchinson 1996, 31–32 for a summary of critiques of Evans-Pritchard's work citing, among others, Beidelman 1966, 1968, 1971; Burton 1974, 1981, 1987; Evans 1978; Gluckman 1956; Gough 1971; Gruel 1971; Hayley 1968; Lewis 1951).

It is through these secondary analyses, more than Evans-Pritchard's work, that the world of Nuer peoples is made static. The Nuer are ascribed certain indelible, not altogether flattering, characteristics, which serve to locate them beyond change. Sanjek (1990a, 39), for example, refers to "Nuer-like non-cooperation." Perhaps the most jarring example occurs in Ruth Behar's offhand indictment of the Nuer for complacency, in developing her argument about agency and resistance in academe: "It was the Chicano and Chicana critics—not the Nuer—who turned around the anthropological mirror, questioning the way they had been represented by outsiders and offering their own, more complex and more lacerating representations, which made salient the question of who has the authority to speak for whom" (1996, 162).

Thus, Nuer are invoked not as participants in their own history and the formation of anthropology, but as place markers in the construction of a discipline (see Appadurai 1988a). Clearly, Behar was not taking into account the systematic ways in which Nuer, and other southern Sudanese, have been denied access to educational opportunities—nor the devastation of the ongoing Sudanese civil war. The Nuer whom Behar describes above are the people represented in Evans-Pritchard's fieldwork in the 1930s. It is the otherness and presumed distance of the Nuer that allows scholars to invoke them with no apparent regard for current contexts.

Hutchinson (1996) and Douglas H. Johnson (1994), among others, have made important contributions to updating the scholarly record with respect to Nuer living in Africa. They document the relative disengagement of Nuer people with their celebrated ethnographic past as late as the 1990s. Johnson describes an incident in southern Sudan when a "Nuer veteran of the Sudan People's Liberation Army showed [Johnson] one of his most valued possessions: a battered copy of Evans-Pritchard's *Nuer Religion*" (1994, vii). Having received the book from SPLA commander John Garang, this man prized his copy even though he could read no English. Hutchinson (1996, 29) reports that Nuer in Sudan in the early 1980s, when she initially did fieldwork there, had virtually no engagement with Evans-Pritchard's work about the Nuer.

> Unlike many peoples of the world, contemporary Nuer images of themselves and their social life did not appear to have been heavily colored by the anthropological discourse. Only one of my university-trained Nuer readers had read any of Evans-Pritchard's monographs—although they had all heard about them. This low readership also appeared to be the norm among members of the Nuer educated elite I encountered in southern Sudan and elsewhere. And as for the 98 percent or more of the contemporary Nuer population that had no access to books (other than, perhaps, a Nuer version of the New Testament), Evans-Pritchard's work appeared to be completely unknown.

Therefore, engagement of Nuer in the United States with the anthropological literature about them appears to represent a watershed. What remains unclear is the role these, and other, ethnographic works will play in the lives of Nuer refugees as this relatively youthful population negotiates the realities of life in the United States and establishes themselves as diasporic transnational communities.

Hutchinson (1996, 351) divides contemporary Nuer populations into three groups: those who have established themselves on the outskirts of northern cities in Sudan, those who have taken refuge in neighboring African countries, and those who have remained in the southern Sudanese war zone. This study adds to the small but growing body of work on Nuer diaspora populations (see Abusharaf 1994, 1997, 2002; Archibald 1997; Clement 1996; Falge 1997; Farnham n.d.; Feyissa 2003; Gray-Fisher 1994; Griffin 1997a, 1997b; Holtzman 1999, 2000, 2003; Power and Shandy 1998; Schechter 2004; Shandy 2001, 2002, 2003, 2005, 2006; Shandy and Fennelly 2006).

Methodological Considerations

This study sketches the outlines of a recent and fluid social p
There are no end points to the migration I describe, except th
ones that I impose for the purposes of analysis. Neither mobility
cess of social incorporation ceases after Nuer people's arrival in the United
States. The findings in this study are derived from data collected between
August 1996 and February 2006 in the United States and during May and
June 2004 in Ethiopia.

Gupta and Ferguson (1997, 12) note that the distinction between the anthropological fieldwork site and home rests on their spatial separation. The
lack of firm geographic boundaries between "home" and "the field" in this
study introduced both challenges and opportunities. I have developed close
relationships with Nuer people over time, and this study has profited enor-
mously from my ongoing dialogue with key informants throughout the analysis and writing. However, there was no comfortable stopping point for this
study. I continue to have contact with the people I describe, their lives continue to unfold, and these new events continue to inform my understanding
of their experiences. Such is the nature of research undertaken without the
sharp (and somewhat artificial) boundaries between "work" and "life."

The dominant research methods in this inquiry are formal and informal
interviews, participant observation, document review, and archival research.
I interviewed approximately four hundred (mostly Nuer) Sudanese refugees
on a range of topics about their lives in the United States and in Africa.
About two-thirds of the interviews were conducted in the United States
and one-third in Ethiopia. Many of the Nuer refugees in this study are from
the eastern Jikany Nuer ethnic group, which includes the Gaajak, Gaajok,
and Gaaguang lineages. Through these interviews, I was able to generate
data, which I maintained in a computerized database, on a total of 904 men,
women, and children, most of them Nuer. The tables in the appendixes provide additional descriptive data on the sample population—documenting
that those interviewed were among the first cohorts of Sudanese refugees to
be resettled in the United States—and represent baseline information that
will be useful in gauging transformation among U.S.-based Nuer.

Given the high degree of Nuer geographic mobility as well as my own
travels, I often had only one opportunity to do a short interview, which was
limited largely to demographic questions. The geographic scope of this study
was expanded further through telephone interviews with Sudanese refugees
and refugee service providers in nine states. The wealth of data I obtained

on individuals in twenty states is critical to discerning macrolevel patterns of social networks, resettlement, and mobility within the United States. I use these data on geographic distribution to demonstrate the myriad ways in which Nuer living in the United States are linked through social relationships that they maintain though various forms of communication, including periodic visits, phone calls, and electronic mail. I present case studies that illustrate the ways in which Nuer mobilize these social relationships and for what purposes.

Participant observation of the full trajectory of refugee migration (for example, Sudan to refugee camp in neighboring country to U.S.) by a member outside the group experiencing displacement is virtually impossible.[5] Therefore, I use life history interviews to explore, in a retrospective manner, the circumstances and conditions that precipitated departure from Sudan. I used additional primary and secondary sources to supplement my understanding of life in Sudan and the refugee camp, and experiences en route to the United States. For instance, I analyzed a set of several dozen essays about flight from Sudan that I was given by an aid worker in Kakuma camp in Kenya written by so-called lost boys (and girls) of Sudan. In addition to interview data, ethnographic participant observation enabled me to explore multiple facets of daily life through a variety of events and interactions in public and private settings, such as formal gatherings among Sudanese for purposes of governance, worship, conflict resolution, weddings, funerals, birthday celebrations, and Christian holidays; informal one-on-one meetings with Sudanese in their homes and in the community, such as in-home visits to socialize, welcome newborns or people recovering from illness home from the hospital, learning to cook Sudanese dishes, and other unstructured meetings; formal and informal interactions between Sudanese and social service providers covering topics such as housing, medical care, clothing, education, cash assistance, and other basic needs. These varied settings provided rich opportunities to observe interactions and events involving both men and women inside and outside of the home.

Most U.S. interviews were conducted in English. In some instances, particularly in casual settings with women, when needed, I relied on informal interpretation from others present. In Ethiopia, I worked with three Nuer research assistants who served as interpreters for about half the interviews conducted there. I began to learn Nuer from a tutor at the outset of my research. Later I took classes offered by a Nuer-speaking pastor in a church for a few American church members and, significantly, Nuer people who spoke but did not read or write Nuer adequately. However, in most cases, my Nuer informants' English proficiency has outpaced my Nuer language abilities.

One of the first phrases I learned from my tutor was his interpretation of how to introduce myself as an anthropologist. I told people *Gora ni chiang naath* (roughly, that I write about the real people, meaning the Nuer). In an attempt to reciprocate for people's generosity in sharing their time and stories, I sometimes helped them gain access to services, usually by assisting with paperwork, when requested and to the extent that I was able.[6] I encountered many Sudanese through my involvement as a volunteer in the day care center for the women's class in English as a Second Language (ESL). Thus, I have changed the diapers of a certain proportion of the next generation of Nuer-Americans. I balanced those contacts with others unrelated to service provision, such as contacts made through a Nuer-language instructor where I was the party requesting services.

To augment my understanding of the experiences of Sudanese refugees from a variety of institutional perspectives, I also conducted in-person, telephone, and e-mail interviews with approximately fifty-five service providers, fifteen individuals affiliated with churches, and twenty international humanitarian-assistance workers in the United States and abroad, including staff of UNHCR and of international NGOs based in Africa.

My primary geographic base was a metropolitan area in the Midwestern United States, which received a large number of primary migrants and has retained a rather fluid population of approximately five hundred Sudanese refugees. Living "among" the Sudanese on a long-term basis was not a viable option for many reasons, the most basic of which is the absence of a geographically consolidated Sudanese community in the primary state in which I conducted my research. Small pockets of residential geographic consolidation are beginning to emerge. However, most of these pockets are located in public housing or designated affordable housing units.[7] The small number of Sudanese women relative to men further reduced the likelihood of a socially appropriate living situation for me as a woman. More significantly, I got married during the course of fieldwork; living in the same city as my husband but in a separate home would have been interpreted by Nuer as untoward social behavior. And finally, many Sudanese move within and among states quite frequently and spontaneously, often breaking their lease.

The frequent and continuous migration of Sudanese within the United States challenges standard anthropological notions of the importance of the setting. I traveled with Nuer people by road to other Midwestern, Southern, and Eastern states for short visits to attend weddings, funerals, graduation ceremonies, or other events. Each event afforded opportunities to reconnect with people whom I had met at previous gatherings and to meet new people. Many factors govern Nuer people's ability to travel to these events, including work, school, and family obligations, as well as resources and transportation opportunities. Therefore the mix of people at each gathering varied dramatically. I attempted to travel from the United States to Ethiopia with a Nuer woman who was planning on returning for a visit, but we were not able to coordinate our schedules, and I ended up traveling there alone. While there, however, my visit was enhanced through connections made possible through my relationships with Nuer living in the United States.

This approach allowed me to examine the unfolding processes in a particular locale over time while gathering comparative data from other selected sites, offering opportunities to generate comparative data on the incorporation of refugees in multiple environments and to document mobility and refugees' perceptions of comparative advantage among different states. These visits also afforded opportunities to live for short yet intense periods of time in the homes of Nuer refugees and provided a way of conducting continuous observation, which is frequently difficult in urban settings (Sanjek 1990b). Another strategy to combat the challenges presented by a geographically dispersed study population was to make use of the same modes of communication that the Sudanese use to stay in touch—telephone, letters, and, increasingly, electronic mail (see also D'Alisera 2004).

To provide some objective assessment to balance the wide-ranging population estimates of the total number of Sudanese refugees in the United States I heard during fieldwork interviews, I obtained a data set from the Office of Refugee Resettlement in the U.S. Department of Health and Human Services, which I analyzed to generate descriptive statistics on the sample of all Sudanese refugees resettled in the United States from 1983 to 1997.

Case studies, rather than life histories, emerged as a more appropriate format to convey the ways in which my Nuer informants spoke about their lives and experiences. In general, people were uncomfortable with formal interview formats that sought to elicit a life narrative. The mode may have resembled too closely the interview required to gain entry to the United States: they present their life story to someone who holds a notepad, a pen, and the power to refuse their resettlement request. For women in particular it was difficult to remove themselves entirely from their child care responsibilities and participate in a formal tape-recorded interview. On the occasions when a woman informant was able to sit down to talk about her life and experiences leading up to resettlement in the United States, the tape recording is punctuated with children's screams for attention, our efforts to retrieve the tape recorder from the child, and interruptions to tend to pots cooking on the stove. These represent common encounters for the ethnographic researcher but merit pointing out for those less familiar with this mode of inquiry. Less formal interview formats with a notepad tended to work much better. Thus, I traded some of the compelling eloquence often found in life history narratives for the benefit of maintaining rapport with my informants.

Overall, my informants freely shared details of their lives before leaving Africa and after arriving in America—only not all in the same interview in an unfolding, linear manner. Malkki (1995) has addressed some of the difficulties in conducting life history interviews with refugees; in particular, she elaborated on her rationale for not triangulating data and implementing other fact-checking maneuvers often associated with sound qualitative inquiry: "Too often, the anthropologist takes on the role of the police detective, discovering what is 'hidden,' assembling 'evidence' to make a strong 'case,' relentlessly probing for ever more information. But sometimes what is called for is not an 'investigator' at all, but an attentive listener. It may be precisely by giving up the scientific detective's urge to know 'everything' that we gain access to those very partial vistas that our informants may desire or think to share with us" (1995, 51).

Related to this are the changing sensitivities and sensibilities involved in writing ethnography about populations who are, as MaryCarol Hopkins puts it, "both literate and proximate" (1998, 57). One could argue that given the recent innovations in global access to information, this concern could apply anywhere. Yet a Nuer person using a public library computer terminal in Nashville, Tennessee, still enjoys greater access to published information than a Nuer person in Gambela, Ethiopia. In addition to the Nuer individuals with whom I have shared parts of this manuscript, upon completion this study will be accessible immediately to the public at large, including those featured in this work. Given this reality, I err on the side of protecting the anonymity of my informants. Writing about such a recent phenomenon is an exciting enterprise; exercising caution with regard to what I write is a limitation with which I contend throughout this study.

God, Gold, Oil, and Water

Causes and Consequences of Conflict

Events in Sudan and refugee camps in neighboring African countries shaped and continue to inform the lives of Nuer refugees living in the United States. Similarly, Nuer in the diaspora have an impact on the lives of Sudanese in Africa. This chapter describes the local, regional, and global conditions precipitating Nuer refugees' departure from Africa and helps to frame linkages between Nuer who remain in Africa and those in the diaspora. Zolberg, Suhrke, and Aguayo (1989) point out that refugee-producing conflicts need to be seen as the outcome of broader historical processes rather than simply a manifestation of internal strife. Within this framework, I highlight economic and ideological forces that render the case of Sudan significant within a larger context of African displacement. And finally, I introduce salient aspects of Nuer life in Africa necessary to appreciate migration-induced transformations.

Historian Douglas Johnson begins the preface to his book on root causes of war in Sudan by noting that "Sudan entered the 21st century mired in not one, but many civil wars" (2004, xi). He, among others, has detailed the interrelatedness and complexity of Sudan's civil wars. Therefore my key aim in this chapter, while acknowledging the importance of these linkages to what I describe here, is to focus on providing a framework to contextualize the experiences of southern Sudanese refugees described in this book. It is impossible to disentangle the so-called North-South conflict from the larger situation; however, it is necessary to focus on certain dimensions to make them comprehensible, particularly to those with only a casual acquaintance with events in Sudan.

Making Peace, Making War

A Comprehensive Peace Agreement (CPA) between southern rebels and the Khartoum government, ending more than two decades of civil war, was agreed to December 31, 2004, and signed, in a formal ceremony, on January 9, 2005 (USIP 2006).[1] The CPA, a collection of agreements, provides for a devolution of government functions and powers, the creation of a new National Armed Forces consisting of the Sudan Armed Forces and the Sudan People's Liberation Army (SPLA) as separate, regular and nonpartisan armed forces with a mission to defend constitutional order, has detailed arrangements for revenue transfers, whereby the government of southern Sudan has been allocated 50 percent of net oil revenues generated from oil fields in southern Sudan, and gives the people of southern Sudan their first opportunity to exercise the right of self-determination (L. Deng 2005). Specifically, the CPA gives the South the right to secede through a referendum to be exercised after a six-year interim period (L. Deng 2005, 7). The CPA has weathered the untimely death of former rebel leader and newly installed vice president of Sudan John Garang de Mabior in late July 2005 and continued upheaval in the Darfur region.[2] Yet it remains unclear whether the peace agreement will endure and, if so, for how long. Johnson aptly captures the predominant sentiment of many of my Nuer informants when he writes, "We live in hope; but hope tempered by experience" (2004, xx).

Thus, causes and consequences of conflict in Sudan are disputed issues. In this setting, politics of the past, politics of place, and the politicization of ethnic and national identity all combine to represent a mosaic of controversy. Charting a path through the, at times, divergent discourses regarding conflict in Sudan will provide a context for understanding the emergence of a Nuer diaspora population.

The population of Sudan is estimated at forty million.[3] While the difficulties in developing reliable estimates for war-induced displacement and death should be noted, an estimated two million were killed by the North-South war that lasted from 1983 to 2005; another four million were displaced, including more than a million living in shanty towns on the outskirts of Khartoum (Hutchinson 1996, 1999); and 600,000 to 700,000 sought shelter as refugees in neighboring countries (UNMIS 2006; Natsios 2005, 93).

A very small percentage of those displaced have gained access to official third-country resettlement placements. However, as this book argues, the effects of third-country resettlement are felt by broad social networks extending out from the individual who is actually resettled (Shandy 2003, 7). North America and Australia have emerged as key destinations for those southern Sudanese who have been resettled as refugees. Sudanese in Canada, Australia, and other places are important to the overall context of Sudanese migration and the maintenance of transnational ties. This study, however, focuses primarily on linkages between southern Sudanese in the United States and Africa. As noted in the introductory chapter, approximately 25,000 Sudanese have been resettled in the United States since the early 1990s when these placement efforts got underway. About a sixth of this population is comprised of the so-called lost boys of Sudan, young men from Kakuma camp in Kenya who had been orphaned or otherwise separated from their families during the war (Bixler 2005; Schechter 2004).

Politics of the Past

Various representations of history in Sudan are linked to larger assumptions and political agendas (Bond and Gilliam 1994). Moreover, the making of war is seldom a transparent process, and Sudan is no exception. J. Millard Burr and Robert Collins (1995, xi), writing the history of contemporary Sudan, note that their depiction was possible largely because of access to documents "most of which are unlikely ever to be made public." Furthermore, members of the Sudanese government and leaders of southern rebel factions, many of them with advanced degrees from European and North American institutions, actively seek to use representations of history to underscore their claims to political legitimacy (see Karadawi 1999).[4] This led some to dub the dimensions of the conflict that pitted southerners against southerners the war of the PhD's.

This politically charged climate is not, as long-time Sudan scholar Wendy James (1991, 299) points out, a setting that is conducive to nonpartisan academic research. Academics are not immune to the larger ideological context in which the United States takes an increasingly politicized stance toward Sudan. Furthermore, warfare in Sudan for more than two decades, as well as lapses in diplomatic ties between the United States and Sudan, render it a challenging environment for U.S. scholars to conduct research. These conditions make Hutchinson's (1996) historical ethnography of money, war, and the state in Sudan such a vital and pathbreaking work. Based primarily on fieldwork conducted just before southern Sudan was catapulted headlong into full-fledged war, her work is an essential link between what Evans-Pritchard reported and that of scholars of the Nuer diaspora.

Malkki (1995) critiques the erasure of historical context in constructing the category of faceless, nameless African refugees. This appraisal is well founded and speaks directly to one of the keys aims of this book: to explore the experience of Nuer forced migration within a broader temporal and spatial context. However, developing one clear understanding of the historical and political conditions feeding conflict is easier said than done (see Karadawi 1999; Terry 2002). And Malkki (1995), in fact, settles for crafting what she calls a "mythico-history" that reflects Burundian Hutus' view of the conditions precipitating conflict and displacement.

This historical overview seeks to provide a framework in which to con-textualize the more particular experiences relayed in this book. Key works that inform this review include a study of war and disaster relief on the Nile by Burr and Collins (1995); Evans-Pritchard's trilogy (1940a, 1951b, 1956); Johnson's study of Nuer prophets (1994) and other work about the causes of conflict (1988; 2004); Hutchinson's historical ethnography of Nuer people (1996) and other related publications (1990, 1994, 1999); Kelly's study of Nuer expansion (1985); Petterson's firsthand account as former U.S. ambassador to Sudan (1999); Jok's analysis of war and slavery in Sudan (2001); Bok's first-hand account of enslavement in Sudan (2003); Duany's (1992), Abusharaf's (1994), and Pitya's (1996) doctoral dissertations; and other texts, which will be detailed throughout this chapter (see, for example, Alier 1990; Daly and Sikainga 1993; Deng and Gifford 1987). I supplement this review with origi-nal interview data to illustrate the linkages with the lives of Nuer living in the United States.

POLITICS OF PLACE

Often the conflict that divided Sudan is described in geographic terms of North versus South, defined as the six northern regions—Khartoum, Darfur, Northern, Eastern, Blue Nile, and Kordofan—and three southern regions— Bahr al-Ghazal, Upper Nile, and Equatoria. The majority population in the North identifies themselves as Arab and Muslim while a politically margin-alized population in the South, including the Nuer, identifies themselves as black African and increasingly as Christian (Hutchinson 1999).

Yet, as numerous scholars have argued, and as the more recent crisis in Darfur illustrates, this geographic distinction glosses over much more com-plex social, historical, economic, and geostrategic processes that contribute to the framing of conflict in Sudan (see, for example, Abusharaf 1994; Burr and Collins 1995; Johnson 1988, 2004; Jok and Hutchinson 1999; Hutchinson 1996). In particular, this depiction creates the false impression that geography and politics are coterminous in Sudan. For instance, noted Sudanese scholar Francis Deng (1972) points out that the Ngok Dinka, located in the Kordofan region, are in all respects affiliated as southern Sudanese, but geographically they live in the northern region. Furthermore, it suggests a united north-ern or southern stance, which Hutchinson (1999, 3) refutes in describing the escalating conflict during the 1990s associated with "South-on-South" violence. The labile nature of politics, definitions of place, and the complex relationship between the two are challenges to understanding the ebb and flow of the conflict. Between 1983 and 1994, the country was divided three times into various configurations of states, provinces, and local government areas. A 1994 constitutional decree redivided the country into twenty-six states (Stock 1996, 921), southern Sudan has ten, an area of 648,052 square kilometers, or a quarter of the total land area of Sudan.

Sudan's vast size, covering more than 2.5 million square kilometers—or roughly 8 percent of the African continent—contributes to its characterization as a crossroads within Africa. Sudan shares borders with Egypt, Libya, Chad, Central African Republic, Democratic Republic of the Congo, Uganda, Kenya, Ethiopia, and Eritrea, and it opens onto the Red Sea.

The geographic placement of Sudan, spanning the customary divide between North Africa and sub-Saharan Africa, challenges accepted categorizations frequently deployed by Africanist scholars. For instance, Ghana frequently is advanced as the first sub-Saharan, or "black African" country to gain its independence from European colonial rule even though Sudanese independence on January 1, 1956, predated Ghana's on March 6, 1957, by more than a year. Indeed, categorizing Sudan as a North African rather than sub-Saharan country can be viewed as a political act, legitimating the position of the Khartoum government. To illustrate this point, two recent doctoral theses produced by Sudanese scholars at U.S. universities, one from northern Sudan and one from southern Sudan, reflect the complex nature of presenting one accepted view of Sudan. Wal Duany (1992, 20), a Nuer political scientist whose dissertation explores the constitution of order among the Nuer, writes, "the Sudan lies in central Africa." Rogaia Mustafa Abusharaf (1994, 1), a northern Sudanese, in her anthropological dissertation on (primarily northern) Sudanese migration to the United States and Canada, writes that her country "is situated in Northeast Africa." A third doctoral dissertation by Philip Pitya, a southerner, on the history of Christian evangelism in Sudan, neatly sidesteps the thorny issue by describing the location of Sudan in technical terms of latitude and longitude: Sudan extends from longitude 38° E to 22° E and latitude 3° N to 22° N (Pitya 1996, 32). The line of demarcation between northern and southern Sudan, drawn by Anglo-Egyptians, follows the tenth parallel (Allan 1996, 921). This chapter will explore the myriad ways in which territory intersects the related domain of politics in this setting.

Evans-Pritchard (1940a, 1951b, 1956) described Nuer people who inhabited the Unity, Jonglei, and Sobat areas, or the Southern Clay Plains, of the Upper Nile region in Sudan, as well as the nineteenth-century processes of Nuer conquest that account in part for contemporary Nuer territorial placement in Sudan. (See also Kelly 1985.) The impermeable quality of the soil results in flooding, which necessitates the mode of transhumant pastoral existence for which the Nuer are well known. Nuer people occupy three-

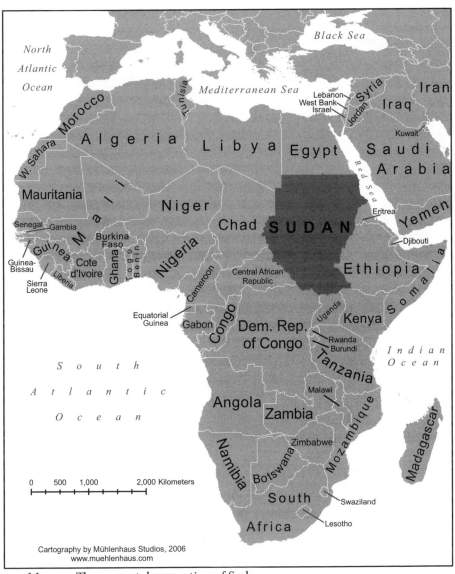

Map 2.1. The current demarcation of Sudan.

quarters of the Upper Nile region; the Anuak, Dinka, Murle, and Shilluk peoples inhabit the remaining quarter (Duany 1992, 29). Malakal, located in Nasir District, is the principal city in the Upper Nile region.

Curiously, given the important role the Nuer hold in the anthropological imagination in terms of people and place, the visual images many have of Nuer and their environs are representations of Ethiopian rather than Sudanese Nuer. Robert Gardner's 1970 film *The Nuer* seemingly captures the southern Sudanese images written about by Evans-Pritchard (1940a); Gardner's film, however, was shot among Nuer in southwestern Ethiopia. (For more on Ethiopian Nuer, see Falge 1997; Feyissa 2003; MacDermot 1972.) According to one of my informants, James Khot, a Gaajok man in his late twenties who was born in Sudan, there are no discernible differences between Sudanese and Ethiopian Nuer: "There is no difference in the language, the way they look, the way they live. Some families have two homes—one in Ethiopia and one in Sudan. When you come from Sudan, you can say you are Ethiopian. It's difficult to identify people in the area." (See also MacDermot 1972, 149.) Notions of Nuer identity that cross national borders may not be problematic to Nuer themselves, but national identity and citizenship become of utmost importance in qualifying for refugee status.

COORDINATES OF DISPLACEMENT: "I AM SUDAN"

A valid issue in discussions of displacement is the extent to which the migrants identify in terms of ethnic group or national membership. Holtzman reports that a Nuer ethnic category, when contrasted with a Sudanese national identity, "is most meaningful to the Nuer themselves." He goes on to note that "being Nuer was much more important than being Sudanese" (2000, 110–11). In contrast, I found that despite a sense of Nuer identity that seemingly transcends national borders, national identity—namely affiliation with Sudan—matters to the Sudanese refugees with whom I worked. They spoke only of South Sudan, Southern Sudan, or New Sudan as possibilities for naming a future, imagined, independent state. What I think this all suggests is that Nuer, Sudanese, and African, while not interchangeable terms, are forms of self-identification that Nuer emphasize in different contexts.

Luke Tap, a Gaajak man in his early twenties who was born in a refugee camp in Ethiopia and now lives in the United States, describes his relationship to Sudan: "I was born in the refugee camp. So, in our culture, when we were in Kenya and we get a kid, we call them Sudanese. We don't call them a citizen of Kenya. And me, too, when I was born in Ethiopia, they did not recognize me as a citizen of Ethiopia. I am Sudan. Both of my parents are

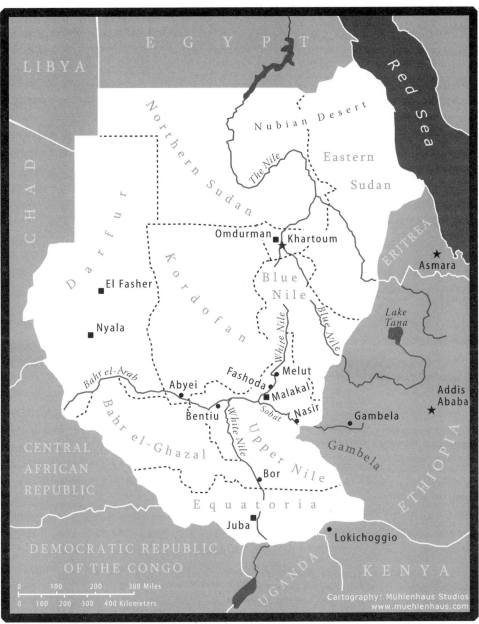

Map 2.2. Division of Sudan.

Sudanese." In another example, Akol, an Anuak man in his thirties, when pressed for his official nationality, said that he was "technically Ethiopian," but that he considered himself to be "ethnic Sudanese" and was resettled in the United States as a Sudanese refugee. His experience is not unique. Within the United States, some of the Nuer who came under the category of Sudanese refugees could be categorized as Ethiopian nationals.

For both Akol and Luke, diasporic identity is linked to territory in profound ways although neither man was born in the country in which he claims national affiliation. To a limited extent, it may be possible to attribute this sense of being "ethnic Sudanese" to shifting borders. The contours delimiting the current Republic of the Sudan were codified in 1899 when Britain and Egypt signed a condominium-rule agreement for the governance of Sudan.[5] Yet colonial and postcolonial gerrymandering to suit strategic political ends renegotiated these national boundaries over time. More important, perhaps, are the ways in which Sudanese identity has been politicized over time.

Locating the Nuer

The following quote from the fourth edition of a noted text on Sudanese history by P. M. Holt and M. W. Daly illustrates that African historiography detailing events and populations in southern Sudan remains inadequately understood: "The southern Sudan contains a bewildering variety of ethnic groups and languages. Unlike Northerners, its peoples are not generally Muslims, nor do they claim Arab descent; although there has been some degree of islamization and arabization" (1988, 3). Southern Sudan needs to be understood as more than a limited refraction of what took place in the North. (See also Johnson 2004, xiv.) There are an estimated two hundred northern ethnic groups, which are typically categorized into five major groupings: Nubians, Beja, Afro-Arabs, Nubans, and Furs (Pitya 1996, 35). Northern communities tend to be united by a common language (Arabic) and religion (Islam). The people of southern Sudan represent approximately fifty ethnic groups but are not united by a common language or religion. Southerners are broadly grouped into three categories: Nilotes, Nilo-Hamites, and Sudanics.[6]

The Nuer are a Nilotic people. They are considered most culturally, physically, and linguistically similar to the Dinka. For Evans-Pritchard, one of the most distinctive characteristics of the Nuer was their lack of a centralized political administration, which he referred to as segmentary lineage organization. Evans-Pritchard describes Nuer political structure as follows:

The largest political segment among the Nuer is the tribe. There is no larger group who, besides recognizing themselves as a distinct local community, affirm their obligation to combine in warfare against outsiders and acknowledge the rights of their members to compensation for injury. A tribe is divided into a number of territorial segments and these are more than geographical divisions, for the members of each consider themselves to be distinct communities and sometimes act as such. We call the largest tribal segments "primary sections," and the segments of a primary section "secondary sections," and the segments of a secondary section "tertiary sections." A tertiary section consists of a number of villages, which are the smallest political units of Nuerland. (1940a, 5)

Duany (1992, 1) notes the division of societies into "state-governed" and "stateless," or acephalous, societies and probes the ways in which Nuer society, as an acephalous society, is so ordered because of the potential benefits of these societies in avoiding despotic regimes.

Evans-Pritchard (1940a, 5) notes that the Nuer differentiate between those who live to the west of the Nile River and those who have migrated to the east of it. This was a relevant distinction among Nuer refugees in the United States, who referred to western Nuer as "the real people." This was particularly true in instances where I would inquire about two different Nuer words with the same meaning. One word was used by western Nuer, and the other was used by eastern Nuer. The eastern Nuer regarded the western Nuer word as more authentic because the area to the west of the Nile is seen as the original homeland of the Nuer. (See also Duany 1992, 28.) My work with Nuer in the United States, which privileged the voices of eastern Nuer, revealed a recognition of difference between eastern and western Nuer; however, I did not find the politicization of this difference that Deborah Scroggins (2002) describes in conflicts in Sudan in the mid-1990s. More interviews with western Nuer—who are far fewer in number in the United States—might have led to a different finding in this regard.

Most Nuer in the United States who have been resettled as refugees originated from lineages situated to the east of the Nile. Consistent with what other scholars have reported, the eastern Jikany Nuer (Jikany Doar) can be broken down into Gaajak, Gaajok, and Gaaguang subgroups (Evans-Pritchard 1940a, 140; Hutchinson 1996). A Gaajak Nuer informant in Ethiopia refined this model by breaking Gaajak into subsections: Cie Reng, Thiang Tar, Thiang Cieng Kang, and Gaguong. Gaguong then branches into Cie

Waw, Cie Nyajani, and Cie Cany. Thiang Tar and Cie Nyajani tend to live on the Ethiopian side of the border. Cie Reng and Cie Waw tend to live on the Sudanese side. Cie Cany are equally likely to come from the Sudanese as from the Ethiopian side.

One reason for greater numbers of eastern, as opposed to western, Nuer in the United States is the proximity of eastern Nuer homelands to international borders—that is, Ethiopia and Kenya. In addition, some eastern Nuer made use of extended family ties with Ethiopian-based Nuer when they decided to migrate. Western Nuer, on the other hand, generally followed established transportation routes northward to Khartoum. Some western Nuer then traveled to Cairo. Hutchinson (1996, 11) provides a detailed map of war-induced migration of Sudanese civilians between roughly 1984 and 1992. Other western Nuer described a perilous journey into Ethiopia, entering to the north of where most eastern Jikany Nuer did, and a stint laboring on Ethiopian farms as a way of securing safe passage across the border and the cash necessary for transport to Addis Ababa. In Ethiopia, while I interviewed many who described walking for days in Sudan, I encountered no one who indicated that they had reached Addis on foot. They described the journey as too dangerous and instead secured the money necessary to pay for bus transport to cross Ethiopia.

Sudanese historian Gabriel Jal, who was interviewed in the 1980s for a documentary film called *Strange Beliefs* (1990), depicting the contributions of Evans-Pritchard to anthropology, notes the significance of the urban-rural split within Nuer society. This was a salient social division in my research as well. Most Nuer I interviewed in the United States lived in rural rather than urban areas before leaving Sudan; others were born in refugee camps in Ethiopia. The small number who were living in towns and cities, such as Malakal in the South or Khartoum in the North, often to attend school, maintained strong ties with rural areas by spending large amounts of time with their relatives in the villages. For example, one of my key informants, who was raised in the city of Nasir, describes visits to his father's village, where he would sit quietly at the edge of the home of the *kuar kuach* (leopard skin priest). He would listen to village problems being mediated. Therefore, while this man grew up in an urban setting, he had profound and detailed knowledge of village events, problems, and daily life. Another informant described the relationship between town and village for Nuer people:

> Even professionals, when they are not at work or they have a break, they can still fish. They can still cultivate. Most Sudanese, they have two lives. When they get breaks they go to visit the village. I used to

wish it would not end when I went to the village. In the village you don't have to worry about things. Professionals get money, but they cannot get all the things they want. So, that is why I fish and cultivate. They get money, but I get other things.

Gordon Duoth, a Gaaguang man in his thirties, spent his teen years in the town of Nasir, rather than the village. He also speaks of life in the rural area in an idealized way, and his concerns about life in urban areas in Sudan echo, at a certain level, the concerns of many Sudanese in coping with life in the United States.

My store, it was removable. When the rain came I could put things in a bag and go away. I sold soap, tea, gum, small things people need. I did this when I lived in Nasir because I see that I need money. At night when I would go to sleep, I would think about needing money. It is stress. In the rural area, in the villages, it is not like this. If you are hungry and someone has food, they will ask you if you want some. In the town, you need money.

Hutchinson (1996) describes the labor migration of Nuer and other southern people to Khartoum to work in the construction industry. The Khartoum government's eviction of these migrants contributed to the escalation of conflict in 1983. In my research with Nuer who had been resettled in the United States, however, I encountered almost no one who reported having worked as a labor migrant.

God, Gold, Oil, and Water

Hutchinson (1999), as well as a number of my informants, identified oil, gold, and water as the three most powerful economic forces that fueled the North-South conflict in Sudan: oil is located in Upper Nile and Bahr al-Ghazal provinces; gold is found in Equatoria; and the headwaters of the White Nile hold great geostrategic importance. I add religion as an ideological force coalescing with economic forces to make the plight of southern Sudanese noticeable to U.S. policy makers.

Clearly, the geographic boundaries associated with control of these resources and the configuration of government can be linked directly to colonial rule in Sudan from 1898 to 1956 (Sarkesian 1973; Abusharaf 1994, 6). However, another view shared both by scholars (for example, Jok 2001) and many of my Nuer informants suggests that Muslim exploitation precedes colonial rule and can be seen in the nineteenth-century raiding of the South for ivory, gold, and, in terms of the most lingering sentiments, slaves. Pitya, for instance, sums up the depth of emotion present in Southern perspectives on events that occurred more than a century ago: "The region was buried under an unfathomable agony, heart-wrenching wretchedness and death" (1996, 46–47). (For a similar sentiment, see also Deng 1972, 7.) Eerily evocative of contemporary depictions of Sudan, this quote underscores the deep-seated and complex nature of identifying the "source" or "root cause" of conflict (Zolberg, Suhrke, and Aguayo 1989).

The precolonial history of Sudan, of which only relevant highlights will be presented here, assumes vital importance in understanding current contexts. (For more detailed accounts, see Burr and Collins 1995; Hill 1970; Jal 1987; Johnson 1994, 2004; Kelly 1985; Pitya 1996.) Similar to what Malkki (1995) describes to explain the Hutu-Tutsi conflict in Rwanda, southern Sudanese assert their primacy to territory based on notions of autochthony and historical representations that depict northern Muslims as immigrants.

The dominant theme in Sudanese precolonial history is the way in which southern Sudan has been engaged in a process of articulation with significant external forces for a very long time. Briefly, this history can be divided into four periods: the ancient Christian and Nubian (3200 BCE–1500 CE), the Muslim (1500–1821), the Turkiyya (1821–85), and the Mahdiyya, or Mahdist (1885–98). Many scholars, relying on written records, situate the beginning of the documented history for southern Sudan as 1839, when the Turco-Egyptians under Albanian Ottoman ruler Mohammed 'Ali crossed the swampy stretch separating the tropical region to engage in large-scale and violent extraction of both slaves and ivory for export to Arabia (Zolberg, Suhrke, and Aguayo 1989, 50; Pitya 1996, 46). Evans-Pritchard (1940a), drawing on archaeological and linguistic data, plots eastward Nuer migration and expansion across the Nile at the beginning of the nineteenth century.

The Muslim period is characterized by the rise of the Funj kingdom, a confederation of ethnic states about which little is known conclusively. The Turkiyya period represents the conquest of northern Sudan by Mohammed 'Ali. Significant in this period is the way in which southerners joined forces with northerners to oppose external forces. In the early 1880s, Mohammed Ahmed al-Mahdi proclaimed a jihad (holy war) against the Turco-Egyptian armies. Slave trading–induced chaos fueled the rise of Mahdi supporters against Ottoman rule, leading to his takeover of northern Sudan. Pitya (1996, 48) depicts the Mahdist period as a time when southerners fought alongside the Mahdist movement "to regain their freedom" from Ottoman rule. Later, however, Pitya (48) asserts, southerners had to stave off Mahdist control to retain their freedom. Nonetheless, Pitya (291) recounts Bari songs emphasizing the sentiment that "the British colonial forces were spoilers, not saviors" in their quest to stop the Mahdi.

The Mahdist period has an enduring historical resonance in terms of Western intervention in Sudan. The Mahdi defeated British general Charles Gordon but died shortly thereafter from typhus. In response to Gordon's fall and the insult this represented for the British Empire, British and Egyptian forces, under General H. Herbert Kitchener, subdued Sudanese resistance, led by the Mahdi's successor, the khalifa ʿAbdullah, in 1898 at a battle near Omdurman. In contrast to the West's general neglect of African history, these events have received a great deal of attention and are etched into the Euro-American popular consciousness by two popularly acclaimed films: *The Four Feathers* (1939), directed by Zoltan Korda (and its 2002 remake, directed by Shekhar Kapur), and *Khartoum* (1966), directed by Basil Dearden.[7] A central theme in both films is the death of heroic "white Christian" Gordon at the hands of "black Muslims"; Pitya (1996, 137) asserts that Gordon's death and the way it is remembered later served as a catalyst for missionary work there, too. Both films speak in profound ways to motivations behind contemporary humanitarian interventions in Sudan (see also Scroggins 2002).

Shortly after Britain's reprisal for Gordon's death, Britain and Egypt signed an agreement on January 19, 1899, to administer Sudan through a joint-power arrangement. Upon signing the condominium arrangement, a systematic process of "pacification" was begun to subjugate the eastern, western, and southern areas that had not yet been subject to European occupation. Johnson (1994) details some of these confrontations and the efforts to suppress the leadership of Nuer prophets.

By the eve of World War I, Christian missionaries were fairly ensconced in these areas. The interwar years saw a consolidation and expansion of evangelistic activity in the South (Pitya 1996, 287), and this topic will be addressed in further detail below. In the South, Sudanese resistance to British rule continued in an overt manner until Britain flexed the muscle of empire: it aerial-bombed a Nuer village in southern Sudan in 1928, effectively quashing anti-British uprisings among "the last indigenous people in British Africa to be conquered by force of arms" (James 1990). Beginning in 1930 in the wake of this rather dramatic series of events, Evans-Pritchard conducted fieldwork among the Nuer.

Johnson observes that the so-called Southern Policy of 1930 "put into words what was already administrative practice" by declaring "that the administration of the South was to be developed along 'African' rather than 'Arab' lines, and that the future of the southern Sudan might ultimately lie

with the countries of British East Africa, rather than with the Middle East."
(2004, 11). Johnson describes the rationale behind these policies as an attempt to quell disruptive foreign influences on "tribal discipline." He goes on
to note that the interwar years had "increased the Sudan government's sensitivity to external subversion and the movement of ideas, but this sensitivity
was sharpened by the new theories of native administration" (29). Notable
features of the Southern Policy were the attempts to restrict travel between
North and South and prohibitions against teaching Arabic and against Islamic proselytizing in the South.

In 1953 Britain and Egypt signed an accord that put an end to the condominium arrangement and granted Sudan self-government in three years.
Significantly, Britain excluded the possibility for self-administration of the
three southern provinces (Johnson 1994, 298). In 1955 southern soldiers mutinied, resulting in several hundred casualties. The mutiny was quashed with
British assistance, but some mutineers escaped and later, in 1963, formed the
guerilla military organization Anya Nya (later called Anya Nya I), meaning
poison.

On the heels of renewed fighting, on January 1, 1956, a five-man council
of state was appointed to take over the powers of the governor general until
a new constitution was ratified, and Egyptian and British troops left Sudan.
Sudan gained its independence. The fighting escalated to civil war that was
to last for seventeen years. An estimated one million southern lives, or one-
quarter of its mid-1950s population, were lost (Akol 1994, 78). From 1959
to 1962 many southerners, including politicians, civil servants, students,
and subsistence farmers, sought refuge in neighboring African countries
(Pitya 1996, 54; Akol 1994; Karadawi 1999). These were the parents of some
of the Nuer who would be resettled as refugees in the United States some
thirty years later. By 1972 repatriation officials estimated that nearly 220,000
southern Sudanese refugees lived in neighboring countries (Akol 1994, 81).

A military coup placed Marchal Abboud in power from 1958 to 1964.
Under his military regime, there was an attempt to Islamize the South.
English-language instruction was abolished, and Arabic was made compul-
sory. Christian missionaries, who provided much of the formal schooling in
the South, were expelled in 1964.

In 1969 another military coup placed Gaafar Nimeiry in power. A viable
solution to address the conflict had been discussed in 1965, but it was not
enacted until the Addis Ababa peace accord, signed by the government of
Sudan and the southern rebels in 1972. The agreement ceded a substantial
degree of self-rule to the South, including control over natural resources.
The Sudanese government relied heavily on international organizations to

repatriate southern Sudanese living as refugees in other countries (Akol 1994, 80).

From 1972 until the early 1980s, the civil war abated in Sudan. Novelist and journalist Edward Hoagland spent three months in Sudan in 1977 and, in his acclaimed book *African Calliope,* reported that the seventeen-year civil war was euphemistically called the Troubles or the Disturbances by Northern Sudanese (1978, 21). Southerners who had been involved in the Anya Nya rebellion told Hoagland that dysentery, malnutrition, and malaria—indirect weapons of war—vied with actual massacres in claiming southern Sudanese lives.

The Addis Ababa agreement began to unravel and culminated in the 1983 imposition of shari'a, or Muslim law, in the South. Hutchinson identifies four political events leading up to this 1983 historical pivot. The Khartoum government sought to modify the administrative boundary between North and South. Government security forces "launched a campaign to arrest and evict thousands of southern Sudanese labor migrants from the capital." The construction site for a Chevron oil refinery was moved from a southern to a northern town. And finally, the North sought to "redivide the south into three autonomous regions" (1996, 3–4). Hutchinson (1996, 4) goes on to explain that the purpose of the recent civil war had been to obtain regional autonomy for a united south; the Khartoum government's actions in the early 1980s threatened to nullify that agreement.

This period coincided with the 1983–85 drought in western and eastern Sudan (see Burr and Collins 1995). History repeated itself in certain respects when government soldiers from the South mutinied once again. These mutineers joined another loosely organized, mostly Nuer, rebel group called Anya Nya II, invoking the earlier Anya Nya movement. This gave rise to the Southern Peoples' Liberation Movement (SPLM) and its military wing, the Southern Peoples' Liberation Army (SPLA). In 1999 an American journalist reported that the SPLA, headed by John Garang, had between twenty and thirty thousand troops (Finnegan 1999, 63).[8]

On April 6, 1985, a military coup overthrew Nimeiry while he was out of the country on a state visit to the United States. Nimeiry spent fourteen years in exile in Egypt before visiting Sudan in 1999 (*New York Times* 1999). A few days after the 1985 coup, northern elections installed Sadiq al-Mahdi, grandson of the late-nineteenth-century ruler, as prime minister. In 1988 Sudan experienced a severe famine following a drought that resulted in approximately 250,000 deaths. The next year, an international consortium sponsored the development of Operation Lifeline-Sudan (OLS) to prevent further mass starvation (see Burr and Collins 1995).[9]

On June 30, 1989, another military coup led by the National Islamic Front ousted al-Mahdi. ʿOmar Hassan Ahmad al-Bashir seized power. Al-Bashir, in turn, installed Hassan al-Turabi as prime minister. Many in the North opposed the government and formed the National Democratic Alliance opposition party. Francis Deng, in a study of displacement in Sudan (1993, 68), summarized the charges against the al-Bashir government as follows: suspending the national constitution; dissolving all political parties, trade unions, and civil associations; and repealing freedoms of the press, assembly, movement, and residence. He also notes reports by Amnesty International that detail the routine torture, ill-treatment, detentions, and extrajudicial killings of Sudanese citizens (see also Human Rights Watch 1994, 1996).

These events coincided with a radical shift in global politics. The years 1989 and 1990 were pivotal in a global context as geopolitical allegiances were realigned to reflect post–Cold War realities. The 1989 military coup also brought a swift change in U.S. foreign policy toward Sudan, opening the door for a limited number of refugees to be resettled in the United States. Clearly, the decision to resettle Sudanese refugees in the United States, getting underway in 1989–90, was as much a political as a humanitarian decision on the part of the U.S. government. Throughout the 1980s, the United States was a major supplier of military weapons to Sudan, because the country was perceived as a key strategic neighbor of Soviet-backed Ethiopia and Libya (Hutchinson 1996; Burr and Collins 1995). On February 26, 1993, the World Trade Center in New York City was bombed by Shaykh ʿOmar ʿAbd al-Rahman, who was linked to some Sudanese agents at the UN (Lobban, Kramer, and Fluehr-Lobban 2002, lxiii). Later that year, in August, the United States added Sudan to its list of alleged state sponsors of terrorism.[10] In 1996 the United States closed its embassy in Khartoum. (For a detailed first-person account of this period, see Petterson 1999.) In 1997 the United States imposed economic sanctions against Sudan. And in August 1998, in the wake of the bombing of the U.S. embassies in Kenya and Tanzania, the United States conducted what was referred to in the media as "a surgical bombing" of a pharmaceutical plant in an industrial section of Khartoum, alleging connections to Osama bin Laden.

The southern rebel groups underwent a dizzying period of divisions and reconfigurations throughout the 1990s, and these events influenced the lives of Nuer in the United States (see below). Johnson (2004, 195–221) and Lobban, Kramer, and Fluehr-Lobban (2002, liv–lxxiv) provide very detailed chronologies of events related to this period, of which only highlights will be presented here. From the perspective of U.S.-based Nuer, a seminal event occurred in late August 1991, when the Nuer soldier and politician Riek Teny Dhurgon Machar, Nuer former Anya Nya II member Gordon Kong Chol, and Shilluk soldier and politician Lam Akol staged a coup against SPLA leader John Garang (Johnson 2004, 202; Jok and Hutchinson 1999; Lobban, Kramer, and Fluehr-Lobban 2002, 170–71), forming the Nasir faction of the SPLA.[11] By 1992 SPLA-Nasir and SPLA-Mainstream were engaged in a civil war. Strife mounted in southern Sudan in 1992 when the Sudanese government attacked rebel outposts. These measures had a downward spiraling effect because they resulted in the suspension of the OLS's distribution of food aid. Around the same time, Chevron sold its oil interests in Sudan to the Sudanese government (Johnson 2004, 202). In September 1993 Machar renamed his group the Southern Sudan Independence Movement (SSIM) (Lobban, Kramer, and Fluehr-Lobban 2002, lxiv); this group was intent on defeating not only the northern government forces but also John Garang and his forces (see also Jok and Hutchinson 1999). In a controversial move in April 1996, Machar and Kwanyin Kerubino Bol signed the Political Charter sponsored by the National Islamic Front in Khartoum (Lobban, Kramer, and Fluehr-Lobban 2002, 170). In April 1997 Machar and others created the Southern Sudan Defense Force, allied with the government, and Machar maintained a political presence in Khartoum when he was appointed chairman of the Southern States Coordination Council. In 1999, Machar created the Sudanese People's Democratic Front and split with the Khartoum government. On January 8, 2002, Machar reconciled with the SPLA (Mainstream). In summer 2004 Nuer in the diaspora (both in the United States and Ethiopia) indicated that Machar was slated to be named second in charge, after Garang, as a part of the impending peace agreement, an event that appeared unlikely to materialize when two weeks before his death Garang named Salva Kiir Mayardit as his deputy. In this position, Kiir was selected as the commander in chief of the Sudan People's Liberation Movement and as Garang's replacement as national vice president. Ultimately, however, after Garang's death Riek Machar was installed as vice president of South Sudan on August 11, 2005.

It is not possible to disentangle the ethnic elements of the struggle from the political ambitions of the leaders of the various factions. It would be far too simplistic to describe southern divisiveness, as is sometimes done, in terms of Nuer-Dinka animosity. Yet the need to convene a Nuer-Dinka Peace Conference in 1999 speaks to the existence of the rift. Peter Burns, a humanitarian-assistance worker who has worked in Sudan and around the globe, spoke of his experience with the Nuer-Dinka divide:

The split between the SSIM (now renamed) and the SPLA has very deep ethnic overtones. I doubt, however, that you will find it a useful exercise to untangle the ethnic from the political, the political from the ambitions of individuals. There is no ethnic conflict without political manipulations. Nuer IDPs [internally displaced people] in Khartoum I spoke with described Dinka domination of the SPLA and the southern government before the war as a key motivation of their split. I have heard Dinka SPLA supporters talking of collective revenge against the Nuer for their treason: "We will drive them into Ethiopia," one of them told me. "They will not come back. This will not be forgiven." I don't know about the massacres in 1992 after the split, but I have been told that much of the killing was on strictly ethnic grounds. (pers. comm, August 26, 2000.)

Clearly, however, any division among southern rebels benefited the northern Sudanese government's aims (see also Hutchinson 1999).

The pace of change, the informal means by which news of the shifting political terrain in Sudan was communicated to Nuer in the United States, and the often unspoken political ambitions of U.S.-based Nuer all combine to thwart clear themes in how, precisely, shifting alliances in Africa are linked to emerging diasporic groups. U.S.-based Sudanese refugees whom I interviewed immediately following the 1998 U.S. bombing in Khartoum expressed general support for what they perceived as an attack on the government of Sudan. Other Sudanese, with close ties to the SSIM rebel faction that was allied with the Sudanese government at the time of the attack feared the impact the bombing would have on Sudanese peace prospects.

Broadly speaking, the division of Sudanese in the United States mirrors ethnic lines in Sudan in terms of Nuer-Dinka animosity. For instance, in the summer of 1998, I had an opportunity to interview noted Sudanese scholar Francis Deng, who is Dinka. Shortly after the interview, I was speaking with a group of Nuer men and began to relay a Dinka myth of origin that Deng had recounted to me. As I was telling the story, the men became increasingly agitated until one man shouted out, "And where is God for the Dinka now?" referring to the famine that was engulfing Dinka areas that summer. The men were offended that Deng had attributed this myth of origin to the Dinka, while they clearly considered it a Nuer myth of origin.

But the evolving situation is more complex than a simple Nuer-Dinka divide, as there are intra-Nuer alliances and hostilities and Nuer hostilities with other groups, such as the Anuak. (For an in-depth discussion of Nuer-Anuak relations, see Feyissa 2003.) For instance, it was not until I was interviewing an Anuak family that I learned that the term *Bar* (which I had been using liberally, having understood that it was a Nuer term for people without cattle) was considered pejorative by Anuak people. When I later brought this point up to a Nuer woman, she began a litany of abuses against her family in Ethiopia by Anuak people.

The various configurations and reconfigurations of southern rebel groups seem to wax and wane in importance in understanding the social and political organization of Sudanese groups in the United States. For instance, from 1996 to 1998 the overwhelming majority of Nuer men and women in the United States whom I interviewed expressed support for Riek Machar. Indeed, a means of casting aspersions on another Nuer was to intimate that their allegiances lay with John Garang and the SPLA. Nuer refugees reported abuse, torture, and death at the hands of John Garang. One Nuer man said, "If Garang hears you make mistakes, he kills you or sends you to jail forever. He would probably kill you. This is what split the SPLA. We have the enemy and die every day, so why do you kill us? He was like Bashir. The enemy." Nuer people I interviewed perceived a U.S. government bias in favor of John Garang over Riek Machar because Garang had completed his doctorate in the United States.

While Nuer in the United States tended to voice support for Riek Machar during much of the 1990s, that support varied with respect to events in Sudan. Machar's alliance with the Khartoum government, which some saw as a tactical maneuver, had worn thin with many of his supporters by late 1999. Some of those same people who had critiqued John Garang earlier began to talk of possibilities for supporting the SPLA. Some of the men I interviewed had served under Garang or Machar or both. Experiences as a combatant were not, however, a topic that informants discussed readily. Therefore, I have very little data on the military connections or service of my informants. (Serving as a combatant can jeopardize refugee status.) Two young Nuer men briefly described being recruited into the SPLA. They recounted throwing their guns into the bush and then seeking access to a refugee camp. Another Nuer man, while we were driving together from Washington, D.C., to Nashville, pointed out the advantages and disadvantages of the terrain we were passing through from a soldier's perspective—hills that would be helpful for snipers, wooded areas that would put those unfamiliar with the area at a disadvantage.

Human Rights Watch perhaps summarizes the difficulty in finding heroes in the tragic circumstances of Sudan in the title to one of their recent books, *Abuses by All Parties in the War in Southern Sudan* (1994). The explanation offered by one Nuer informant suggested that ego and political agendas outweighed the needs and concerns of refugees: "The Government controls towns. Rebels control other areas. The leaders are all there to fulfill their dreams." (See also Jok and Hutchinson 1999; Scroggins 2002.)

Education, Religion, and Politics

This study singles out education, religion, and politics for analysis as a particularly salient constellation in contemporary Sudanese politics, as they all relate to displacement. Indeed, these three variables are inextricably intertwined. Against the backdrop of political and economic marginalization of southerners presented thus far, these variables are relevant to understanding the displacement of Nuer refugees and their incorporation into the United States.

It is challenging to disentangle the threads of religious persecution of the minority Christians by the politically, economically, and numerically dominant Muslims. Anti-Muslim sentiment among my Nuer informants ran high. For example, driving in a car with a Nuer informant behind someone with a pro-Allah bumper sticker incited a diatribe against all believers of Islam and the religion itself. Paul, a Gaajok man in his late twenties who was attending college, implied that Islam symbolized much more than a belief system: "Most of the southern Sudanese here are Christian. They oppose Islam because of their treatment by Arabs. If the Arabs didn't treat the southerners badly, there would be a lot more Muslims in Sudan." Similarly, Johnson notes that "the current drive to Islamize the South has produced more Christian converts in the last decade than the entire colonial missionary enterprise did during the first half of the twentieth century" (2004, xvi).

Therefore, religion and education have gone hand in hand in Sudan: missionary spheres were drawn up for the Nuer regions, and for southerners religious missions are important in understanding education. Religion and education are linked to politics in Sudan, as educational credentials function as a filter limiting access to opportunities. Johnson notes the inequities in the ways in which southern Sudanese were slated for incorporation into an independent Sudanese state were linked intimately to educational opportunity. "Out of an estimated population of nearly half a million, the Nuer had only one college-level graduate, no more than half a dozen secondary school students approaching completion of their education. The 'Sudanization' of administration prior to independence meant the appointment of northern Sudanese with no previous experience in the South, rather than the elevation of the Nuer to self-government" (1994, 298).

Limited access for southerners to education is reminiscent of apartheid rule in Namibia and South Africa, where the black segment of the population was excluded systematically from opportunities linked to social mobility. Yet it is religion as a basis of persecution that renders the situation in Sudan distinct from other settings where a majority population oppresses a minority population. In contrast to Rwanda, Burundi, or Liberia, for example, the religious element of the Sudan conflict makes those who flee fit the category of what Zolberg, Suhrke, and Aguayo (1989) would call "classic refugees." Whereas international refugee law may not recognize hunger as a justifiable reason for refugee status, it does recognize the right to religious freedom.

Apart from distant sixth-century roots of early Christianity, in Sudan modern Christianity got underway in the twentieth century. Historically, the most influential among evangelistic Christian movements in Sudan have been the Anglican Church Missionary Society, the American United Presbyterian Mission, and the Roman Catholic Mission (Pitya 1996). Pitya (1996, 99) notes that the first contact between missionaries and Nuer, Shilluk, Dinka, and Bari peoples came at the end of 1849.[12] One Roman Catholic priest, from this first expedition to the South, remained and lived among the Bari people for two years. Two other Catholic missions were opened in the next few years among the Bari and the Dinka, but evangelistic work was hampered due to upheaval caused by the extraction of slaves and ivory (Pitya 1996, 101). From 1849 to 1881, successive waves of Catholic missionaries attempted to start and sustain missions in the South with little success. The last wave was marked by the arrival of the Verona Fathers in the 1870s (Pitya 1996, 104).[13]

The onset of condominium rule ushered in a new era for missionary activity in Sudan. Banned from evangelizing in the Muslim North, Christian missionaries focused their efforts on the South. Although evangelization was not permitted in the North, a number of Christian schools and hospitals were established there.

Despite numerous attempts by Catholics in the nineteenth century, however, it was not until the beginning of the twentieth century that Christian missionary activity got solidly underway in southern Sudan. In terms of internal borders, in addition to the divide between North and South, southern Sudan was carved into a configuration of "spheres of religious influence" that were apportioned for evangelical activities by various Christian denominational missions to avoid overlap and potential conflict. In addition to the return of the Catholics, Protestant missionaries entered the arena. Presbyterians in particular were well regarded by colonial authorities because of their educational work (Pitya 1996, 165). The goals of the government and the missions, however, were often at odds.

Missionaries consolidated their evangelistic activities in mission stations, and their agendas encompassed evangelization, Bible translation, the study of local languages and customs, education, medicine, industry (such as masonry), agriculture, and domestic duties (Pitya 1996, 167). Upon arrival in the early 1900s, the missionaries began to study southern Sudanese languages and customs (Pitya 1996, 253).[14] And in a statement evocative of claims made about promises of access to education that have been used as an incentive to recruit child soldiers in contemporary southern Sudan (see Scroggins 2002), Pitya goes on to note that "the missionaries perceived education as the handmaiden of evangelism" (1996, 176).

Religion, education, and other mission-based activities were conflated. In colonial Sudan, infrastructure, including hospitals and schools, was developed in the northern part of the country, while development in the southern part was left in the hands of Christian missionaries and eventually funded, in part, by the British authorities (Pitya 1996, 293; Sarkesian 1973, 6; James 1991).

Of particular relevance for Nuer areas, the American United Presbyterian Mission established a mission at Nasir in 1902 and their first formal school in the South in 1903 (Pitya 1996, 264). They established a second mission at Nasir in 1911 (264). English eventually was made the official language in southern Sudan, and became the language of instruction in the intermediate schools (342).

The British colonial authorities became heavily involved in southern Sudanese education in 1946 and 1947. Shortly after independence, the government took control of all southern mission schools, and in 1962 there were further limits on both foreign and Sudanese Christian evangelism, culminating in the 1964 expulsion of foreign missionaries (Pitya 1996, 52). Many of the schools in the South were destroyed during the war from 1955 to 1972. Akol reports that "most schools were not operational and consequently the majority of children had limited or no education" (1994, 85). Before the resurgence of the conflict in Sudan in 1983, 18 percent of the appropriate age group was enrolled in secondary school, and 50 percent of the appropriate age group was enrolled in primary school (Kabera 1989, 33). These statistics do not differentiate North from South, and large discrepancies would presumably exist between the two. Furthermore, these statistics represent estimates before the ensuing seventeen years of war. In fact, only a handful of men whom I interviewed had attended tertiary educational institutions before leaving Africa, and most of them had attended university in Egypt. I encountered only two men who had completed their studies before coming to the United States—one chemical engineer and one medical doctor. Both of these men were facing long years of retraining to obtain the necessary credentials to be licensed in the United States and are typical of immigrant groups that are deemed underemployed.

Pitya (1996, 365–69) suggests a number of factors that contributed to the increase in Christian conversions from several hundred southern Christians in 1913 to an estimated one to two million southern Sudanese Christians today. He traces rapid expansion of Christianity in Sudan to the period between 1928 and 1947. The East African Revival Movement, later known as Barakole, which had begun in Uganda in the late 1920s, had an impact in Sudan. A second revival movement among high school students in southern Sudan also created converts. (To place this conversion process within a wider theoretical context, see Peterson and Allman 1999.) Greater cooperation, increased communication, and collaboration among Protestant missionaries resulted in more converts. Protestant-Catholic rivalry spurred missions to work harder at evangelization efforts, and in the 1940s the first Sudanese deacons and priests were ordained.

In her earlier work, Hutchinson (1996) notes that the most recent conversions, since the missionaries were expelled in 1964, should be seen as an event fueled by internal forces in Sudan; however, her current research focuses on the ways in which renewed missionary efforts are related to the existence of Nuer diaspora groups in the United States and contribute to contemporary violence not only in terms of Muslim-Christian hostilities, but within Christian groups themselves. In particular, she is charting the escalation of intra-Nuer violence along newly formed ecclesiastical divisions that correlate in disturbing ways with Nuer segmentation (Hutchinson 2000).

This chapter has provided a framework for understanding the linkages between the lives of Nuer in the United States and those remaining in Africa. It has sought to contextualize the "North-South" conflict within a broader historiography. It has highlighted the importance of pre-colonial, colonial, and post-colonial forces, with special reference to the interwoven issues of education, religion, and politics. It has also described the key factors fueling the conflict in Sudan and the conditions precipitating departure for the Nuer described in this book. This chapter, while not endeavoring to be exhaustive in its treatment of historical forces shaping contemporary Sudan, has attempted to telescope in to pinpoint key historical events, particularly during the tumultuous 1990s, as identified by commentators in the U.S.-based Nuer diaspora. Through an examination of the causes and consequences of this conflict, it is possible to place individual Nuer lives described in the case studies that follow within a larger context of devastation, and the accompanying uncertainty and rapid social change. Nuer experiences take shape as strategies, but ones that are conditioned by the circumstances in which they are lived.

3

Constructing Refugees

It is useful to consider the following juxtaposed images, both representing contemporary Nuer realities:

> A Nuer youth lies prone alongside two other boys on the dusty clay ground on the outskirts of a village in southern Sudan. A man crouches over him with a razor blade. Beginning with the right side, the man makes six parallel cuts from each side of the youth's forehead to the center. This ritual scarification, which has been outlawed in Nuer areas since the 1980s, still marks entry into manhood for many Nuer youth.

> In Des Moines, Iowa, another Nuer youth sits in pained concentration in front of a computer screen in a license branch, taking an exam for his driver's license. Still weak in English, he struggles to recall the multiple choice response sequence he memorized to pass the exam, in this American rite of passage into adulthood.

The emergence of a Nuer diaspora in the United States feeds a growing effort to rethink anthropological associations of people and place (Appadurai 1991; Gupta and Ferguson 1997; Piot 1999). "The Nuer" no longer refers solely to a purportedly isolated people inhabiting the Nile valley but also to the latest wave of newcomers to American cities like Saint Paul, Omaha, and Nashville. Spatial and temporal contexts assume greater significance, leaving notions of a Nuer people outside time and space in their wake. In the words of Sharon Hutchinson, "in a world where people, products, and ideas increasingly refuse to stay put, who is to say for certain where one sociocultural matrix begins and another ends?" (1996, 28).

It is certainly possible that the two young men described above could be brothers, even twins. How does one brother remain in the southern Sudanese war zone while the other starts a new life in a vastly different society half a world away? How is one categorized a refugee, the other an internally displaced person? How does a rural migrant from southern Sudan overcome apparent obstacles, such as immigration restrictions and airfare, to migrate to the United States?

The refugee system through which Nuer migrants have passed is a bureaucracy and is characteristically, as Paul Gilroy (2000) would say, "counter-
anthropological" in its antirelativistic stance. This one-size-fits-all approach
ostensibly applies the same set of criteria to migrants from Bosnia, Cambo-
dia, Somalia, Russia, and Sudan. The bureaucracy produces, or constructs,
refugees, sometimes selecting one brother but not the other.

By moving between microlevel and macrolevel analyses, it is possible to
explore the interplay between the refugee system and the Nuer migrants
who negotiated certain obstacles in working their way through this system.
In subsequent chapters I introduce detailed case studies that add texture to
this model. By way of introduction, this chapter describes the mechanics
of refugee flight and resettlement by setting out the maze through which
refugees who are resettled in the United States must pass. I probe the engagement of forced migrants with the international bureaucratic apparatus
conferring refugee status. I argue that the structuring nature of refugees'
engagement with this apparatus is central to understanding the demographics of the Sudanese refugee population in the United States, and the related
social dynamics. In particular, this chapter addresses how Sudanese refugees
learn how to leave. What is the flow of information that teaches them how to
move through the system? What does it take to move through the system?
What are the barriers refugees encounter, and how do they work their way
through them?

By characterizing Sudanese refugees as socially and politically constructed, I seek to point out the ways in which their suffering conveys neglect
by the rest of the world. Furthermore, by describing their active participation in seeking third-country resettlement, I draw attention to refugees' involvement in securing their own and others' survival. In so doing, I attempt
to move beyond the narrow stereotypes of African refugees by portraying
them as actors in this process.

Estimates of Displacement

One of the challenges in recognizing refugees is counting them (Helton
2002). A confounding factor in describing the larger social context in which
Nuer refugee migration occurred involves obtaining accurate regional population estimates of refugees in Africa. As noted previously, the current population of Sudan is estimated at forty million, with an estimated nine million in southern Sudan. The U.S. Committee for Refugees and Immigrants
(USCRI 2005), a nonprofit organization that produces an annual report on
the status of the world's refugees, estimates that five to seven million Suda-

Table 3.1. Sudanese Refugees in Neighboring African Countries, 2003, 2005

Host Country	2003	2005
Central African Rep.	35,000	20,900
Chad	15,000	225,000
DR Congo	70,000	45,200
Egypt	20,000	23,000
Eritrea	1,000	—
Ethiopia	90,000	90,500
Kenya	70,000	67,600
Uganda	170,000	—

Source: USCRI 2003, 2005.
Note: All figures are estimates.

Table 3.2. Refugees from Other Countries Living in Sudan, 2003, 2005

Country of Origin	2003	2005
Chad	—	5,000
Eritrea	280,000	191,000
Ethiopia	2,000	15,000
Uganda	5,000	7,900
Other	—	7,000

Source: USCRI 2003, 2005.
Note: All figures are estimates.

nese currently are displaced within Sudan, whereas 703,500 live as refugees and asylum seekers in other (mostly neighboring) countries. The situation is made more complex, as the label Sudanese refugees, when loosely applied, can refer to both refugees from Sudan and refugees from other countries living in Sudan. On the surface, it may appear paradoxical that Sudan exports refugees to other African countries while acting as host to refugee populations from neighboring countries, such as Ethiopia, Eritrea, and Kenya (see Karadawi 1999). Yet, as noted throughout this study, hosting refugees is both a humanitarian and a political act and sends a strong message of disapproval to the government from which the refugees are fleeing (see Zolberg, Suhrke, and Aguayo 1989). The following tables help frame regional displacement in Sudan and surrounding countries. Table 3.1 provides data on 2003 and 2005 USCRI estimates of the distribution of Sudanese refugees in neighboring countries. Most remarkable is the surge in numbers of Sudanese refugees in Chad between 2003 and 2005, reflecting the escalation of the conflict in the Darfur region in Sudan. Table 3.2 details the country of origin for African refugees living in Sudan in the same time period, based on 2003 and 2005

USCRI figures. The difficulty of counting refugees reappears in later discussions of "tracking" refugees after resettlement in the United States.

The Refugee Filtering System

UNHCR recognizes three options, or what it calls durable solutions, to address the situation of refugees in the world. The first is voluntary repatriation to the country of origin when circumstances permit; the second is integration into the country of first asylum; the third and least frequently used is third-country resettlement. The UNHCR model is an ideal type rather than a real scenario for Nuer refugees who tended to participate in serial migrations, rather than one-time, unidirectional paths of "flight."

The resettlement of Sudanese refugees in the United States depends on a regulatory scheme that resembles a cone-shaped filter: rigidly orchestrated rituals and rules, in the form of policies, function as a series of gates through which diminishing numbers are allowed to pass. For Africa, this means that roughly 3.3 million refugees (USCRI 2005) are winnowed down to twenty thousand, or 0.6 percent, per year for U.S. resettlement. The twenty thousand resettlement cases that the United States accepts annually for the entire African continent seems modest, unless one contrasts it with the previous ceiling of seven thousand. There has been a 250 percent increase since the mid-1990s. The slim chance of becoming an African refugee designated for resettlement in the United States makes it a "durable solution" for some, but a symbolic gesture for many more.

Thus Sudanese refugees in the United States represent a minute percentage of those displaced by the conflict. The distinction between refugees and internally displaced persons, or IDPs as they are known in forced migration parlance, has received increased international attention. David Keen (1992, 31) describes the contrast between resources allocated to IDPs and refugees who have crossed a border: in 1987 foreign aid spent on displaced persons in Sudan amounted to only $2.15 per capita, but $557 per capita was spent on refugees fleeing other countries to live in Sudan. Francis Bok (2003), Sharon Hutchinson (1996), and Jeremy Loveless (1999) describe the bleak conditions under which southern Sudanese IDPs live in Sudan, particularly in squatter settlements on the outskirts of Khartoum. A humanitarian aid worker who had spent time in Sudan said that a commonly heard observation was, "If you're going to run, head for the border."

While refugee camps are established ostensibly to address de facto refugee situations, their existence undoubtedly functions to attract those weighing

Table 3.3. Sudanese Refugees in Camps in Ethiopia, 1999, 2003

Camp	Refugees in 1999	Refugees in 2003
Bonga	12,700	18,092
Dimma	8,000	16,433
Fugnido	25,000	31,692
Shirkole	15,000	18,414
Yarenja	—	4,345

Note: All figures are estimates.

survival options. Beginning in 1983, UNHCR established camps and centers for Sudanese refugees in Ethiopia, which emerged as the primary country of first asylum. Sudanese also fled to other countries bordering Sudan, such as Egypt, Ethiopia, Kenya, Uganda, the Democratic Republic of the Congo, Central African Republic, and, more recently with the Darfur conflict, Chad and Libya. The overthrow of the Mengistu government and ensuing instability in Ethiopia in 1991 displaced Sudanese, causing them to return to Sudan or leave for other countries, such as Kenya and Uganda (F. Deng 1993, 66).

A UNHCR staff member based in Ethiopia gave me an overview of the manner in which humanitarian assistance for Sudanese refugees unfolded there:

> Itang was the original camp opened to deal with the Sudanese influx in 1983. Fugnido was the second camp to be established in 1987. Dimma camp was established in [1989]. All three of these camps were evacuated in 1991 as a response to the change of regime in Ethiopia. At that point, the majority of the refugees returned to Sudan. The refugees began returning to Ethiopia in large numbers in 1992. Itang was not reopened; however, Dimma was reopened in 1992 and Fugnido in 1993. Bonga camp and Shirkole camp were opened in 1993 and 1998 respectively.

These camps are comprised of ethnically and nationally heterogeneous groups. A 1996 United Nations Development Program (UNDP) report, for instance, noted that the total population of Fugnido (spelled *Pugnido* in the report) was host to 43,237 inhabitants, 70 percent of whom were Nuer.[1] Map 3.1 identifies active and defunct refugee camps in Ethiopia and Kenya through which the refugees described in this study passed en route to resettlement in the United States.

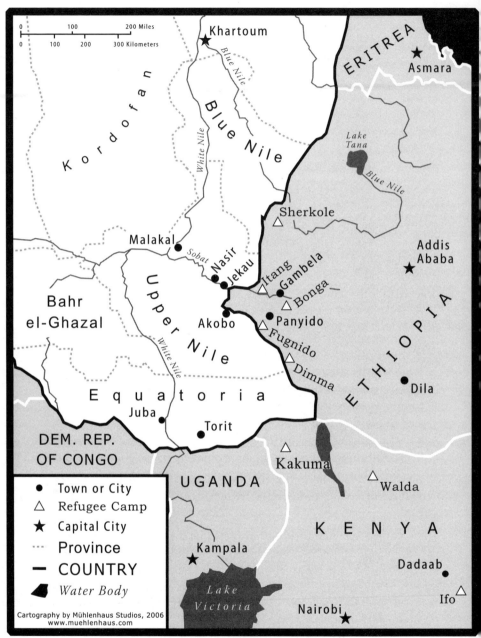

Map 3.1. Refugee camps in Ethiopia and Kenya.

Gaining Entrée into the United States

As noted previously, the Organization of African Unity's definition of *refugee* is broader than that used by the United States. Similarly, third-country resettlement is only one of the three possible "durable solutions" to address refugees' predicament. Occasionally, the United States agrees to accept specific cases of humanitarian need put forward by UNHCR. In general, however, the United States decides to accept particular refugee groups in accordance with larger geostrategic interests.

The parameters governing the process whereby a population is designated a priority for U.S. resettlement are not transparent. Moreover, it is often only in retrospect that the full articulation between U.S. foreign policy and refugee admissions crystallizes.[2] It is still not fully clear why the U.S. government focused on Sudan beginning in 1990 after ignoring, even fueling, the crisis in Sudan in the 1980s. Burr and Collins (1995) admit that many of the documents referred to in their study of contemporary Sudanese events may never be made public, making it unlikely that an official rationale will be published in the near future. The theories offered during the course of my research ranged from a Nuer work ethic to U.S. racial politics to pure serendipity. Mat Wal, a twenty-seven-year old Gaaguang man working as a security guard and hoping to enter a community college program in computers, held this view: "Anthropologists are sent to learn about cultures and assess which culture is best. When officials decide who to allow into the United States they refer to these writings to decide who to let in. They chose the Sudanese because they work hard." A Washington-based, high-level refugee services administrator expressed the view that the increase in African resettlement in the United States, beginning with Ethiopians in the 1980s, was the result of lobbying by the Congressional Black Caucus in the wake of large numbers of Soviet Jews resettled during the Reagan administration. And finally, a refugee policy analyst provided the following anecdote about the resettlement of a Somali group to illustrate that resettlement policy may not stem from any master plan: A U.S. immigration official was traveling abroad with her son. Her son joined in a soccer game with refugee youth in the neighborhood near the hotel where the official and her son were staying. In this way, the plight of this particular group came to the attention of the U.S. official. Upon this official's return to the United States, it was decided in Washington that this refugee group was appropriate for resettlement in the United States.

Table 3.4 provides data on what I consider the first cohort of Sudanese refugee admissions to the United States, between 1983 and 1997. During this

Table 3.4. Sudanese Refugee Arrivals in the United States, 1983–97

Fiscal Year	Number of Refugees
1983–84	4
1984–85	0
1985–86	3
1986–87	0
1987–88	2
1988–89	1
1989–90	6
1990–91	59
1991–92	6
1992–93	126
1993–94	253
1994–95	1,288
1995–96	583
1996–97	282

Source: U.S. Office for Refugee Resettlement; tabulated by author.
Note: Total = 4,306.

time a total of 4,306 Sudanese refugees were resettled in the United States; virtually all (4,288) were resettled after 1989. These data support the assertion that the sharp increase in the flow of refugees of Sudanese origin to the United States parallels a shift in U.S. foreign policy toward Sudan (see chapter 2).

This study, as noted earlier, focuses on refugees who arrived after 1989; in fact, the earliest arrival date I encountered in interviews was 1992. Limited available data from the Office of Refugee Resettlement (ORR) on the few Sudanese refugees arriving between 1983 and 1989 are provided in the appendixes. (For a full discussion of the history of the limited flow of, mainly Northern, Sudanese immigration to North America, see Abusharaf 1994, 2002.)[3]

Learning to be Chosen

Once a refugee group is selected for resettlement, the Immigration and Naturalization Service (INS) confers refugee status on eligible individual applicants. The INS has final and absolute control over who is admitted to the United States as a refugee; however, in an interesting hegemonic twist, the U.S. government does not act alone. Refugee resettlement in the United States has been called "one of the United States' broadest and most enduring public-private partnerships in behalf of humanitarian objectives" (Holman 1996, 16). INS officers, in conjunction with staff from various international organizations, implement the screening infrastructure, which includes an interview, mental and physical health screening assessments,[4] security name check, as well as verifying U.S. sponsorship. Transport to the United States, arranged through the International Organization for Migration, conveys the expectation that refugees quickly will assume a productive role in U.S. society after resettlement. The refugee must sign a promissory note to repay airfare, which for Nuer people ranged from $800 to $1,000 per person. Repayment is ensured by linking future resettlements to this revolving fund; if refugees default, it limits or delays future refugee resettlements. This can be a powerful incentive for many refugees who are awaiting family reunification; according to refugee program staff, refugees across groups typically do not default on these loans.

The screening interview merits particular attention as one component of the selection process where refugees can hope to influence the outcome. Refugees have little influence on whether the U.S. government selects a particular group for resettlement; similarly they have limited control over their medical screening.

Within the refugee apparatus, the INS applies a set of criteria to evaluate the refugee's eligibility for resettlement. It is ambiguous who constitutes a refugee in a situation of famine, war, or terror orchestrated by a state or resistance movement. The INS officer's role is to impose a bureaucratic order on this chaotic situation by deciding who meets the criteria for admission to the refugee resettlement program (see Smith 2000).

The refugee's role, from the perspective of the system planners, is to describe truthfully his or her life experiences and await judgment. Refugees who attempt to tilt the process in their favor by manipulating information are accused of fraud and depriving a more deserving candidate of the opportunity to resettle in the United States. This perspective is based on the erroneous conceptualization of "refugeeness" as some objective, black-and-white state devoid of gray areas. When the definition of who is and is not a refugee begins to blur, it becomes increasingly difficult to justify whom to accept for resettlement and whom to deny (Keen 1992, 33).

Sudanese refugees, either as families or individuals, met with a screening committee on a case-by-case basis. All members in a particular case were interviewed at the same time. Refugee cases are prioritized according to specific, preestablished criteria.[5] Refugees whom I interviewed had no understanding of how their case had been classified. The UNHCR staff member in Ethiopia whom I interviewed by e-mail offered the following explanation, which details the criteria used to determine third-country resettlement for Sudanese refugees.

Our approval rates in Ethiopia have varied widely. Our resettlement programme for significant numbers of Sudanese began in 1997. For the U.S., approval rates for Sudanese were 30 percent in 1997, 75 percent in early 1998 and 95 percent in late 1998.[6]

Individuals with protection problems in country of asylum and medical conditions, which would benefit from treatment abroad, are given first priority for resettlement.

She went on to describe the plight of populations that have since been labeled warehoused, or populations of ten thousand or more restricted to camps or segregated settlements or otherwise deprived of UN refugee convention rights in situations lasting five years or more (USCRI 2005).

We also have a "solutions" category in which refugees are put forward for resettlement, not for protection or medical reasons, but because they have been in country of asylum for a significant period of time, have no prospects of returning home in the near future, and are looking at a life of relief handouts in a refugee camp.

The following example illustrates the divergent ways in which refugee system representatives and participants interpreted the process. For policy makers, refugee status is conferred at the level of the individual. For refugees, membership may be a status to be achieved on the behalf of a corporate group. Simon Deng, a thirty-year-old Gaajok man in the United States who was attending college, described his resettlement selection by saying that he had been chosen by the U.S. government "to come to America to take care of Nuer who remained in Africa." In his view, he had been given access to "an opportunity to make money; [his] task [was] to work hard to achieve success for [himself] and for [his] family in Africa."

The filtering mechanism governing U.S. resettlement exerts considerable influence in shaping and defining the refugee group as a whole; in many respects engagement with this bureaucratic apparatus generates the raw material from which groups reassemble a social structure in diaspora settings. The apparatus sets its own standards in terms of the values ordering society and defines and legitimates the most basic human relationships, such as certain kin and affinal ties, while discounting others. For instance, nuclear family groupings are privileged over extended family groupings. A classificatory sibling, for example, is not accorded the same degree of consideration as a biological sibling. To draw from the two examples at the beginning of the chapter, if the two young men had been brothers as reckoned in U.S. kinship terminology, they could have been resettled together. If the two had been brothers according to Nuer kinship systems, they would have been considered separately.

The literature pertaining to refugees is replete with examples of refugees struggling to translate their concepts of family and reality into a format that is comprehensible and compelling to the INS gatekeeper (see, for example, Welaratna 1993, 112). Attempts to "translate" culturally specific relationships into what refugees think INS officials want to hear can backfire and refugees may be accused of falsely representing their situation, which may delay or prevent their resettlement (see Meredith 2000; Smith 2000).

The ways in which refugees translate their experiences into a narrative for refugee resettlement gatekeepers is a sensitive area. The ways in which refugees negotiate "truth" is a highly touchy topic, as recent immigration law reforms have widened the scope of crimes punishable by deportation, which in the case of refugees can mean *refoulement,* or involuntary repatriation. While not the focus of my research, an unintended by-product of this work has been the generation of data on the ways in which "identity markers" are strategically manipulated or invented to conform to what INS gatekeepers are seeking in determining refugee status. This strategic manipulation can be viewed as discernible instances of refugee action. Third-country refugee resettlement, despite the appearance of a top-down bureaucracy at work, is an area of contested terrain. The realm of identity markers—name, date of birth, and documented kin or affinal tie—is one site where this battle can be observed. An examination of these negotiated realities begins to reveal effective strategies on the part of refugees seeking third-country resettlement. Altering identity markers is one strategy within a context of limited options and extreme social transition.

Collective and individual pasts become powerful commodities in the struggle for asylum or third-country resettlement as well as the repatriation and reintegration of former refugees. Information in these contexts is strategically manipulated by, for, and about refugees to encourage refugees to adapt to their new environs, to return home, or to secure third-country resettlement. These strategic manipulations of information, or refractions of reality, span a continuum from outright manipulation of fact to differences in interpretation or perception. Hu Ying, in a response piece to Aihwa Ong's 1996 article in *Current Anthropology* poses the question, "When does 'strategy' of survival become 'manipulation'?" She also suggests that strategies test our own liberal tolerance in "the apparent betrayal of [the person's] own culture" (1996, 757). For example, a U.S. caseworker told me that she and her colleagues are not bothered when they learn of instances of refugees' outsmarting INS agents, but they experience twinges of discomfort at the possibility of a refugee having taken the resettlement slot allocated to someone else.

Nuer men and women whom I interviewed spoke about refugees in the United States who had assumed the identity of another person to secure third-country resettlement. However, I had limited opportunities to interview people who spoke to me regarding this sensitive topic in terms of their own experience. In most cases, I can only present the explanations offered by those living in the United States. In one case, during fieldwork in Ethiopia, however, I attempted to secure an affidavit from an individual whose identity had been assumed by a cousin who had been resettled in the United States, but we were unable to meet due to security issues in western Ethiopia, where he was staying. In all cases that I encountered directly or indirectly where one individual took the resettlement place of another, there was reportedly no animosity. Informants noted that the actual person whose case was selected for resettlement may have been unable to travel to the departure site in Africa at the appropriate time for any number of reasons, including a lack of funds or illness. The perceived loss for the individual was seemingly a matter of gain for the corporate group. One Nuer man in his thirties explained it thus: "It is okay to take whatever name comes up; the other person will take yours when that one becomes available." (For an example of a similar practice among Kosovar refugees at Fort Dix, New Jersey, see Gozdziak and Tuskan 2000.) Francis Bok (2003), a young Dinka man who escaped enslavement in Sudan and who was resettled in the United States as a refugee, describes in his autobiography an alternate way in which one could end up with a different identity: to leave Sudan he secured a Sudanese passport on the black market. His name, Francis Piol Bul Buk, had become Francis Fioul Bul Bok, which now is his legal identity in the United States.

Given the legal sensitivities associated with this practice, it was not possible to assemble adequate data to investigate specific social patterns associated with membership in, for example, agnatic groups. Certainly, a common name shared by patrilineally related cousins could facilitate this manipulation of information. However, the consequences of this practice, if discovered by the INS after resettlement, are grave. A refugee service worker advocating on behalf of a Sudanese refugee ensnared in possible deportation proceedings relayed that the INS assumes the worst and alleges that the refugee who arrived under guise of another person's identity may have murdered the person whose name was used for resettlement. Attempting to legally change identity markers such as name or age after resettlement is the principal way these cases of usurped identity come to the attention of INS. The ritual associated with resettlement confers an identity that is for the most part nonnegotiable. The INS threatens to deport, on the basis of fraud, refugees who admit to having altered their identity markers. The practice of returning a refugee to his or her country of origin (refoulement) is contravened by international law; however, some legal loopholes reportedly exist. I know of several documented and pending cases in which the INS has threatened to deport the Nuer individual in question.[7]

More significantly, these instances of attempts to change documented identity after arrival indicate the extent to which some of the Nuer I worked with truly constitute the first wave. It is highly unlikely that subsequent cohorts will make the mistake of attempting to change their legal documents after arrival in the United States, given the threatened INS sanctions.

More common among Nuer refugees arriving in the United States is living within the framework of a new reality that they helped to construct through their engagement with the refugee resettlement apparatus. One way many southern Sudanese refugees cope with this newly constructed identity is to deploy multiple identities, such as name, marital status, age, and sibling relationships, in various situations. Malkki, in her study of Hutu refugees, acknowledges a similar dynamic: "refugees lived at some level within categories that were not of their own making, but they also subverted these categories, to create new ones" (1995, 7).

Survival in situations of war and refugee camps may well have depended on their capacity to negotiate membership in clan, ethnic, and national groups in response to various situations. There is no reason why this should change in a diaspora context. My ethnographic data suggest that there was no specific formula for gaining access to resettlement. For example, interviews elicited the following responses when I asked Nuer informants how they were selected to come to the United States while others remained in the camps. "Everyone from southern Sudan with no passport is considered a refugee. It depends on the life story you tell and the medical checkup," said one man. Another summarized the interview by saying, "You want to win!" Still another told me, "It's like an interview for a job."

When I probed what was important to convey in the life story, Nuer refugees offered conflicting descriptions. For instance, depending on one's particular situation, there were three scenarios relating to age. Most common were younger individuals who hoped to be resettled; they therefore increased their age to qualify for resettlement as adults—for example, a sixteen-year-old applied as an eighteen-year-old. Second, an individual seeking resettlement as an underage family member would have claimed to be younger than they actually were. Third, and least common, was assuming the identity of another person who may have been older, younger, or the same age. Accordingly, there were equivalent variations in scenarios relating to kin and affinal ties: one's younger sister became one's child.

Many described the learning curve associated with understanding INS criteria. In a tragic commentary on how devastation can seem normal, the biggest mistake people made, informants told me, was to invent the extraordinary in order to be eligible for resettlement: "People feel they need a reason, so they tell the person interviewing them that they killed someone and if they return to Sudan they will be put in jail." The Nuer men who worked as interview interpreters in the camps, who had some level of English proficiency gained through formal schooling or simply living in Kenya, reported that they had coached people on what they believed was a better approach: "We told the community, we need to tell them the reality. Don't say you killed someone; just say you were caught in the crossfire." Holtzman describes a similar dynamic: "As they learned what the interviewers wanted to hear, the Nuer felt compelled to alter their stories accordingly" (2000, 26).

Another illustration can be seen in the case of a man whom I will call Ahmed Deng Bol. He had a son, whom he named according to customary Nuer practices Jal Ahmed Deng.[8] According to the Nuer men who relayed this story, the "U.S. lawyer" told the other Sudanese men to take Ahmed outside and get him to eliminate Ahmed from his and his son's names or the lawyer could not help him. Ahmed was claiming religious persecution in Sudan as a Christian, but his and his son's names were Islamic. Ahmed reportedly did not want to change his name because all his documents said Ahmed Deng Bol. "When Ahmed was turned down, people cried and prayed," my informants told me. Eventually, he changed his name and was accepted for resettlement.

Some perceived the refugee selection process in a way that is at odds with the official rendition of events but is very meaningful in its own right. Despite the carefully scripted selection process described thus far, a couple of refugees attributed their refugee status to having won "the lottery." I was well into my research before I thought to probe this perception from a policy level. Most southern Sudanese in the United States arrived through standard refugee resettlement channels on a temporary resident alien card, rather than through the annual immigration diversity lottery sponsored by INS.[9] Refugees receive a card—the I-94—which grants them temporary entry into the United States until they receive their green card, or permanent residency, which allows them to work in the United States without being an American citizen. After five years, they are eligible and encouraged to apply for U.S. citizenship.

Perhaps this interpretation of resettlement opportunities through metaphors of chance should be credited with unusually keen perspicacity rather than mere misinformation about a process whose rules must seem, at best, idiosyncratic. Yet, the immigration lottery system appears to loom large for at least some refugees as a way of making sense of the fact that they are living in the United States while others they left behind are still living in the situation from which they fled. I assisted some Nuer in the United States to complete applications for the last immigration diversity lottery on behalf of friends and family still in Africa. It is unknown the extent to which this element of chance helps to mediate psychological dislocation pertaining to their own relative prosperity and well-being vis-à-vis those who were left behind. Bok (2003, 202) describes the range of emotions as guilt, anger, sadness, and confusion about what to do. For some refugees, particularly those who arrived in the United States under guise of another person's identity, the element of being in the right place at the right time is central to how they make meaning of their experience. For others, this is seemingly an area of internal conflict.

On Placement and Incorporation

From the perspective of Nuer refugees, incorporation into U.S. society is simply one more point on a larger trajectory of migration. The process of incorporation is open-ended and will endure throughout the life span of each individual, their offspring, that of the next generation, and, perhaps, beyond. Similarly, incorporation into the United States does not signal a severing of ties to Africa.

In theory, the process by which refugees adapt to a new country varies dramatically across refugee groups according to divergent social, cultural, historic, and economic backgrounds as well as the different economic and social milieu they enter (Haines 1996, 28). In practice, as illustrated by the case of Mary Chuol, a widowed Gaajak woman in her twenties, refugees are often perceived as a homogeneous category. Mary was the first Sudanese to be placed in a midsize northern town. The agency that managed her resettlement placed her in a home with a Ugandan refugee whom the resettlement caseworker had asked to communicate household necessities to Mary. The Ugandan woman used rudimentary Kiswahili to indicate that food was prepared. Mary, who didn't speak Kiswahili, laughs when retelling the story because the American assumed that because they were both from Africa they could communicate.

Country of origin, the most common nomenclature used to define refugee groups, is often a poor predictor of alliances. Many refugees fleeing civil conflict situations have negative attitudes toward compatriots from other ethnic groups. Kathleen Heldenbrand (1996) recounts the experience of a Shilluk family from Sudan who was resettled in a Midwestern U.S. city. The caseworker assigned to assist the family was also Sudanese; however, he was an Arabic-speaking Muslim. The Catholic Shilluk refugee could understand Arabic but, given the nature of religious tension in Sudan, he found it exceedingly difficult to interact with the caseworker. Nuer are most culturally similar to Dinka. Yet Bok notes that "the ancient tensions between the Nuer and Dinka have followed us to America, making socializing difficult" (2003, 173).

African refugees are incorporated into U.S. society within a particular racial and cultural matrix (Ong 1996). Race and economics coalesce to position Nuer refugees on the lowest rungs of the socioeconomic ladder. Not surprisingly, perhaps, educational achievement appears to be the most dynamic way they are attempting to alter their situation.

The economics of refugee incorporation are relevant not only to the lives of individuals and families but are a key policy issue as well. Refugees are caught in the ideological crossfire between the federal and the state government; immigration to the United States is brokered at the level of the federal government, yet incorporation of the immigrants into the economic and social spheres is left up to individual states (Holman 1996, 23).

A similar paradox can be seen in the ways in which refugees and immigrants are socially constructed for popular audiences. To merit international humanitarian assistance, refugees must demonstrate compelling need—recall the "flight" scenario—leaving behind all material possessions. Yet to overcome anti-immigration sentiment in the United States, refugee arrivals must quickly transform into "productive" citizens. In fact, refugee resettlement placements are governed by a "success" formula that captures this ideal.

Placements, brokered by voluntary agency representatives, occur on Tuesday mornings in New York City. More than one refugee services worker who had observed this process described it as people who sit around a table and "do horse trading" (for example, "I'll trade a Somali family for two Bosnian free cases"). Refugees are allocated based on the size and demographic composition of the group and the organization's "success" rate with previous cases, as determined by the organization's percentage of eligible cases who are employed. Eighty percent of "free cases," or those without documented family connections residing in the United States, must be employed in order for the organization to remain eligible for further placements.

In addition to placement responsibilities, voluntary agencies (*Volags* in refugee parlance) provide assurance of sponsorship to the overseas resettlement office and manage the first phase of incorporation into the host country.[10] Family reunification is a deciding factor in determining resettlement destination, and these cases are sent, when possible, to where the sponsoring family member resides at the time the paperwork is filed.[11] Often, a long delay between when the paperwork is filed and the family member's arrival in the United States confounds this process, especially if the sponsoring individual has moved.

An agency's New York representative communicates with a network of affiliates across the United States, and the affiliate assesses the applicant's case in conjunction with the likelihood of securing a sponsor—an individual, church, or organization—to oversee the immediate transition. At this point, notice is sent to Africa; three to six weeks after sponsorship is assured, the refugee is supposed to arrive in the United States. However, the refugee service worker who provided me with this overview also noted that resettlements coming from Africa were less "reliable" than those from Europe or Asia. She went on to note differentials within the United States in terms of support for African refugees: "In terms of community resources, people have been less generous with the Sudanese. The Bosnians get more. It is simply attributable to racism. There is a requirement of sponsorship to accept the person. So, all resettled refugees . . . have some sort of sponsor. It may involve churches getting together to cosponsor rather than just one individual or group."

Upon arrival in the United States, refugees are given minimal support. Immediate requirements for the voluntary agency are addressed in their "month one checklist," which includes medical services, refugee health requirements, notification of the right to apply for the resettlement of other family members, and repayment schedule for the travel loan. Refugees resettled among family members receive services for fewer months than if they were a "free case," prompting some families I worked with to encourage family members applying for resettlement to try to come as a free rather than "family reunification" case.

A special category among Sudanese refugees are "unaccompanied youth." Those not accompanied by a parent or other adult relative receive full care until the child reaches the age of majority, a status that varies by state, or is reunited with a parent (Holman 1996, 19). Differentials in the way a "youth" or a "minor" are defined in particular states contributes to some degree to interstate migration to take advantage of higher age cutoffs for benefits, particularly access to education. The topic of the resettlement of unaccompanied minors is of increasing importance given the resettlement of a cohort of

Sudanese youth that journalists have dubbed the lost boys of Sudan. In 2000 the United States began accepting 3,800 Sudanese refugees from Kakuma camp in Kenya who had been orphaned or otherwise separated from their families (see Bixler 2005; England 2000; Schechter 2004; Simmons 1999). These groups are considered especially vulnerable because they have spent their formative years away from home and have few, if any, ties with their families, presuming they are still alive.

Refugees encounter myriad reactions by the host community to their resettlement. Jo Ann Koltyk (1998), for instance, describes the points of friction and tension wrought by induced and rapid multiculturalization associated with the mushrooming Hmong community in Wausau, Wisconsin. David Haines (1996) describes the different faces American society presents to different refugee groups at different points in time. One differentiating factor between earlier and later waves of Sudanese refugees to the United States is the economic milieu into which they were incorporated. The earliest cohorts, arriving in the mid-1990s, encountered an economic boom. Those arriving in the period leading up to and just after September 11, 2001, were met with a different set of circumstances. The following example, recounted by a Sudanese refugee, describes what he calls a scapegoat syndrome and provides insight into the situation refugees encounter during less prosperous times. The twin cities of Fargo, North Dakota, and Moorhead, Minnesota, experienced catastrophic flood damage in spring 1997. Lutheran Social Services, a voluntary agency located there, agreed to suspend refugee resettlements in the community during the flood relief effort. Through some misunderstanding in conjunction with erroneous reporting in the local newspaper, the Fargo-Moorhead community was told that a large number of Somali refugees had been resettled in Fargo-Moorhead during this period. Angry debates ensued that speak to the broader issue in refugee resettlement: how do we reconcile the act of helping outsiders when existing community members need assistance? A critical question in refugee debates is the extent to which refugees should be provided domestic assistance not available to other U.S. residents (Holman 1996, 24). The Personal Responsibility and Work Opportunity Reconciliation Act of 1996, otherwise known as welfare reform, exacerbated tensions in this arena by excluding refugees from benefit cuts applied to the noncitizen foreign-born population.

These questions go beyond the scope of this study, but the issue is central to the way in which refugees are incorporated into American society. Once again, it becomes important to distinguish refugees from other migrants. A refugee services provider in California whom I interviewed spoke of his office's public awareness efforts to educate the public about the distinction between undocumented workers and refugees. Again, we hear the common refrain: immigrants are pulled out of their country by better opportunities; refugees are pushed by conditions beyond their control. This speaks to some of the ways in which the "push" explanation is a part of a broader ideological framework governing access to the United States or other Western countries.

Perhaps bowing to anti-immigration sentiment, the federal government steadily has been decreasing the amount it contributes to support recently arrived refugees. The Refugee Act of 1980 codified what had been a rather loosely applied refugee model for incoming Cubans and Indo-Chinese. In 1980 federal support extended up to thirty-six months after arrival (Holman 1996). Cuts in 1991 reduced the time limit to eight months (Holman 1996, 24).[12] Diminishing federal assistance, in conjunction with the devolution of other public assistance programs to the state level, has implications for refugee populations that have unusually high levels of interstate migration.

A Demographic Profile of Sudanese Refugees in the United States

The previous discussion on the strategic manipulation of identity markers has important implications for descriptive statistics generated by agencies, such as the Office of Refugee Resettlement, on basic demographic characteristics of this population. This becomes central to our understanding of southern Sudanese as a refugee group in the United States as the gap between everyday existence and the accompanying paper trail widens. Thus the paper trail documents a reality not of the Sudanese refugees, but of the interplay between the refugees and the institutions with which they come into contact. Studies of refugee groups that rely exclusively on these data encounter serious limitations in their capacity to produce valid findings. The data in this chapter are presented with that caveat in mind; however, these data represent the closest approximation of a universal census of Sudanese refugees in the United States. As indicated earlier, there are no official means by which refugees are tracked after arrival in the United States.

Similarly, attempts by ethnographers and service providers to construct a reliable and valid census of the entire Sudanese, or even the Nuer, population are hampered by many difficulties, including internal migration within the United States. Even those who work most closely with Sudanese groups note the difficulty in achieving reliable census population estimates. In the words of one service provider, "Every time we try to do head counts, people are moving or visiting."

Sudanese refugees reported that they were resettled in groups varying from six to seventy-five individuals. Almost invariably, arrival in New York City, gateway to the United States, signaled a fragmenting of the group. In a wrenching sort of dispersal, groups would be divided up and sent to far-flung locations—Des Moines, Rochester (New York), Seattle, Dallas, Sioux Falls, Las Vegas, Nashville. The demographic composition of the Sudanese population in the United States continues to evolve. (See appendixes for further breakdowns of data on Sudanese that arrived between 1990 and 1997.)

GENDER

The imbalance in the ratio of nearly three adult males (1942) to one adult female (718) of the 1990–97 sample of 2,660 Sudanese refugee resettlements to the United States is striking, even though it echoes the situation for other refugee populations.[13] Since the gender ratio of children is roughly equal, I deliberately omit them from this analysis to highlight the gender difference within the adult population. (The larger sample size would dilute the significance of this finding.) In marked contrast to popular notions of refugee groups being comprised predominantly of women and children, this finding merits special attention. Absent from the ubiquitous observation that refugee groups are composed of a majority of women and children is that most refugee populations are relatively young, particularly in Africa, where roughly half the population is under age fifteen. For instance, if a population were 25 percent adult male, 25 percent adult female, 25 percent male children and 25 percent female children, 75 percent of the population would be classified as women and children. Women and children as populations of special concern in refugee situations lies not in their numerical dominance but in their vulnerability in conflict situations (see Nordstrom 1999).

The imbalance in the ratio of male to female adult refugees suggests that the selection of refugees for resettlement in the United States is gendered. Nuer informants proposed the following reasons to explain the higher proportion of males to females: male youth were pressed into service as soldiers; women, particularly those with children, were less likely to have kept pace with the repeated migrations from Sudan to Ethiopia, back to Sudan, and then to Kenya; and crossing the border was not an equal-opportunity endeavor—women were less likely to have the necessary cash to cross the border into Kenya. This experience is illustrated in one of the case studies presented in the next chapter where a son was chosen over daughters to receive the pooled family assets to attempt the journey, via the refugee apparatus, to America.

AGE

Throughout this study, I refer to many of my informants as individuals in their early, mid-, and late twenties; this age group represents nearly half the first cohort of Sudanese resettled in the United States. Based on reported year of birth, the estimated current age for resettled refugees (excluding U.S.-born children) ranges from three to seventy-two. More than 95 percent of the Sudanese population who arrived through fiscal year 1997 at the time of resettlement were younger than forty-two.

GEOGRAPHIC PLACEMENT

Refugees differ from other immigrant groups by being figuratively and literally "placed" in preselected destinations in the United States (Forbes 1985). Beyond the official U.S. government "scatter approach policy," which deliberately tries to disperse refugee groups to diminish the impact on any one resettlement site, any patterns associated with this resettlement would have to take multiple factors into consideration. Between 1990 and 1997, 4,288 Sudanese refugees were resettled as both individuals and domestic units in thirty-six different states. Similarly, within states refugee placements were dispersed across counties. During that period, Texas received the largest proportion of Sudanese refugees, approximately 17 percent. South Dakota received approximately 12 percent; California, Minnesota, Iowa, and Tennessee each received between 5 and 9 percent; each of the remaining twenty-eight states received fewer than 5 percent. Map 3.2 illustrates this distribution.

The migratory process described here is unique because of the ways in which engagement with the refugee apparatus allowed Nuer to bypass the process of migration described by other scholars, which involves successive steps of migration resulting in greater distances and longer duration. Many of the individuals discussed migrated from rural southern Sudan to suburban Middle America via short stays in refugee camps in neighboring African countries. Similarly, many of these migrants lacked the necessary educational background to qualify as immigrants to the United States under other circumstances. The refugee apparatus was a key mechanism in facilitating this migration.

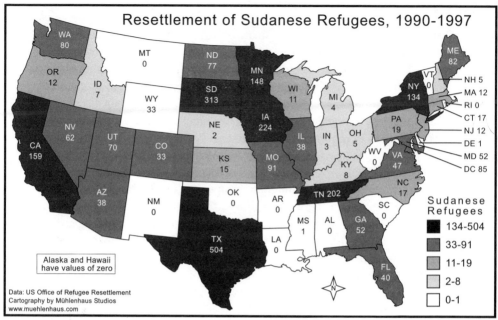

Map 3.2. Distribution of refugees.

4

Flight Patterns

When the British want[ed] to give independence to the Sudanese they were afraid because they have no education. They thought if they have too much education, they will know it is their country. In Sudan, you cannot follow higher education if you are not Muslim. The problem for us was education. We thought if we come to America, we can get education. Then we can help others.

In Sudan, I witnessed so many dangerous things: the inhumanity of the state, discrimination in terms of religion, persecution of women and children by government militia. It involved close family and put my life in danger. Young people who think of their futures see a denial of further education because of being a southerner. The only job option is to teach. I made a plan even if I don't know what the end of it is and God was listening. Sudanese are refugees, but they are also individuals. They marry even if it is too dangerous to raise kids. Peoples' lives were in danger. They were running to a place to raise kids.

These words, spoken to me by two different Nuer men in their twenties, who had been resettled in the United States through refugee channels, attest to the complexity of the Sudanese refugee situation on a number of levels: life in southern Sudan is tragic; education, religion, and politics intersect in ways that marginalize southerners; refugee resettlement is a transnationalized strategy—there is an expectation that those who obtain resettlement opportunities will assist those who remain; the experience of refugee migration does not eclipse individuals' attempts to pursue basic human life cycle goals, such as marrying and having children; and education is a central variable in the quest for a better future. In sum, the men's words illustrate the observation by Zolberg, Suhrke, and Aguayo (1989) that refugees are products of the intersection of perilous conditions within their own country and the promise of possibilities beyond its borders.

The individual experiences of flight, engagement with the refugee bureaucracy, and resettlement in the United States contextualize future linkages between home and the diaspora. Thus a single refugee group, loosely united through language and culture, can have quite different versions of "the refugee experience." The divergent paths that Nuer people have taken to

the United States illustrate the intense interplay between macrolevel structural and institutional frames and individual, situational action.

The term *flight* engenders a perception of a swift, and perhaps unthinking,
transit between two distinct geographic spheres and is depicted as devoid of
social and cultural significance. This study questions that characterization
by elucidating the extent to which many southern Sudanese, particularly
those born in the past forty years, never have known a society unmarked by
upheaval. Given the protracted nature of conflict in Sudan, war and life in
refugee camps constitute a normative existence for many southern Sudanese
(Malkki 1997). It is impossible to claim that displacement suspended the
flow of social and economic life. Rather, rebuilding is a process that is woven
throughout the experience of upheaval and migration that may indeed serve
as a mechanism for coping with rapid change and suffering.

Refugees emerge as *bricoleurs* who construct meaning out of past experiences and current conditions. James Clifford (1997, 23) notes the importance of the process of transit between two geographic locales: to fully
comprehend being there, we must also examine getting there. This pertains
to the experience of Nuer refugees, as it is in the process of getting there
that the instances of refugee action can be discerned most clearly. The cases
described in this chapter refute the concept of individuals scattering willy-
nilly; the people I describe were also moving strategically toward something.
Tragically, in many cases that something may have been simply the raw elements to sustain human life—food, water, health care, some degree of security. Yet this does not negate the fact those individuals acquired information
about the limited array of options and acted on that knowledge.

The following two cases describe, in detail, the two points of origin and
paths of flight that were most common in the stories I heard from Nuer refugees in the United States: Nuer born in Sudan subsequently left for refuge
in Ethiopia; or Nuer born in a refugee camp in Ethiopia migrated to Sudan
under deteriorating conditions in Ethiopia. Yet these were not the only paths
of flight, and these cases are followed by alternative experiences that point
to the limitations in trying to develop a "typical" Sudanese refugee profile.
Similarly, as indicated earlier, the paths taken by eastern Sudanese differ
markedly from those whose geographic location made Khartoum a more
viable destination (see Hutchinson 1996).

The individuals depicted in the stories below participated in a ping-pong
series of moves involving migration to Sudan from refugee camps in Ethiopia—the reverse of what one would expect. Participation in serial migrations illustrates the extent to which the category of refugee is mutable: upon
crossing the border to Sudan, Nuer ceased to be statutory refugees and

became internally displaced people (Keen 1992, 31). It also points to
tions in understanding "strategies" refugees deployed as a part of so-
of grand design. Strategies in this context refer to the action of marshaling
resources at hand, in tandem with a set of values, beliefs, and goals, toward
some desired end. Strategies do not refer to an overarching roadmap—too
much was changing and continues to change at too rapid a pace for that degree of control over their experience. However, repeated attempts, tolerance
for risk, and the limited array of alternative options contributed to a context
whereby a small stream of Sudanese refugees actively sought and gained
resettlement opportunities.

Points of Departure, Paths of Flight

For many Sudanese refugees, as the following story illustrates, flight from
the country of origin was not a one-way linear journey. The promise of improved conditions in Sudan or, as was more likely, the deterioration of conditions in the country in which they were seeking refuge, such as Ethiopia,
prompted a retracing of steps back to Sudan. Therefore flight was often a
recurring ordeal whose effects were felt most acutely by those who were
physically least able to travel (the very old, very young, and infirm.)

Like other forms of migration, refugee flight may appear to be the act of
an individual, but it is often a journey undertaken on behalf of other family
members. In a Sudanese context, where successive waves of refugees have
crossed the border to Ethiopia or other African countries seeking security,
flight becomes a collective strategy, extending back in time over multiple
generations and geared toward creating opportunities for present and future generations. Once refugees have been resettled in the United States,
they can begin the lengthy process of petitioning for family members to join
them. They can also send remittances to the family through individuals traveling back to Africa, informal banking networks, or standard money-wiring
services, such as Western Union. The story of David Bol illustrates a number
of themes central to understanding the experiences Nuer in America underwent during their journey.

INVESTING IN SONS

David Bol is an engaging young man in his early twenties. He is quick to
smile, particularly when playing with his three young, U.S.-born children.
The upbeat sense of normalcy with which he conducts his daily routine—
work in a box factory, school to complete his GED (high school equivalency
diploma), and interactions with his wife and children—belies his tumultuous

journey to the United States. David married his wife, who is Nuer, in the United States. David estimates his age to be about twenty-four. Even though he was born in Itang, a refugee camp in Ethiopia, he is not sure of the exact month, day, or even year of his birth. When required to establish a birth date for himself for documentation purposes associated with resettlement, he chose January 1 because people told him it would be easy to remember.

When David left the camp, at about age fourteen, to go to Sudan for the first time, in the wake of the fall of the Mengistu government in Ethiopia, he was a man in Nuer society. In Itang, he had undergone *gaar*, the ritual scarification marking his entry into manhood. David was born in Ethiopia because his parents had left Sudan in the 1960s; his father had fought with the southern Sudanese rebels, Anya Nya, against the government and had not returned when others repatriated during the 1970s. David describes his own journey to Sudan:

> We ran back to Sudan in 1991. . . . In the Upper Nile Region. We stayed there about four months. The government came with helicopters or jets and bombed people at the area where there are refugees, because the refugees are everywhere in southern Sudan . . . everywhere. So, they used to bomb people. And the United Nations came and put the[ir] flag down where the people are. They put the flag down so the Sudanese government would stop bombing people.

David left Ethiopia for Sudan on foot with his father, mother, the father's third wife, two younger brothers, and two younger sisters. David recalls the long journey, the meager amount of food, and his mother's insistence that the children eat what little there was. David's mother died during the hard trek from lack of food and ensuing weakness. Of his father's three wives, she was the first to be married and the second to die; the second wife, a victim of disease, had died earlier in Itang.

The UN negotiated with the rebels who had captured Ethiopia and asked that the refugees, who had fled, be allowed to return. The new Ethiopian government protested the return of the refugees because of connections between the people in the camps and rebel fighters from Sudan. Eventually, David and the surviving members of his family were allowed to return to a new refugee camp in Ethiopia called Dimma.

Life was very difficult in Ethiopia after the change of government in 1991. One of the biggest hardships was a lack of food and the means to procure it. David's father was worried that the whole family would die in the camp, leaving no mark of their existence in this world. He sought to diversify his options for perpetuating the family name by sending one of his children to Kenya to seek passage to America. As David explained,

> My father and my young mother [his father's third wife], I call her mother too, and my two brothers and two sisters, we were in the refugee camp in Dimma. So, there was a way, people in the city of Addis Ababa heard that there was a way for people to go to America. So, my father, he called us when he heard that message. How could we do that same way there in Kenya to go to America? Can we get one among you, my kids, to go to America. When some people die here, we will have our son in the world. We will keep our name in the world. When we die here, he will keep our name in the world.

In recounting his story, David reflected on why his father had chosen him over his sisters to leave, "I don't know why, but in Sudan, they believe in boys and ignore girls." He claimed to not know why his father had chosen him over his two brothers. David is, however, the eldest living son. David's father sold the family's clothes and blankets that they had been given by the UN, to provide money for David's journey. The family's sacrifices to facilitate David's journey to Kenya and eventually to the United States can be viewed as an investment resembling other scenarios in African life, where a family or a village might pool resources to send one promising individual to university. Clearly, what distinguishes this case is the crisis situation in which it occurred, which afforded few alternatives. Nonetheless, remaining in Ethiopia, with its tragic hardships was, albeit unfavorable, a genuine alternative, as evidenced by the many who did remain. Thus, an understanding of migration to Kenya and eventually the United States must take into consideration the ways in which those who made the journey embraced risk; while it was hazardous to remain in Ethiopia, it was nonetheless more dangerous to migrate.

> My father sold out two blankets, and including my blanket and my brothers' blankets and the one blanket of my sister . . . five blankets. For one blanket we get 40 Ethiopian money [birr, 40Br is about $5]. So together we get 200 and something [about $23]. I don't know, I forget. It has been a long time. They told me that I can go. I buy a ticket for 25 Ethiopian money for the bus [$2.86]. I get out from Dimma without shoes and without jacket, only a T-shirt and one pant.

The trip that ensued from Ethiopia to Kenya was indeed perilous and involved relying on all available social networks. David boarded a bus heading for the capital, Addis Ababa, where he met some boys that he knew from primary school in the refugee camp. His friends advised him to take a certain route even though they had heard that rebels often hijack vehicles on that road. His friends even drew him a map. As predicted by his friends, David's vehicle was hijacked.

> I remember there was one place called Agar Miriam, a town in southwest Ethiopia. There were rebel people, Ethiopian people. They attack people in the road. They kill them and take out their loads. That day when I reached Dila they had killed three cars. So, the government caught me. They say, where are you from? I say I am from Sudan. They like Sudan because they were refugees in Sudan. They like Sudanese. They said they wanted to take me to the base of soldiers. We will find out the way you can go there tomorrow. They give me food. They give me a blanket. I eat well, and they give me a good place to sleep. In the morning, they pass my case to the boss. They say, where are you going? I say to that town; I have two brothers there.

The following day the rebels let him continue on his way. When he reached a town where he had unspecified "relatives" they talked to the Kenyan drivers who were bringing in food from the UN. The drivers let David wear a UN driver's uniform so that he would not be detected when rebels stopped the UN trucks en route at the border to Kenya. The Kenyan truck drivers provided the information needed to make the final leg of the journey.

> They [the truck drivers] were returning to Kenya. When we reach Kenya, we have a very, very, very strong government in Kenya. We don't have a way to take you to the refugee camp by this truck if you don't have an ID or registration card. So, we can take you to the office of the United Nations here. So, it is too tough. You can go to the police station of Kenya, and they can give you a letter, and then you can go to the registration office of the United Nations. If you don't do that then the United Nations registration office can do nothing. They say to bring a letter from the police station is very hard. They say, we don't know what to do with you. We bring you to Kenya, but we don't know what to do for you. I say, God will do something.

In an extraordinary example of the use of even formal regulatory institutions in making his way to the camp, David had to agree to an arrest by the Kenyan police, which was staged by a person who worked in the police station. The arrest was a prearranged event intended to allow him access to the refugee camp, as he had entered Kenya by irregular means.

They put me in the jail, where there are a lot of Kenyan people
jail who are talking: You goddamned guy, where are you coming
I keep quiet. . . . [The friend of the truck driver who was helpin_
talked to the boss of the police station. They say, Why do you leave
the refugee camp in Ethiopia? And I say, You know there is a problem
in Ethiopia. We were living for a long time in Ethiopia until the new
government came in Ethiopia, and we don't have enough things to stay
in Ethiopia. So my father sent me out of Ethiopia. A lot of refugees are
killed in the camps in Ethiopia, and they have the disadvantage for the
food, too. We don't have enough food. So, my father sent me out. If
you die there, you do. But if you don't die, you keep our name in the
world.

After hearing his story, the police gave him a letter and transported him to
the camp the next day. When he arrived at the refugee camp, Walda, there
were other Sudanese, but no Nuer people. And finally, David describes his
role in the process of chain migration; as soon as he got access to a telephone, David called his friends in Addis Ababa who had suggested the route
that he had taken.

So when I reached there I find somewhere to call Addis Ababa. I reach
in the refugee camp, and I told them the path I came. And I posted
them a letter. And they came. A lot of people they came by that way.
So, we were there in 1992 about twenty-six Nuer people. And those
twenty-six people live in America now. I think three of those people
went to Canada.

David's story provides rare insight into the lived experience of refugee migration. First, in a crisis setting, he mobilized all available networks of kinship and friendship. For example, he does not rely on a specific, established
social grouping, such as agnatic kin. This approach suggests that no two
experiences of Nuer refugee migration will be exactly alike. However, those
who come later have the advantage of benefiting from the cumulative experience of their predecessors.

David's experience illustrates the ambiguous web of authority a resettled
refugee in the United States might encounter during his journey—that of
his father, and of Sudanese, Ethiopian, Kenyan, and U.S. authorities. It also
demonstrates the extent to which his very survival was linked to his ability to
circumnavigate bureaucratic obstacles within a complex web of interwoven
nodes of authority. Clearly, these formal regulatory mechanisms governed
his migration experience in important ways. At numerous points along the

way, as happened to other Nuer migrants who made the same journey, he could have been killed, incarcerated, conscripted into the SPLA, or sent back to Ethiopia or Sudan. Yet, significantly, during some encounters with these regulatory mechanisms, he was able to deploy human relationships to help him achieve his goal. Under direction from his father, he negotiated successfully through potentially catastrophic encounters with Ethiopian rebels, Kenyan border guards, Kenyan police, and UNHCR officials.

In contrast to notions of refugees bereft of all personal belongings and material goods, it is significant that David's family had clothes and blankets they had obtained from a UN aid program to sell to provide resources for David's journey toward resettlement in the United States. Also noteworthy is that David's family, while certainly not part of the very small number of educated elite in Nuer society, were neither among the poorest of the poor. David's father's military service and multiple wives signal that within a context of impoverishment, they had access to some resources. David's story underscores the importance of the question posed by scholars of migration across geographical settings: what kinds of households possess the capacity to migrate, given the right conditions? (Baker and Aina 1995, 12; Portes and Rumbaut 1996.)

In these ways, David's case also illustrates the ways in which refugees learn how to leave. David's family first learned about possibilities for resettlement opportunities in the United States while in Itang. Later, in Addis Ababa, people in this social network even supplied him with a map. And when David eventually arrived in the camp, he relayed information about his successful journey to people back in Ethiopia; he both telephoned and sent a letter.

David's experience does not fit the common depiction of refugee flight. A "Sudanese" refugee, he was born not in Sudan but in Ethiopia. He spent his entire childhood in a refugee camp because of his parents' decision to migrate before he was born. He sought resettlement in the United States, not necessarily because he was being persecuted for specific religious beliefs, but his life was nonetheless in danger. And surely, with his father's history of having fought against the government of Sudan, David's life could well have been in danger had he sought to return to the only country where he had citizenship, Sudan. Similarly, the fact that David, as the oldest living male child, was chosen among his siblings to undertake the journey is significant culturally and illustrates one of the ways in which the migration process is gendered.

It is relevant that despite the hardships associated with life in the refugee camp in Ethiopia, David did in fact grow up there, and he underwent gaar there. Karen Jacobsen (2005) documents the prevalence in the literature of the notion that refugees who spend significant amounts of time in camps develop a "dependency syndrome," which is thought to hamper their later abilities to be self-sufficient and remain gainfully employed. The degree of industriousness with which David approaches his own future, and that of his children, runs counter to this theory in important ways. David is a significant provider in the form of remittances for his family members who remain in the camps in Ethiopia. He has submitted affidavits on their behalf for them to join him in the United States and is awaiting the processing of their applications. His father, however, has indicated that he is too old to come to the United States and will remain in Africa.

Finally, David's story contrasts in significant ways with those commonly told to government and humanitarian aid officials. When I compare David's description of his experiences with a set of several dozen essays about flight from Sudan that I was given by an aid worker in Kakuma camp in Kenya written by the so-called lost boys (and girls) of Sudan, I am struck by the role of David and other Africans as heroes. In contrast, in the essays written by the Kakuma youth, they represent themselves as victims, with international aid workers and God figuring prominently in their salvation.

INVESTING IN EDUCATION

The next story presents the case of a Sudanese man who was born not in a refugee camp but in the eastern part of Sudan. By being born in Sudan, his experience more closely resembles the scenario of the ideal "Sudanese refugee." In contrast to what one might expect during the height of the war in the 1980s, Thok Ding describes a childhood in rural southern Sudan largely unmarked by war and violence. Eventually this gives way to tragedy and departure from Sudan. While I have no data to support a direct connection in terms of information flow between David and Thok, Thok's experience of deciding to set out for Kenya after receiving a letter from other Nuer who made it successfully to the refugee camp in Kenya suggests a possible sequential link in the migration chain. Similarly, the fact that Thok already had a family member living in the United States when he arrived supports this observation that he followed the lead of others. Both Thok and David refer to letters or maps as an information source in learning how to leave; this underscores their relative privilege as literate people in a context of shrinking educational opportunities for Nuer in the 1990s.

Thok Ding, in his mid-twenties, was born in Upper Nile Province, Sudan. When I first interviewed Thok, he told me of his desire to go to medical school. Several months later, he still hoped to pursue the math and science subjects that he likes, but he had shifted his goals to a perhaps more realistically attainable career in computers. Thok lives alone and works part-time as a parking garage attendant, which also allows him to study to complete his GED. He is a somber young man, and life seems to weigh heavily on his shoulders.

His first memory is of going to the forest to take care of his calves. He describes leaving home in the early morning with other boys his age, taking food with him to eat while he was grazing the cattle and protecting the calves from wild animals. When he was a bit older, in his early teens, he underwent the ritual scarification ushering him into manhood along with other boys who were the same age. The man who performed the scarification made six horizontal cuts from each side of Thok's forehead to the center, beginning with the right side. The other boys with whom Thok underwent scarification are still keeping cows and farming in southern Sudan. After undergoing the painful gaar ritual, Thok said he could be free. "You are independent. That means you can do whatever you like. You can have a woman. You can have a home by yourself. You can live away from your parents."

After Thok became a man, the government troops attacked his village, killing his father. Thok left Sudan after this sad event, traveling on foot for three days with his mother and siblings and their cattle to an Ethiopian refugee camp called Itang. Thok's first formal education opportunity was in Ethiopia, where he attended a mission school. He advanced quickly, skipping several grades. Seventh grade stands out for him as the real beginning of his education. When he passed a national exam, he was transferred to Gambela, another camp, to attend school, leaving his mother and siblings behind. Food scarcity made life in Gambela very difficult. Thok remembered that students were given only three "measures" of grain per month. They would grind the grain to flour, cook the mixture with water, and eat it plain, without a stew. (The addition of stew is significant, as it not only imparts flavor to the dish but also crucial nutrients.) While he was attending school in Gambela, war broke out in Ethiopia. Thok rejoined his mother and siblings, and together they returned to Sudan. Thok did not elaborate on these events saying only that he left his family members in Sudan to travel to Addis Ababa on his own to meet up with friends. "Some people went to Kenya, and they wrote us a letter telling us that there is a chance here to get a form to go to the U.S." In Addis, Thok was given assistance from UNHCR, and he used the money to buy a bus ticket to travel from Ethiopia to Kenya.

Again, Thok did not elaborate on the process by which he entered the camp in Kenya. But approximately ten years after Thok first fled Sudan, he, along with twenty or so other Sudanese refugees whose cases had been processed, boarded a plane for the United States. Before leaving Kenya, he knew that he was going to a place called Sioux Falls to join the son of his father's mother's brother, Samuel Tap. Samuel had not sponsored Thok officially, but the agency was still attempting to place Thok in a location where he had "family." In recounting his experiences, Thok spoke of the intense fear he felt upon arriving in New York City and being separated from his fellow Sudanese traveling companions—his only link with the life he had known up to this point. An airline representative directed the twenty refugees, who spoke limited or no English, toward approximately ten different airline gates, each bound for a different far-flung destination—Minneapolis, Nashville, Houston, Las Vegas, Des Moines, San Diego, Kansas City. Thok was the only one going to Sioux Falls.

Arriving in South Dakota at night, some twenty-six hours after leaving Nairobi, Thok was met by a representative from the volunteer agency responsible for his resettlement, Lutheran Social Services, and a pastor. His memory of that first night is dim, but he recalls being given shampoo, a toothbrush, and some strange food. LSS took him to Samuel Tap's home, where he spent his first night in the United States.

Thok's LSS caseworker encouraged Thok to get a job as soon as possible. John Morrell and Company employed a steady stream of newly arriving immigrants in its Sioux Falls, South Dakota, plant. Thok actually had experience from Sudan and Ethiopia slaughtering cattle, but these were not really skills that transferred to an American-style kill floor. Other Nuer men and women worked at Morrell, but it was Thok's caseworker who helped set up his job interview. He was hired immediately even though he spoke very limited English. Thok remained in Sioux Falls for twenty-one months. For most of that time, he worked forty-five to fifty hours per week as a meat cutter for Morrell. Despite the long hours and the physically demanding work, he expressed no complaints. His experience contrasts with some researchers' assumptions about the unpleasantness and health risks of work in such occupations and demonstrates that these attitudes are not necessarily shared by those who may see this work as the most attractive means available to generate income within a limited set of options.

Thok left South Dakota in the car he had purchased from his earnings to travel to Minnesota. When I asked why he chose to go to Minnesota, he replied, "People get to school, and you get everything—cash assistance, medical [insurance]—everything if you are in school. And in Minnesota there are a lot of jobs and other things." Currently, Thok is single, lives by himself in Minneapolis public housing and is struggling to complete one remaining subject to attain his GED diploma. For the moment, he is satisfied with his job as a parking garage attendant; sometimes he works as many hours as they will allow him, often seven days a week, because he can study when not waiting on customers.

DIVERGENT PATHS TO RESETTLEMENT

David's and Thok's experiences leading up to third-country resettlement from Kenya represent the general migration trajectories that I heard the most frequently and are consistent with what Holtzman (2000) and Abusharaf (2002) report. While this is changing with the increase in family reunification cases from Ethiopia, it was less common to hear of early resettlement cases directly from Ethiopia. Responding to claims of abuse by the Ethiopian government, UNHCR did resettle some refugees directly from Ethiopia. James Kiek, a Gaajok man in his late thirties who was one of the oldest Nuer people I met in the United States, arrived directly from Ethiopia and described his experience: "Refugees collected in capital cities; accidents happened [referring to violence against the refugees]. UNHCR condemned the Ethiopian government [and sent us to America]." It was, in fact, the lack of resettlement opportunities from Ethiopia that prompted people to undertake the dangerous journey to Kenya.

While Sudan-Ethiopia-Sudan-Ethiopia-Kenya or Sudan-Kenya were the most common migration scenarios I heard, some came to the United States via Cairo, as Bok (2003) describes in detail. Still others came to the United States via a more circuitous route, as illustrated by the following two examples: Yien Kak, a young Gaajak man now in his late twenties left Sudan in the 1980s for Ethiopia. Like the experiences of the two men above, he was forced to flee Ethiopia. Yet instead of returning to Sudan he made his way westward across the continent to Liberia. He lived in Liberia for a few years, supporting himself as a rather successful petty trader. Conditions deteriorated in Liberia during the late 1980s and escalated into full-blown civil war. Yien left Liberia with other refugees for the Ivory Coast. He had learned French as a part of his trade business, which had taken him to other francophone West African countries. In the Ivory Coast, he applied for and obtained third-country resettlement as a Sudanese in the United States.

Another case demonstrates an even more dramatic experience. Peter Dak, a Gaajak man in his late twenties, described being forcibly conscripted into the Sudanese Government Army in his teens shortly after undergoing gaar. The Sudanese government sent him to Iraq, where he stayed for eight years, working in a factory. Peter vividly recalled Iraq's war with Iran, the death of Khomeini, Iraq's invasion of Kuwait, and the U.S. war with Iraq. When the Iran-Iraq war ended, he said that Saddam Hussein opened the road to Jordan and told those who wanted to go to leave. Peter had hoped to go to Italy, where a family member resided, but the United Nations in Jordan sent him to Libya instead. Peter did not want to stay in Libya, so he boarded a truck bound for Niamey, Niger. He did not remain in Niger, because he did not speak French. From Niamey, he took a bush taxi to Lagos, Nigeria, where he encountered international relief organization workers who gave him a small amount of money to attend school. Peter made this journey with a friend with whom he remained for four years in Nigeria. From Nigeria he applied for and secured resettlement in the United States. This is by any measure an extraordinary story. It is, however, consistent with a story that I heard from another non-Nuer southern Sudanese man and is also recounted by Holtzman (2000, 19).

Women, Children, and Resettlement

Flight and departure were gendered processes. In the previous chapter, I drew upon official immigration data to show that approximately three Sudanese men, age eighteen or older, were resettled for every Sudanese woman. When I asked Nuer informants why there were so many more Nuer men than women in the United States, people explained it to me in two ways. From a Nuer woman's perspective, when you leave Sudan, your destination is decided by "where you can reach by foot." A Nuer man explained: "More men than women leave the country. They cannot take children because there is no food, no water, and other dangers. We want to test it first to see how many die on the way."

Culturally derived notions in Western societies, embodied in the phrase *women and children first,* point to expectations about which segments of society are the most vulnerable and deserving of intervention and resources. (For a similar dynamic explained by Somali men in Finland, see Alitolppa-Niitamo 2000.) From a Nuer perspective, it was incumbent upon males to first test what, from all accounts, was a dangerous and unknown situation. However, while some married men did leave their wives behind, others traveled with their wives. Significantly, in order to conform to U.S. notions of the family, men with multiple wives were able to designate only one as a spouse for resettlement purposes. Having more than one wife not only offends both dominant religious and gender-role sensibilities in the United States, it is illegal; thus, I generated little ethnographic data on polygyny. It would seem likely that men might try to categorize a second wife as a sister or daughter; however, as described in the previous chapter, children over the age of eighteen and siblings are very low priority in terms of resettlement policy.

Nuer women are a key part of a complete depiction of Nuer refugee experiences in America. The following case describes the experience of a woman who was resettled at the same time as her husband. Nyamal Chuol, a Gaajak woman born in the early 1970s in Upper Nile Province, left Sudan with her husband, a Gaajok, for Ethiopia, where they had their second child, a son. Nyamal had married around the age of fourteen; her first child had died of snakebite in Sudan. Nyamal, her husband, and their son were resettled as one "case" from Ethiopia. They were first placed in Texas but later moved to Tennessee to join "relatives." Eventually they moved to Iowa for higher wages. There they had a third child. Nyamal had never attended school before arriving in the United States, where she participated in a women's ESL class. Currently, Nyamal and her husband are working in a dry-cleaning shop and a fast-food restaurant, respectively, and they stagger shifts to ensure that one of them is always home to care for the children.

But the experiences of Nuer women refugees on their own in the United States are different. Born in Sudan in the late 1970s, Nyadien Puoch came to the United States as a widow and remarried after arriving. Nyadien lost her mother at a young age and was raised by matrilateral kin, as her father was a soldier in the Anya Nya I rebel movement and hadn't properly wed Nyadien's mother with the requisite transfer of bridewealth cattle. Nyadien describes her life as a child in Sudan:

> When I am little, then we go outside to play with a lot of girls and a lot of boys. We go outside and play in the village. . . . I was seven or eight or even five. I was there. Before that I was in the city. And when my mom is dead, my mom's parents they go there and take us in the village. . . . We play at daytime and at nighttime too. I mean after dinner. The girls and boys play. They have a lot of songs. And when the time you go to bed, the mom calls you. And then you go to bed.
>
> When we go to the river, we say there is a lot of crocodiles, and the moms don't like us to go there. When we go there, maybe they come to call you. I like to play in the river. When I hear my aunt saying, Nyadien! I go far away, and then she doesn't see me and she goes back in the village. After then I come out.

Nyadien describes her household duties and seasonal migration associated with animal husbandry.

> I made *kop* but not all the time.[1] My aunt is cooking a lot. But she doesn't allow the little girls to cook all the time. . . . Sometimes I milked the cows, like this [milking gesture]. And when it is a little cow, I feed it because I put the water inside its mouth—the baby cow. Yeah. And

then in the August/September we go to a different town, because we have two towns. One is summer. One is winter. When we go in the winter, I let the cow outside in the yard.

Nyadien first left Sudan in 1987. Her mother's brother was in school in Itang; he and his wife needed Nyadien to care for their children. According to Nyadien, 1987 was not a time of difficulty in her village: "He needed me to take care of his kids. That's why I go there. We don't have a problem. We have a lot of corn." The situation changed in 1991 because of fighting between Anuak and Nuer people. Many Nuer people, including Nyadien, returned to their village in Sudan. "We have a war—Bar [Anuak] and Nuer. . . . Because in 1991 we have a problem in Itang. Before we get food in Itang, a lot of people go to [Sudan] from Itang to collect corn in the village. When they came back, the Anuak people, they killed them [the Nuer]! On their way! We have a way that you walk and that way all the time [refers to the path that they took]."

Nyadien's future husband, although he was from her village in Sudan, first noticed her while living in Itang. He wrote a letter to her mother's brother indicating that he wished to marry Nyadien after he finished high school. The problem for this young suitor was that, although he had a sister, his sister's husband was dead, and the young suitor therefore did not have bridewealth cattle to marry Nyadien. A second man, with cattle, proposed marriage, but Nyadien refused him because she loved the young man from Itang. Her father became involved at this point, even though he had not paid cows for Nyadien's mother, and insisted upon a bridewealth payment of twenty-five cows. Eventually he told Nyadien that she could marry her young suitor after he paid a portion of the cows, but he must eventually pay all twenty-five. By this time, her husband had joined the migration of young men from Ethiopia to Kenya.

Nyadien traveled to Addis Ababa, where she met her husband's father's brother, who was to accompany her across the border into Kenya. Together they took a bus, but at the border with Kenya they had to get through Kenyan authorities. Nyadien described this interaction: "Maybe you lied, and then you say 'I will come back tomorrow.'" Nyadien's husband was waiting for her in the camp. They waited until she had her first period before sleeping together, but they did not conceive a child. They spent one year together in the camp before her husband succumbed to illness and died. Nyadien had already been approved for resettlement on her husband's application, so when the time came she was sent to the United States on her own. Nyadien is Christian, so the levirate, or marrying her husband's brother, was not an option for her. But she described this as a possibility in Sudan: "In my country, we have that culture. If you [a man] have a brother and your brother gets married, and then your brother is dead and he has a wife, you go in the bed with your brother's wife. If you have a brother, and there are two brothers, the one is dead and the [other] one goes to bed with the woman. No problem."

Nyadien, in addition to providing a woman's perspective on the refugee experience, echoes Thok's experience of a childhood not unlike that described in earlier ethnographic literature (Evans-Pritchard 1940a,b, 1951b, 1956), seemingly unmarked, at least directly, by the upheaval precipitated by conflict since the mid-1950s. This seems particularly paradoxical given that both Nyadien's and David's fathers were soldiers in the rebel army.

Nyadien's emphasis on concerns over the basic problems of birth, puberty rituals, marriage, and death, even in the midst of what most would think of as extreme civil conflict and upheaval, is elaborated on in fine-textured ethnographic detail by Hutchinson (1996). While Hutchinson emphasizes the ways in which Nuer are coping with rapid social change, the experiences of childhood described by Nyadien and Thok seem disengaged from, or at least do not focus on, this reality. Yet this quickly shifts when Thok loses his father and home and Nyadien journeys across the border to a refugee camp in Ethiopia.

And like both Thok and David, Nyadien relates her story to food availability. Thok and Nyadien both had opportunities to cultivate or keep livestock in Ethiopia; Nyadien's camp even had a designated agricultural plot. David, on the other hand, stayed in a camp where refugees could not cultivate their own food, prompting David's father to send him to Kenya for fear that the family would starve. And, in the second camp where Thok stayed as a student, food scarcity was a problem.

Unlike both David and Thok, Nyadien notes extended family members in her story and was in fact raised by matrilateral kin; her father appears only later, at the time of her marriage to collect bridewealth cattle. And unlike both David and Thok, her migration across the Sudan-Ethiopian border for the first time was not precipitated by violence or a crisis. Yet access to education in Ethiopia is related to all three stories.

These cases demonstrate the ways in which Nuer refugees, if not active players in the conflict in Sudan, were social actors in securing their own and their family's survival. The camps served as an active site for cultural and social production, allowing individuals to establish networks of kin, affines, friends, and acquaintances that could be used in times of crisis and mobilized after arrival in the United States.

Conditions in the Camps

Refugees in camps await repatriation to their country of origin after the conflict ends, integration into the country of asylum, or resettlement in a third country. These "warehouses" for forced migrants provide marginal levels of protection from attack and, as demonstrated in the case studies, of food supply. Nyadien Puoch described the fighting between Nuer and Anuak people. (For more on Anuak-Nuer relations, see Falge 1997; Feyissa 2003; MacDermot 1972.) All the individuals described in the case studies, with the exception of Peter Dak, who was in Iraq, identified the lack of security and changing political system in Ethiopia as a factor prompting their decision to seek out third-country resettlement in Kenya.

Ethiopian refugee camps were considered vastly superior to Kenyan camps as a place to stay. Kenyan camps attracted Nuer refugees from Ethiopia because of their reputation as a point of access to U.S. refugee resettlement. Rather than deploying a risk aversion strategy, Nuer refugees embraced risk en route to a more permanent solution to their predicament. This experience was not confined to Nuer refugees. Other southern Sudanese, such as Anuak people, described their efforts to leave Ethiopia to go to Kenya. One Anuak couple and their friend told me about searching the ground for bits of gold in southwestern Ethiopia, which they later traded at the Kenyan border to bribe their way into Kenya. Nuer people I queried about the same practice told me that they knew Anuak people who had done this; they countered that Nuer people did not look for gold in this Anuak area because they would be attacked or chased away.

Thomas Pal, a Gaajak man in his early twenties, compared Itang camp, in Ethiopia, with Kakuma, Ifo, and Walda camps, in Kenya:

> Itang is a very good camp because there is a river and big trees. Refugees can go to the forest and bring wood. You can farm and sell things. You go to the river to fish and shower. You can sell the fish. Kakuma has no river, no forest. They stand in line and get wood from the UN. There is no good camp in Kenya. Ifo and Walda have no river. Itang has a river and a good forest. You can go to the bush and build a house. In Kenya they have tents and it is too hot to live in tents.

Clearly, mediating factors, such as camp conditions and closings in Ethiopia and access to the means (information and cash) to migrate, influenced decisions; once the camps were reopened, however, the decision to leave the relative security of Ethiopian camps for Kenya becomes very significant, as camps in Kenya were considered particularly dangerous. Gordon Gatkuoth, a Gaaguang man in his mid-twenties who left Ethiopia for a camp in Kenya, offered a description of the perils of Kenyan camp life:

> The refugee camp where we were staying, Walda, was attacked by reb-
> els. We lost five people. They were killed. There were rebels of the
> Ethiopian people. There were rebels from Somalia too. Another time,
> they killed one guy at night. They come at night when we receive ra-
> tions from the United Nations. If you don't want to give them rations,
> they will kill you. If you get rations, in the nighttime, rebel people will
> take it. It's a very, very big problem. If you don't give them food, they
> will kill you. If you give them food, tomorrow you do not eat. That's
> when we decided to go to America. If you stay here [in the camp], you
> may die.

The decision to leave either Sudan or Ethiopia for Kenya was not easy. Ethiopia, with its food scarcity and intermittent security problems, for many Nuer was an improvement and offered better chances to survive than did Sudan. The decision to leave for Kenya, however, was a bold choice: to trade the hardships they knew for those they did not.

Learning to Leave

Common to studies of migration is the notion that people learn to leave. There is a learning curve associated with understanding how the system works and what it requires to pass through the system. Three dimensions of this system are the kinds of information required, the means by which it is transmitted, and the social relationship among those who share this information. Given anthropological understandings of Nuer social organization, some might expect to find patterns associated with relations of kinship and patrilineal descent. While my research findings do not exclude this possibility, the ethnographic data seem to support a crisis-mode approach: during times of scarcity or adversity, people mobilize every possible social relationship. Therefore, it is most appropriate to think of Nuer social networks in the broadest possible sense: relationships forged along bloodlines in villages, matrilateral and affinal ties, age-set or school mates, and, particularly, those with whom one lived in refugee camps. The refugee camps, in particular, served as unique sites of social interaction where people who might not necessarily have an opportunity to come into contact are suddenly living together in quite intimate circumstances. Refugee camps serve as fruitful terrain for expanding social networks.

Studies of refugee populations tend to downplay the learning curve associated with leaving. This tendency may be due to a number of factors, including an attempt to control the "image" of refugees being resettled into a politicized U.S. context, where immigration seems increasingly a flashpoint political issue (see Foner 2003). It may also be part of an effort to protect informants.

Holtzman (2000, 26), in his study of Sudanese resettlement in Minnesota, has already broached the topic of Nuer people's efforts to manipulate the system to gain access to resettlement channels. Similarly Bok (2003) has described his own efforts in using the black market to secure a passport with which to exit Sudan. I also seek to illustrate the ways in which Nuer refugees were actors in their resettlement process. In so doing, my intent is not to disclose "secret" behavior but rather to describe what Susan Coutin, in a theoretical discussion of clandestinity (2005), calls known, yet hidden, practices. It is important to preface this section with the fact that my informants were extraordinarily forthcoming about, even proud of, their engagement with the resettlement apparatus. From their perspective, the system was not designed to sort out "authentic" from "inauthentic" refugees. Rather, it functioned as a filter that allowed a limited number to pass, but the criteria by which some people were accepted and others denied were never clarified and therefore appeared arbitrary (see chapter 3).

The refugees described in this study were among the first cohorts in the process of learning to leave. David Bol, for instance, told me that he was the first Nuer person to arrive in Walda camp and described how he transmitted this knowledge to other Nuer people in Addis Ababa.[2] Thok Ding represents a second link in the chain, because he received information from people in the camp before setting out for Walda. Similarly, Nyadien Puoch joined her husband in Kenya after he had already made the journey.

Yet the experiences of these three individuals should not be viewed as an established set of practices. Interviews elicited numerous, and at times contradictory, perspectives on what it took to move through the system. In general, informants agreed that it was important to fit in with the interviewer's notion of a Sudanese refugee. That notion, depending on the interviewer or even the day, remained an elusive piece of knowledge. Similarly, the journey across the Ethiopian border into Kenya was full of dangerous unknowns—the Kenyan police, Ethiopian rebels, and Somali bandits (as my Nuer informants would call them). Matthew Kuach, a Gaajak man in his early thirties, explained, "It depends on their mood at that time. If you fail, you won't know why you failed. You can make a mistake. The interview is a very short time. They make their decision in a very short time. There is no right answer, but they know in their minds."

Informants indicated that they understood that religious persecution and being Christian formed a part of the identity of the "ideal Nuer refugee." The case of Ahmed Deng Bol illustrates this point (see chapter 3). A generalized inability to fend for oneself as marked by limited English, low levels of education in general, particularly literacy, also seemed to be desirable resettlement traits. Nyang Kuon, a Gaaguang man in his late twenties who is fluent in Arabic and had attended a year of university in Cairo, summed this educational situation up: "It's easier for someone with a little education than higher education to come here. They have pity for them. Immigration thinks once you have education, you can solve problems for yourself. They feel sorry for people who couldn't speak English and had to use an interpreter. If they made a mistake, the immigration [service] would just say it was the mistake of the interpreter." In response to this perception, some Nuer men who had traveled out of Sudan for education or other purposes deliberately destroyed their passports and other documents before their encounter with UNHCR staff.

If this perception is true, it presents a paradox in light of pressures on the refugee resettlement program in the United States to transform refugees into economically self-sufficient and productive members of society in the shortest time possible. While this may point to a lack of a consistent Nuer understanding of how best to influence the resettlement system, it also points to the limitations in trying to posit any sort of bureaucratic conspiratorial agenda.

Being far from Sudan and a national minority within the group seeking resettlement—as were Yien Kak in Ivory Coast or Peter Dak in Nigeria—seemed to improve a person's chances for resettlement selection. Peter Dak said,

> In West Africa, they came to visit and took all twenty-four or so Sudanese. They took them to USA. There were more than one hundred Liberians, but they took only four who had relatives in the USA. They had a lot of Liberians in the USA, but they didn't have a lot of Sudanese and they had slots open. They didn't have a resettlement office in Nigeria. They came from Nairobi. Even if you make a mistake, they take you. We did the short interview, but it didn't matter if we made mistakes.

Age was one of those variables that people struggled to get right. Informants misrepresented their age by increasing or decreasing their actual years depending on their specific situation. It should be noted that few were in a position to even know their "actual years," as measured by the system employed by refugee officials. For the most part, age was not recorded in southern Sudan, where births are related to events, such as a birth after a set of twins, during a time of drought, or during a journey. John Wiyual, a Gaajok man, does not know his age but believes he was born in the early 1970s.

> For Sudanese, it is better to be older when you talk to Immigration. They think people who are older are better [able] to take care of themselves. If you don't have a family member to come to join, it is better to say you are older. Me, I don't even know how old I am. If you know the year you are born, you are lucky.

These experiences of relatively young Nuer men and women who arrived in the United States in the 1990s and are now in their twenties and early thirties, challenge popular and even some scholarly depictions of what is referred to as refugee flight. First, migration for most of the cases described was not a linear journey; rather it involved a series of migrations. Second, the migration of these first cohorts to be resettled in the United States could be characterized as exploratory and relatively dangerous; this appears to be one of the variables influencing the three-to-one ratio of Nuer men to Nuer women in the earliest waves of Nuer refugee migration to the United States. Third, as found in other forms of migration (Portes and Rumbaut 1996), David Bol's use of UN blankets to secure the cash necessary to cross into Kenya indicates that it is not the poorest of the poor who decide and are able to migrate.

In the maze of possible origins for the journeys of Nuer refugees and the many possible nonlinear permutations of that migration process, rapid communication has enabled individuals to provide information, monitor routes, and gain access to social networks that could be mobilized quickly. It must therefore be understood that refugee migration is shaped and motivated by more than a reaction to war-induced violence.

Negotiating Nuerness in America

What it means to be Nuer is best understood as a long and continuing process of contestation, reconfiguration, and elaboration. For anthropologist Keila Diehl, "any study of refugee culture also necessarily problematizes the culture concept by exploring the processes of cultural maintenance and reconstruction required when a group of people (and their practices and beliefs) are unhooked from the reinforcing context of 'their' place" (2002, 8). Among Nuer in the diaspora this process is influenced heavily by the gendered and generational demographics of the group described earlier. Migration offers possibilities for reconfigured power relationships in Nuer social organization, where previous avenues to leadership are supplanted by new opportunities. Access to education, community leadership positions, and Christian churches all serve as important vehicles for social reconstruction.

Who Decides What It Means to Be Nuer?

Social relationships among southern Sudanese in the United States were forged along blood lines, in larger kinship frameworks, including marriage, in natal villages in Sudan, in refugee camps and schools outside Sudan, and during passage to the United States. This reflects some characteristics of Malkki's "accidental communities of memory" (1997, 91) and other characteristics of more classic anthropological notions of localized groups. Malkki's concept emphasizes the importance of social bonds generated under seemingly abnormal circumstances, which for many displaced populations have actually become the norm.

Holtzman identifies two main kinds of kinship relations that link Nuer groups and individuals: "*Mar* describes an actual kinship relationship between individuals which can be directly traced through a line of relatives. Brothers, sisters, parents, uncles, aunts, and cousins are all *mar.*" He also notes, "*Buth* refers to relationships between lineages though actual links between individuals cannot be traced" (2000, 42). To this I would add the importance of natal village (*cieng*) relationships, which, given the upheaval in Sudan over the past decades, may or may not coincide with buth and mar relationships.[1]

Nuer social organization in the United States is most appropriately characterized by its fluidity. Nuer families have felt the truncating effects of civil war and the filtering effects of engagement with the refugee resettlement apparatus. Ongoing resettlement, particularly for family reunification cases, continues to alter the composition of social groups. Individuals have also encountered differing constraints and opportunities after arrival in the United States. All these factors contribute to a system that best can be described as in flux.

Therefore, control over what it means to be Nuer, the observation of Nuer "tradition" (which many of my informants referred to as Nuer law), and even the Nuer language itself is, at times, hotly disputed. The informants I worked with were aware of Paul P. Howell's book *A Manual of Nuer Law* (1954). However, references to Nuer law in my interviews never elicited this specific reference. Nuer law was invoked in instances where I might have expected people to refer to Nuer tradition. Nuer were also fond of the word *culture* and used it often to describe differences between U.S. and Nuer social norms. The RV journey described earlier clearly demonstrates that diasporic Nuer are aware of and have access to books written about them. Yet I never encountered a specific incident where these texts were invoked to settle a dispute.

The following example illustrates the process of contestation over what it means to be Nuer in the United States. It calls into question who has the authority to represent the group to outsiders. While this is a function of intragroup power dynamics, it also points to relations between the group and outsiders. Doreen Indra (1999), for instance, notes that in refugee situations, the voices of men are often privileged, providing a gendered and static perspective on "the" culture.

During a conversation with four Gaajok men in their twenties and one in his thirties, I posed a question about child-naming practices. John Duoth Reath indicated that he would possibly name his future son Peter John Duoth. That seemed consistent with my understanding based on interviews and observations of naming practices among Nuer in the United States. Therefore I was surprised when John's response was greeted by heated dissent from the other men. Gatdet Riek, the oldest man in the group, who was in his late thirties, insisted that naming the child after its grandfather is a Dinka practice. When a third man, Gordon Pal, insisted that his family named children in this way, Gadtet accused him of "having Dinka" in his family tree. Gadtet, who seemed to outrank the others by virtue of age-based seniority, had the last word: Nuer only "name the child after the grandfather some-times." But, Gatdet added, even the Dinka create new names. The expres-sion on Gordon's face, although he remained silent, revealed that he stood by his original assertion but chose not to challenge Gadtet. This notion of having inferior knowledge or understanding about Nuer tradition was re-peated on another occasion when Wal Buom, a Nuer man, was recounting his genealogy for me. William Tharjiath, Wal's friend, interrupted, insisting that Wal had made a mistake after the eighth generation. William corrected his friend, explaining that Wal's faulty version was due to "having Dinka" in his lineage. The incorporation of Dinka people into Nuer genealogies is a well-documented practice in the ethnographic literature and did not appear significant in explaining emergent forms of Nuer social organization in the United States. Yet it appears to affect notions of legitimacy with respect to representations of Nuer cultural practices.

Another example of the contested nature of remembered Nuer cultural practices can be seen in a case where a Nuer man is accused of killing his father's brother's son in a fight in Tennessee. During a discussion shortly after the incident among Nuer men, one Nuer man described what would have happened if the same killing had taken place in Sudan: "If someone has killed someone, the government will put the killer in jail. Compensation will take place. A fine will be taken by the government—three years in jail." He continued to give an overview of killing: "There are three ways of killing a person: accidentally (*guac*); war/revenge/fight (*thong*), meaning compensa-tion; intentional killing (*bhim*) and the government will settle the case. Pay seventy cows—sometimes they [the victim's family] will refuse compensa-tion. And not having cattle is not an excuse for not paying compensation." At this point, the discussion turned into a rapid-fire argument among the six Nuer men seated in the living room contesting the specifics of this descrip-tion of Nuer "law."

Clearly, as demonstrated in the examples above, divergent perspectives exist on some fundamental aspects of Nuer life and death. Hutchinson (1996) has documented similar variation in Nuer social life in Sudan, where she attributes cultural variation to differentiation between eastern and west-ern Nuer and their articulation with external processes. This theme was less dominant in my study, perhaps due to my heavy reliance on eastern Nuer groups, who are by far numerically dominant in the United States. One ex-planation may be due in part to histories of displacement: people who char-acterize themselves as Gaajak, Gaajok, or Gaaguang (eastern Jikany Nuer) may be a generation removed from life in southern Sudan having grown up in a refugee camp in a neighboring African country.

Contestation over what it means to be Nuer and who decides is exacerbated by the relative lack of Nuer elders in the United States. As noted earlier, in many Nuer U.S. communities the oldest people are in their forties. These individuals do take on limited roles in terms of community arbitration in a relatively informal sense. One man in his twenties put it this way: "Elders are chronologically young, but they have addressed the emotional issues and the public issues." But the elders in the United States are themselves working through the changes associated with life in a new environment in which they are ill prepared to care for themselves, let alone others. One Nuer woman in her early twenties explained the experience of older Nuer people in the following way: "Elderly people say they are sorry to come here. They are crying a lot. They feel bad."

In light of this, it becomes very difficult to describe the "typical" Nuer refugee in the United States or to provide a comprehensive, yet succinct, depiction of "Nuer culture." This runs counter to the efforts of international humanitarian workers and domestic human services providers (health care clinicians, social workers, employment counselors) to achieve "cultural competence" with a wide spectrum of populations and who tend to rely on cultural snapshot–type documents that provide a thumbnail sketch of the particular culture. Arguably, these efforts represent good intentions with respect to recognizing cultural difference but remain inadequate to understand evolving cultural systems.

Expressions of Patriliny

A central question for anthropologists familiar with the Nuer ethnographic record is the extent to which segmentary lineage organization is correlated with processes of reconstituting social organization in the diaspora. The examples below point to the polyvalent nature of responses to questions on this topic. Timothy Kuach, a Nuer man in his early thirties who had taken an introductory anthropology course in the United States in which they had studied about the Nuer, suggests that it is far too early in the establishment of a Nuer diaspora to discern these relationships. "In Sudan, when a lineage gets too big, a section will break away and go live somewhere else. It is because of food. Here, it takes time to build a lineage. In future, there will maybe be a Nebraska lineage, a Minnesota lineage. But it is too early."

Most of my U.S. informants considered themselves to be Gaajak, Gaajok, or Gaaguang (see chapter 1). The usual response to my queries about lineage affiliation was surprised laughter that I was aware of these matters. One of my informants pointed out that most states had people from a mix of these lineages. For instance, in Tennessee, there were more Gaajok than Gaajak. In Minnesota, there were more Gaajak than Gaajok. Gaaguang were, reportedly, not in the majority in any of the states. Timothy Kuach asserted that for some seeking leadership positions in mutual assistance associations (MAAs), this may hold some importance, but it did not matter for him. Rather it would be more important what the prospective leader "said, thought, and did."

I do not imply that lineage membership is irrelevant. For example, I attended a graduation celebration in Omaha, Nebraska, honoring Nuer youth who had completed high school degrees. I met a number of people who had come to visit from many states—South Dakota, North Dakota, Minnesota, Iowa, Tennessee—representing Gaajak, Gaajok, and Gaaguang people. Upon returning home, I received a call from a Gaajok man inviting me back the following weekend for a second party to honor Gaajok students who had not been included in this event, which my informant said was for Gaajak students. When I brought this matter up with my Gaajak hosts, with whom I had traveled to the event, they laughed but agreed that there had been some breakdown in communication; there had been talk of having a second party. Another Gaajok man, Hoth Chuol, who is attending community college, explained the Gaajak-Gaajok divide in terms of educational opportunities in Sudan:

Gaajok got education before the Gaajak. They think we dominate them. Gaajak in Minnesota are quiet because they are in the minority. Gaajak are quiet in Tennessee when there are more Gaajok. Sometimes people refused education [in Sudan]. They didn't see the value. Gaajak are not willing to go elsewhere if they are transferred. People *resist* government, especially forced movement—for example, a job transfer. For young graduates, jobs in public service are assigned randomly. Gaajak refuse to move. Gaajok don't refuse and therefore move ahead. Education in Sudan is free, including food and uniforms. All graduates get jobs working for the government. Lots of people work as tax aides.

As noted earlier, Farnham (n.d.) identified specific patterns relating to lineage membership in a struggle for control over an MAA. My findings, however, suggest that lineage membership is more negotiable than biologically determined ties of descent are sometimes conceptualized to be. For instance, I encountered married couples in which one spouse was Gaajak and the other Gaajok. Moreover, I recorded three cases where a Nuer man or woman who claimed membership in a particular lineage (for example,

Gaajok), was identified by others as a member of an entirely different lineage (for example, Lou). When I pursued the matter with one individual in question, he replied nonchalantly that biologically he was Lou but after growing up in a Gaajok area, he "felt more like a Gaajok."

Evans-Pritchard, writing about kinship, also noted that any Nuer "can establish kinship of some kind—real, assumed, by analogy, mythological, or just fictitious—with everybody he comes into contact with during this lifetime and through the length and breadth of kinship" (1951a, 368). Therefore, their patrilineal social structure is more accurately understood as an idealized model of society (Gough 1971; Mair 1962, 124, 133–34). The ways in which patriliny is expressed in the everyday and life cycle events of Nuer-speaking refugees in the United States proved a more fruitful line of inquiry. This section provides examples of informants' understanding of lineage membership, marital exogamy, and the naming of children.

When broaching the subject of Nuer social organization, it is useful to define Nuer notions of what constitutes the family and how that social grouping appears after being filtered through the resettlement mechanism. Refugee selection defines a family in classic nuclear terms—husband, wife, and unmarried minor children.

Nuer adults, who were born either in Sudan or in a refugee-camp situation in another African country, continue to calculate descent along patrilineal lines, symbolized through naming, as described by Evans-Pritchard more than sixty years ago. This finding is significant because it differs from what Sudanese scholar Mohamed Salih (1994, 117) reports for the patrilineal Moro in Sudan. Most males and females, age eighteen to forty-two, whom I interviewed regarding family history could supply me with the names of at least seven, and up to thirteen, ascending agnatic generations. In contrast, few were able to provide me with more than two ascending matrilineal generations. This does not, of course, negate the importance of matrilateral ties in patrilineal systems. Rather, it simply affirms agnatic ties in establishing identity.

The relevance of agnatic ties can be seen in a number of spheres. First, the fact that the identity of one's pater (socially recognized father) is not in doubt has importance in contemporary legal contexts for refugees seeking asylum. A child carries the name of his father, his father's father, his father's father's father and so on. As explained earlier, the Nuer system of naming calculates up to thirteen or more ascending generations of men. To non-Nuer, it may appear that a small number of names are used repeatedly. For instance, if I ask a Nuer person if they know a John Chuol, they may say yes, but we could be thinking of different people. But in a Nuer system, I could ask if they know John, son of Chuol, son of Bol, son of Hoth, son of Diew, son of Guek, son of Deng, and so on. This is an effective system for pinpointing an individual's social identity (even if this does not coincide with biological reality). Significantly, if one's father or grandfather fought with the Anya Nya I rebel movement, it would be entirely possible for the Sudanese government, perhaps with the assistance of a Nuer informer, to identify that individual. This has important repercussions for Nuer refugees who are at risk of being refouled, or sent back, to Sudan, as I learned in consultation with an immigration attorney on behalf of a Nuer man threatened with deportation.

The ability to recount seven ascending agnatic ancestors was also important among my Nuer informants because that is the number of generations they should consult in selecting a marriage partner to avoid transgression of incest taboos (*ruaal*). This accords with what Hutchinson (1996) reports with respect to a contraction of generations in determining incest taboos.

THE NAMING OF CHILDREN

The enduring nature of patriliny in Nuer social organization can be seen in the naming of children born in the United States to Nuer parents. Naming children represents a deceptively simple act that sheds light on how Nuer parents choose to continue past practices or adopt those commonly found in U.S. society. Analyzing naming practices is one way of documenting the degree to which Nuer in the diaspora are actively seeking to maintain a Nuer identity. (See also D'Alisera 2004.) Most Nuer parents reproduce the patrilineage in both a biological and a social sense by retaining customary naming practices that ascribe agnatic descent group membership. This naming practice represents a conscious and deliberate choice because Nuer naming practices run counter to norms within the United States.

To employ a hypothetical example, a son born to a man named John Jal logically could be called Jok Duoth. It may appear that a rupture has occurred in transferring the father's name to the child. Upon closer examination, it becomes apparent that this is not the case. The full name of the father, reckoning seven generations, is John Duoth Jal Deng Kurjiok Wal Wang, whose son is Jok John Duoth Jal Deng Kurjiok Wal. Seldom does the U.S. bureaucratic system accommodate individuals with more than three names. Service providers, in a rather crude cultural translation, interpret Nuer naming practices to be children taking their father's middle name as their surname. While this observation is not untrue, it is a significant reduction of the larger reality.

The force of everyday processes whereby immigrants and refugees are made into subjects of a particular nation state is strong and persistent (Ong 1996, 2003). In addition to the majority of cases of naming practices described above, I also have documented a limited number of cases where Nuer parents, perhaps influenced by a desire to accommodate or assimilate, have opted to use the father's third name as the child's surname. It is difficult to predict the impact this divergence from customary practices will have on calculating patrilineage membership among subsequent generations of U.S.-born Nuer children.

It has been argued that the segmentary nature of the Nuer lineage system has an inherent capacity to absorb change. The Nuer lineage system has incorporated non-Nuer, such as the Dinka, into their genealogies. This could translate into a quite favorable prognosis for the ability of the lineage to endure changing circumstances.

The introduction of Christian names in Sudan is one example of the way in which the form is maintained, albeit redeployed with new content and meaning. The example of John Duoth Jal illustrates the way in which Christian influence was grafted onto the lineage over time. John would have adopted this name later in life, at the time of baptism or confirmation. He will pass this baptismal name onto his children. This process has interesting implications over generations; if naming practices are retained in the present form, John Duoth Jal's son's surname will be Duoth and his grandson's surname will be John. Christian names may be conferred at birth, but it is more likely that they are bestowed during a church ceremony later in life. All the children whose births I documented in the United States were given Nuer rather than Christian names. One Nuer man explained why: "They don't want their children to get lost. They don't want to get confused with African Americans. To have my names as a Sudanese gives me my own opportunity. If they want to give special opportunities for Africans, I will be one. Your name can help people recognize quickly that you are not American. I'm a Sudanese. I want to be proud of being Sudanese."

Another example of the form's ability to incorporate change is in the choice of the child's first name. While the second through the thirteenth names are prescribed by the names of the pater, the choice of a child's first name represents a window of opportunity to introduce new content onto an accepted form. The choice of a name could be influenced by any number of factors, including birth order among siblings, within a set of twins or after a set of twins; names from ascending generations from either the (rare) maternal or the (usual) paternal line; or events, experiences, or circumstances surrounding the pregnancy in the lives of the parents. Typically among Nuer refugees, the name of the child is chosen by one or both parents living in the

United States, but these choices may be influenced by other family members still residing in Africa through letters, telephone calls, or via messengers traveling between Africa and the United States. A common name among Nuer children in the United States is Jal (feminine Nyajal), meaning journey or migration.[2] Another common name is Chol, meaning something that replaces that which is lost or missing, as in a child born after a sibling who died. I also encountered several girls and women named Nyakor, meaning daughter of war.

Many of these names are a representation of the chaos and trauma endured by these refugees. Other names are representative of a more hopeful future. One couple named their daughter Nyalaat. The Nuer do not hesitate to produce neologisms; the root *laat*, derived from the verb to work, was chosen, the young mother told me, "because her father is working at Denny's."[3] The parents of another little girl named her Tethloat, meaning happiness. Indeed, a person's full name marks more than biological descent. It represents a history of significant events in the life of the family over generations, such as migration, famine, drought, disease, loss, and, perhaps for this generation of Nuer, a chance to begin again.

Reestablishing Authority

Reestablishing authority is an important component of social organization in the diaspora. Evans-Pritchard's seminal work on Nuer patrilineal descent and segmentary lineage organization is a useful starting point for this discussion. Evans-Pritchard took the controversial stand of distinguishing descent from kinship and cemented the divide by addressing the topics in separate monographs (1940a, 1951b). Patrilineal descent, as commonly defined in anthropology, is the tracing of group membership through ascending generations of males. As noted earlier, Nuer are categorized as an acephalous society, one that is not organized around a centralized authority (see Duany 1992; Evans-Pritchard 1940a). In such societies, lineage forms the basis of social organization. Hutchinson, however, notes that by the early 1980s during field research, the Nuer "had been drawn from an indigenous society allegedly devoid of institutionalized rulers into a bewildering spiral of local government authorities, district councils, party bureaucracies, regional assemblies, and national parliaments—all of which were constantly being reshuffled, reorganized, and disbanded" (1996, 25). While arguably not so far removed from historical Nuer political processes of segmentation and fission, this articulation with the state introduced possibilities for state-appointed political leadership about which local Nuer communities had little say.

Like the processes of state intervention in local leadership issues in Sudan, resettlement in the United States launches the Nuer into renewed engagement with government bureaucratic structures in delimiting community leadership and authority. Resettlement in the United States transfigures avenues to power, challenging gender and generation structures that are present, although transforming, in Sudan. Against a backdrop of how race and education work to situate recent Nuer refugee arrivals at the bottom of the U.S. socioeconomic heap, I single out for discussion mutual assistance associations and churches to illustrate the ways Nuer seek to transform their circumstances.

RACE, EDUCATION, AND STATUS

Immigrants to the United States are incorporated into a particular social and economic matrix, depending on their educational level, job skills, degree of English proficiency, and race (Ong 1996). For some, while they may be earning more money than ever before, they will likely experience a downward shift in social status with respect to the larger society. For many Nuer male refugees in the United States, higher status seemed linked to "desk," or white-collar, employment. In reality, given their low levels of education upon entering the United States or the ways in which their academic credentials were devalued upon arrival, most Nuer were employed at the lowest levels of the workforce in jobs that are hard to fill with U.S.-born workers. The almost certain loss of status upon arrival in the United States is a common experience for many refugees and immigrants.

Ong, in her study of differentials within Asian groups arriving in the United States, notes that "hierarchical schemes of racial and cultural differences intersect in complex, contingent ways to locate minorities of color from different class backgrounds" (1996, 737). Race is an overarching variable in the organization of U.S. society that tends to function to locate those with darker skin at the lowest rungs of the socioeconomic ladder. Therefore it is significant that race did not emerge as a more dominant theme in how Nuer people described their experiences in the United States. In fact, when race came up in conversation or interviews, I was usually the one who introduced the topic. My experience, as a white American, diverges markedly from that reported by Abusharaf (2002, 164), a northern Sudanese, who notes that "racialization as a Black people in a White-dominated society" is a central feature of Sudanese incorporation into North America. For those

I interviewed, it is likely that Nuer who currently do not see themselves as victims of racial discrimination in the United States will alter their perspective over time as their number of encounters with a broader spectrum of Americans increases. Prejudice, as John Rex and Robert Moore (1967, 12) observe, can be seen in the structure of social relations and the role of participants' expectations of others within this system.

The following example provides one illustration of how Nuer approach racial categories and relations in the United States. In Luby's, a Nashville cafeteria that my Nuer hosts had brought me to for lunch, I was surprised at my host's openness with an elderly, white, Southern employee who was offering refills from the coffee trolley. When she arrived at our table, my Nuer host smiled at her broadly, reached up to chuck her on the chin, and asked, "Little mama, how is my little mama today?" The woman's eyes widened as she pulled away from his hand. My Nuer host kept smiling and shaking his head saying, "My little mama," as the woman's hand shook pouring coffee into our cups before spinning around on her heel to wheel her trolley to the other side of the dining room. My host had approached her as an elderly woman; the woman had approached him as a black man.

When Nuer mentioned issues of race or ethnicity it tended to be about their relationships with other Sudanese, African Americans, or Mexicans. (For a discussion of Nuer relations with Mexicans and Somalis in a meat-packing plant town in rural Minnesota, see Shandy and Fennelly 2006.) One Nuer man in his early thirties, when asked if he felt white people discriminated against him in America, explained, "In the Sudan, black people oppress other black people." Another Nuer man in his thirties said, "African Americans say, Hey man, how come you dark? You are too dark! African Americans see West Africans or Somalis as closer to them. Somalis and West Africans don't get the question, why are you too dark?" Holtzman (2000, 115) reports similar interactions between Nuer and African Americans. Nuer, who are often resettled in impoverished neighborhoods in the United States, encounter African Americans involved in drugs and other illegal activities and tend to make broad generalizations based on these experiences. Nuer cite the fact that a Nuer child and a young Nuer man have been killed by African Americans—the child by a hit-and-run incident in Minnesota and the young man in a convenience store robbery in Tennessee. This prompted one Nuer man to say, "The African Americans took one of ours when he was working night shift. We let the U.S. government take care of that one. Back home if they [someone] did it [killed someone] on purpose, they would kill him." The only time I heard a Nuer person suggest that they were being discriminated against based on their race by whites was when I was trying to assist Nuer families to find affordable housing. While helping one Nuer family find an apartment, the wife asked, "Maybe they are not calling us because we are black?" Her husband countered that it was because of their "accent in English" and asked if I would make the initial call to see if anything was available.

On a population level, social service providers have observed that Sudanese are treated differently than other refugee populations whom they have been involved in resettling in the United States. First, they assert that it is discriminatory that much smaller numbers of African refugees are resettled than European refugees. Second, there are allegations of racial discrimination over the lengthy delays in resettling African refugees' family members, again in comparison with other refugee groups. Finally, some refugee service providers in the United States assert that there is a generalized reduction in community support—from individuals and institutions—for facilitating the resettlement of Sudanese as compared to non-African groups, such as Bosnians or Kosovar Albanians (Gozdziak and Tuskan 2000).

"DON'T EAT THE EDUCATION HERE!"

Nuer in America display a strong desire to pursue educational opportunities. This correlates in important ways with the ongoing struggle for an independent South Sudan and the history of marginalization within the larger Sudanese political economy. In this respect, education is both a personal and a political issue. In particular, Nuer encourage each other to pursue educational opportunities while in the United States in order to "bring something back" when they eventually return to Africa.

For example, Peter Dak, a Gaajak man who had completed his GED in the United States, summarized a longer speech at a celebration marking some Nuer students' high school graduation in Omaha:

> Don't threaten your teacher to give you good marks. You must work hard. Don't buy a gun and go to school. Boys, don't put rings in your nose and ear. When you are a man, you take those things out. Parents of kids, you go to church. The church will tell you how to manage your kids at home. People are not qualified to be pastors, but they are appointed. Americans know we have a low education. Take the education back home like the missionaries. Don't eat it here. Take it back home.

While it is not possible to provide reliable data on the educational attainment of all Sudanese or even Nuer refugees before their arrival in the United States, for reasons described earlier, human services providers suggest that, relative to other refugee groups, such as Bosnians, Somalis, or Vietnamese, the Nuer as a population arrive with lower levels of education. Sarah Schmidt, an American caseworker who worked intensively with southern Sudanese refugees since 1994, estimated from her approximately fifty Nuer clients that Nuer tended to have zero to five years of formal education before arrival in the United States. Sarah's caseload, however, was disproportionately comprised of women. Drawing on my sample of Sudanese not linked to service provision, which had more men than women, I estimate the median to be approximately six years of formal schooling before arrival in the United States. (Recall the case of Thok Ding, who joined school at a later age and skipped grades.) Only a handful had attended college or completed a tertiary degree before arrival. I encountered no women who had a college degree, and the few men with a tertiary education had undertaken studies in Egypt.

Education, training, and professional credentials are often not recognized at all or perhaps acknowledged as inferior to that obtained in the United States. This is certainly true of the limited number of Sudanese refugees I have interviewed who had professional training in fields such as medicine and engineering. Joseph Mut, a Gaajok man in his late twenties, was a chemical engineer in Sudan. He passed licensing exams in the United States, and he displays the licenses proudly on the wall in his apartment. Yet, like the medical residency requirement for graduates of foreign medical schools, he must do additional training at a U.S.-based institution to qualify fully for positions commensurate with his training in Africa. When I interviewed Kiir Wal, the only African-trained southern Sudanese medical doctor I had heard about, he was just beginning the lengthy process of what essentially amounts to retraining in the United States.[4] The U.S. population of Nuer may be skewed as a function of differing international criteria for refugee resettlement. Sharon Hutchinson (pers. comm., 2000), for instance, noted that Nuer in Australia, where immigration policies require English proficiency, seemed to have higher education levels than Nuer in the United States.

Sarah Schmidt and Jane Bunson, U.S. caseworkers, have noted differentials in education level between Nuer and Dinka refugees. Peter Dak, a Gaajak man, agreed with their observations, explaining that Nuer tended to have fewer years of formal schooling in Sudan than their Dinka counterparts. However, he asserted that this was not a result of oppression by Dinka, but rather Nuer attachment to cattle. Dinka, in his view, were more likely to send their children to school, while Nuer parents were more likely to keep their children "in the forest caring for the cattle." Peter also pointed to the gendered dimensions of educational access. Dinka parents were more likely to invest in the girls' education than Nuer were. And, indeed, one of the few Sudanese women I have met with a high school education obtained in Africa is Dinka (and married to a Nuer). James Khot, a Gaajak man who was born in Sudan and had attended high school in Ethiopia, described the disadvantage of being rural in gaining access to schooling: "Schools are not available; you have to be close to town or have relatives in the town to go to school. Others don't go to school because they don't like it. Some live in Khartoum, where there are lots of schools, but they don't go."

Whatever their background or access to schooling in Africa, education is attractive to Nuer in America. Those with only a few years of primary school are striving to obtain a GED. When I relayed information about well-paying ($20–30 per hour), part-time work as an interpreter to one young Gaaguang man, he told me that he was already working part-time and would prefer to not take on the additional employment because he wanted to study. Women with no previous schooling are struggling with the alphabet in ESL classes. Nuer men who had access to tertiary education in Egypt are striving to complete four-year or advanced degrees. Despite being slotted into U.S. society in a disadvantaged position, many Nuer refugees are attending community colleges and universities with the help of U.S. federal financial aid in the form of grants and loans.

The Nuer man who gave the high school graduation celebration speech in Nebraska went on to extol the virtues of education for all members of the community, no matter their age. To the elders, he said, "Go to school, even if you [only] graduate the GED, you can get good jobs with GED. You are not too old. If you go to school to learn ESL, you can talk to your doctor, your lawyer, your church and tell your secrets. You don't need an interpreter, who will tell other people your secrets." This quote also highlights the issue of privacy within the community. Sudanese who are illiterate or who do not speak English must rely on interpreters to help them with their most intimate encounters with health care clinicians, social workers, and attorneys.

EMPLOYMENT

Those Nuer with little education have access only to jobs the U.S.-born population does not want. Undoubtedly, some Nuer find jobs through social networks; however, they do not appear to dominate any particular occupation or service jobs in the ways in which other immigrant and refugee groups have in the past (see Lamphere, Stepick, and Grenier 1994). Factory worker, security guard, parking lot attendant, fast-food server, and nursing home assistant are some of the occupations in which Nuer work.

Like other immigrants in the Midwestern United States, many have worked, for at least some time after arrival, in meat and poultry packing and processing. Meat and poultry plants readily provide jobs to newcomers that are among the most dangerous in the United States. A particularly contentious aspect of shari'a (Islamic law) in Sudan is *hudud*, or amputation of limbs and death by stoning for infractions such as adultery, stealing, or drinking alcohol. This adds a particular twist to the experiences of Sudanese refugees who have lost fingers and hands due to accidents at their meatpacking and processing jobs and may influence their decision to return to Sudan. David Lam, who had lost his hand doing this work, explained: "In Sudan, such a disability is difficult. Under Islamic law, people who are punished for stealing have something cut off. So, people who have a disability like this are considered thieves. They are looked down upon. People with such a disability like this are looked down upon by the Arabs." Another Nuer man who lost his hand in an accident in a meat-packing plant in Iowa told me that the only payment he received for his accident was worker's compensation. Joseph Mut, who began working in the slaughterhouse his first week in the United States, provides another perspective: "I worked for a week killing hogs. The hogs made a lot of noise when they were slaughtered. I couldn't sleep that whole week from nightmares. I asked to be moved to another department and worked cutting out the heart and organs. The work is very hard, but people are hired at up to $9 per hour."

Unquestionably, work in meat or poultry plants is arduous and dangerous. But, for Nuer, as for other immigrant groups, it may provide opportunities and serve as a stepping-stone to other employment. Nyabar Jok, a woman in her late twenties who spoke some English as a result of time spent in Kenya awaiting resettlement, applied for numerous jobs, but she was repeatedly rejected. Eventually, however, she obtained a job at a beef-processing plant. In contrast to the nightmarish experience reported above, she said that she liked the work and that the money, $8.50 per hour, was good. She enjoyed the independence associated with earning a good hourly wage. (For similar experiences among Southeast Asian workers in Kansas, see Benson 1994.)

Nyabar's experience is an interesting example linking occupation to gender relations and the structure of domestic units. Nyabar had left her husband temporarily to live with her cousin (mother's sister's daughter) in another state. She cited her inability to get a job where her husband lived as her reason for leaving. The economy where her husband lived was quite good, so he found it to be a poor excuse. She created additional pressure by telling him that she was unhappy to be living so far away from family. He "consented" to her departure eventually and, because she had no money of her own, paid for her bus ticket. Nyabar never returned to her husband.

Within a year of her departure from her husband, she had begun to see another man.

Low education levels upon arrival situate Nuer in ways that circumscribe employment opportunities in the United States. Nuer refugees nevertheless negotiate these barriers to create "white collar" employment opportunities within a context of changing Nuer social organization.

Mutual Assistance Associations and the Professionalization of Ethnicity

Leadership positions in the Sudanese community organizations provide few opportunities for desk jobs. The U.S. Office of Refugee Resettlement encourages refugee populations to establish MAAs that are incorporated as 501 (C)(3) tax-exempt organizations. In Minnesota, for example, Nuer first established an MAA under the aegis of an existing Ethiopian organization until they established their own tax-exempt status, relying on an attorney's pro bono services. Such organizations typically are governed by a board that meets every three months and in emergencies. The MAA director is usually not a voting member of the board. Holtzman (2000) and Farnham (n.d.), who studied these governance processes more systematically, describe how both Minnesota and California MAAs emerged as hotly contested political spheres that vied for control over state dollars designated for the Sudanese community. These observations are consistent with reports from other states, where southern Sudanese populations have reported MAA leadership conflicts that have degenerated into violence, as one American who works with refugee groups described:

> The Nuer have experienced five years of stability. And then, last year, there was dissent and lawsuits. This process is similar to other refugee groups. The dissent degenerated into violence. Some in the group did not hesitate to resort to violence. . . . The current dissent began when there was a split as a result of community elections. The dominant group didn't allow the elections to take place. The breakaway group held the elections anyway and voted out all of the other board. They then hired lawyers to handle the case. The board is comprised of five members. The new elections resulted in a recount of the votes. Attorneys threw out some of the ballots because they couldn't read them. One guy was beaten up as a result of the process. The dissident group filed a civil rights suit against my office. They said the old board was given $30,000. The records were subpoenaed, and it was shown that they were only given $2,200. Next, they were not giving the new group

the right to serve the population. It is still a mess. It is still bubbling and boiling. Americans are drawn in, and they quickly get in over their heads. They lose control of their involvement.

The existence of one "Sudanese" MAA does not preclude the establishment of others in the same state. However, multiple organizations then must compete for a limited pool of resources through a proposal process. Arguably, this fragmentation undercuts efforts to establish a presence within the larger pool of refugee groups, such as Hmong, Somalis, and Bosnians.

Control over funding is often a source of conflict. In one state, MAA governance issues turned particularly ugly when the Nuer executive director, who did not enjoy popular support, allegedly embezzled funds to pay his own attorney fees, for allegedly having raped a Nuer woman employee. It has not been possible to resolve the case, which was featured briefly on a local television station, because the former executive director fled the state while out on bail and remains at large. Leaving the state under allegations of MAA financial mismanagement was a pattern I documented in several states. In this particular situation, the high drama brought the case to the attention of the state attorney general, who intervened because state dollars allegedly had been embezzled, and there was talk of the American board members who oversaw the organization being implicated in a lawsuit. The state attorney general's office sent representatives to a "community" meeting to elect a new board of directors. An uninformed local police officer also attended. Problematic for these "community" meetings is defining who comprises the community (Crehan 2002). From a state perspective, the Nuer are a part of the Sudanese community. Clearly from the material presented thus far, while Nuer consider themselves Sudanese, they may not see the value in being lumped together with northern Sudanese or even other southerners, such as Dinka, Anuak, or Shilluk people. The notion of community based on national origin is especially problematic for settings, such as Sudan, that has been engaged in a civil war. Postmeeting conversations with Nuer often include reflection on who was absent from the meeting. Broadly speaking, non-Nuer southerners and Nuer with a college-level education are often absent from these meetings. One college-educated Nuer man who was in graduate school explained that those with higher levels of education relied least on the community and did not see the advantage of engagement with MAAs, supporting the earlier assertion that MAA leadership can serve as a fast track to white-collar employment.

Nuer and U.S. Churches

Among Sudanese refugees in the United States, Christian identity serves as a vehicle for social reconstruction and renegotiation. From the moment refugees are met at the airport by their sponsoring agency, religious institutions manage their integration into the host society (see Shandy 2002). In the United States, many of the voluntary agencies that contract with the U.S. government to implement its refugee resettlement program are Christian based, including Lutheran Social Services, Episcopal Migration Ministries, and Catholic Charities USA. While these programs are obliged to and do operate along secular lines, Christian churches and congregations act as sponsors, and volunteers are often recruited within these bodies to assist in easing refugees' transition to the United States. These volunteers are vital to the resettlement experience in that they are the ones who familiarize individual refugees with the essentials of quotidian life in an environment that is vastly different from the one with which they are acquainted. For example, in addition to hosting refugees in their homes, volunteers associated with these religious institutions have gathered clothing and household materials; helped people find low-cost clothing and cars and secure employment; and provided instruction in how to ride a bus, do grocery shopping, and operate a microwave oven.

There have been mixed responses within congregations to incorporating these newcomers. For some church members, these experiences have provided opportunities to look far beyond the confines of their suburb, city, or state. These experiences have even prompted some church members to travel to East Africa and, remarkably, even to Sudan. At one extreme, Scroggins (2002, 350) describes how "a Minnesota housewife" became caught up in the movement, flew to Khartoum to deliver aid, and eventually married southern rebel leader Riek Machar. For other church members, the Sudanese newcomers have been unwanted intruders causing dissent within the church.

Two key features of American Christianity that Sudanese refugees appear to be tapping into are voluntarism and denominationalism. Disappointment over both regular attendance and what I call denominational drift was a recurrent theme in my interviews with American church members. The denominational array of Protestant churches present in the United States did not exist in Sudan in the 1980s and 1990s, when these refugees left their country. Dee, an American who attended a Presbyterian church, noted, "In general, churches have been able to provide space, manpower, money, and promises of help, without fully thinking through what that entails" for

Sudanese refugees. She went on to observe that "Sudanese jump ship for promises of aid from somewhere else. And Americans feel burnt when this happens." Bella, another Presbyterian woman, described this in poignant detail when she described her friendship over several years with a Nuer man and his family. The family had shown up one night unannounced at the church after a long bus journey from another state where they had been re-settled initially by a voluntary agency. It was the dead of winter and they had arrived without suitable clothes for the climate; members of Bella's church mobilized and assisted the young family with housing, clothing, transporta-tion, and a job. One day, without alerting anyone, the family loaded their minivan with some of their belongings and left. Bella got teary in recount-ing the story, saying that she would have been saddened if they had told her that they were leaving, but she was deeply hurt by the fact that they had not said goodbye to her or any of the other church members. She later learned through church channels that the man had been offered an opportunity to serve as a pastor in a Covenant church in another state.

This movement from the Presbyterian to the Covenant Church is grounded in the, perhaps predictable, way in which Sudanese pastors who ministered to congregations in Africa frequently have found their creden-tials and achievements devalued in the United States. This seems particu-larly true in the Presbyterian Church, which was among the first to send missionaries to Sudan in the nineteenth century, particularly to Nuer areas (Pitya 1996). Many Sudanese refugees were Presbyterians or Seventh-Day Adventists when they arrived in the United States. Individual Presbyterian churches, like other Christian denominations, have welcomed the south-ern Sudanese as persecuted Christians and offered them moral and mate-rial support. Presbyterian churches, however, have been hampered by their governance structure in allowing Nuer to serve as official pastors. According to Sheila Sundren, a Presbyterian pastor who works with other immigrant populations, the Presbyterian Church, is more rigidly structured than other Christian churches; it struggles to incorporate these "other-language" pas-tors and makes exacting requirements for those who have not attended a Presbyterian-approved seminary in the United States. "In churches where there are pastors from other countries, the English-speaking pastor is always the senior pastor. The other-language pastor is paid less. The power dynam-ics are always there." Sheila characterizes Presbyterian immigrants who seek to be pastors for U.S. congregations as falling into a category officially called laboring within the bounds, and perhaps more descriptively, falling between the cracks. These relationships manifest themselves in inequities of power and compensation. Significantly, Sudanese who were pastors in Africa lack the requisite educational background to serve as Presbyterian pastors in the United States. An African service provider in California put it this way:

> A lot [of Sudanese] came here and are Presbyterian. They felt that they were not welcomed by the church. They came with elders and deacons, but there was no place for them in the church hierarchy. Truly, when pastors and deacons were ordained in Africa, it was by American missionaries. They don't understand what happened to them during their long hours of flight on the airplane from Africa. It was a disturbing thing. In Africa, there was a pastor in the refugee camp. He was asked to go through training again in America. In San Diego, we are handling this by recognizing the Sudanese pastor as a visiting pastor.

An American service provider in Texas noted that a Nuer man "had to walk on water to be accepted into the seminary." The Nuer face a conundrum in engagements with the Presbyterian Church in America: by virtue of being Christian, they were denied opportunities for education in Sudan. Due to little education, they are prevented from obtaining pastoral training in the United States.

Some Nuer have responded by attending other Protestant churches with a less stringent set of rules governing access to pastoral positions. These institutions provide material and emotional support, but perhaps most significantly they provide space in which Sudanese can undertake social and political organizing necessary for community building. While Sudanese do disperse for weekly church attendance, they gather at interdenominational services around the holidays.

Sudanese refugees represent an important twenty-first-century case study in migration. The extraordinarily rich ethnographic record, with respect to the Nuer, provides us with an ideal opportunity in which to observe and document processes of social transformation within a transnational social field. Nuer migrants depicted in this chapter originate from a range of backgrounds. The arrangement of their domestic units varies widely and transforms dramatically as additional family members are resettled from Africa to the United States. And the specific geographic location in which they are placed here, as well as the presence of other Sudanese available to greet them upon arrival, all conjoin to provide a highly idiosyncratic mosaic of experience.

Yet certain generalizations emerge from the ways in which specific aspects of Nuer society transform. Education, community leadership brokered by engagement with the state, and access to churches all surface as important avenues to renegotiated authority structures in the diaspora. This rendering of the experiences of Nuer migrants in the United States expands our understanding of who constitute "the" Nuer and points to trends that may materialize into patterns over time.

6

Gender Relations

The Transnational Sandwich Generation

Slipping off my shoes and rapping on the Nuer family's apartment door, I smiled in anticipation of being overrun by the couple's two boisterous young children. When Nyawal Chuol opened the door, I understood quickly that something was wrong. Compared to the usual din, the small, one-bedroom apartment that Nyawal shared with her husband Nyang Deng and their two children was subdued. Nyawal explained that during the night they had received a phone call from Ethiopia informing her that her mother's sister's daughter had been in a motor vehicle accident. Nyawal was very worried about her sister. Yet she also was concerned with the dilemmas she now faced in maintaining her family in the United States, sending enough money to Ethiopia to pay for her sister's medical care, and continuing to meet the existing obligations she and her husband had to his family. Nyawal's dilemma represents an important dynamic in the Nuer migration experience by underscoring the intersection of transnational linkages with gender and generational relations. It also provides insights into the contentious realm of Nuer marriage in the United States.

In the transnationalization of Nuer marriage and courtship the renegotiation of gender roles and generational relations are key sites of contestation where African-based elders' authority is challenged yet still perpetuated by U.S.-based Nuer men and women. Marital tensions linked to familial investment of remittances are a growing source of conflict for Nuer married couples in the United States. Here I seek to carve out some conceptual space to move beyond the superficial demonizing discourse some Nuer males use to disparage segments of the Nuer female population. In these cases, men refer to those women who do not conform to their version of Nuer society's gender-role expectations by refusing to "settle down" as tourist women.

Migration, which often alters the demographic composition of social groups along gender and age lines, provides opportunities to reconfigure authority structures and social relationships. As noted earlier, for resettled Sudanese in America, engagement with the refugee resettlement apparatus has resulted in a skewed demographic profile, where the population is predominantly male. Similarly, most Nuer in the United States are relatively young. Absent from Nuer gender relations in the United States, therefore, is the proximate influence of traditional elders.

The experience of migration between Africa and the United States introduced a whole complement of new variables with which Nuer migrants have had to contend. The conditions under which the Nuer lived in Sudan are not, for the most part, replicable in the United States. Obvious changes include the nature of work, the economics of daily life, and living arrangements. These changes have precipitated ongoing shifts in other domains such as gender roles and generational interactions.

A fundamental shift in Nuer gender relations in the United States is women's increased access to education and income-generating opportunities on par with their husbands. In Africa, Nuer women are certainly not described as meek. However, processes of commoditization of land and labor, war-induced destabilization, and a truncation of kinship ties due to displacement and increased mortality rates elevate women's vulnerability in these settings. In contrast, even Nuer women with little or no formal schooling before arrival in the United States find themselves equipped to contribute to the maintenance of family in the United States and in Africa. What this signifies, I suggest, is a new, transnationalized version of the "sandwich" generation, where one cares for and supports one's family of origin on one continent and one's family of procreation on another.

Ways Elders Exert Control

One half of the transnational sandwich equation can be seen in the ways elders in Africa exert control and command resources from Nuer in America. The institution of marriage is the principal avenue through which African-based elders accomplish this. This control is seen most vividly through the transfer of bridewealth, the selection of marriage partners, and the naming of children.

Age still matters within Sudanese families. One man whose father was killed in Sudan spoke to me about the weighty responsibility of being head not only of the family residing in the United States but also of the remaining family members in Africa. In another setting in a living room full of men in their late twenties, a man in his late teens served us food and drinks. The men joked that since he was the youngest he would be the "woman," illustrating the complex interplay of gender and generation. The difference, however, was that in contrast to what Nuer women typically do, when he finished serving us he sat down and joined us rather than retiring to another room. This scenario of a young man preparing and serving food is reminiscent of settings in cattle camps in Sudan, where males would fend for themselves when away from mothers, wives, and sisters.

A divorced Nuer woman in her late teens with a two-year-old son, Nyajok, noted that her mother and siblings were in Sudan; she said that she had tried to get her mother to come to the United States, but she refused. After finishing high school, Nyajok hoped to return to Africa to visit her mother; however, she is not interested in returning to Africa to live because "there is no future there." And, she appreciates "the freedom in America." Since she came to the United States when she was fourteen, she has enjoyed significant autonomy from family control. Nyajok notes that if she were living in Africa, she would have "to do everything mother says." But here, she makes her own decisions, including divorcing her husband, who is in his early twenties and who cares for their son.

SELECTION OF MARRIAGE PARTNERS

Those familiar with the Nuer as described by Evans-Pritchard are undoubtedly curious about the ways in which marital alliances are brokered among such celebrated cattle-keeping people in the seeming absence of cattle. While there are exceptions, Nuer men are marrying Nuer women. I have documented one case where a Nuer man in Georgia reportedly married a woman from Thailand. Some Nuer men married Ethiopian women while still in Africa and resettled with them in the United States.[1] At numerous gatherings, I have observed a handful of young Nuer men with American girlfriends, black or white. Since these gatherings are, for the most part, segregated by sex—the women and children in one area and the men in another—the American girlfriends stand out as they sit with their boyfriends in the men's area.

Many Sudanese men reported being married and awaiting the arrival of their wives from Africa. Marriage in this context could mean a consummated marriage, which resulted in children, or simply a girl who was promised to a particular man when she reached an appropriate age. Both types of marriage are legitimate for Nuer. However, the latter form of marriage is more difficult to document for immigration authorities.

Other men are single and will rely on family members to broker a marriage for them or will adopt the dominant practice in the United States and choose their own wife without the intervention of their parents or family members in Africa. Tut Jak, a single Gaajak man in his late twenties who has attended college in the United States, asserted,

Marriage is a matter of decision. If we were in villages in the South, we would be married by now, but here we are free. There we are told, Don't marry girls who are Anuak or Dinka. We are encouraged to marry girls from Africa whose backgrounds they [parents in Africa] know well. We are very traditional. Me, I am the elder one. My family needs my services. If I marry someone who is not Nuer, she may control the money. Or she may be surprised [in the sense of looking down on them]. It's not that they hate others, but my wife is the one that must give them the services they need—clothes, cooking with them. We dominate women there. My brother did it. My father did it. I won't do it. I will teach my wife my own culture so she won't be surprised. I will alert her.

The geographic dispersal of the Sudanese in the United States adds an interesting and challenging dimension to courtship. Deng Kurjiok, an unmarried Gaajak man in his mid-twenties, lived in a total of six different states during his first four years in the United States. He said that traveling throughout the United States to live in various locales was important to his marriage strategy. In his words, "you have to find a friend before you can have a wife." There are very few unmarried or unbetrothed Nuer women in America. However, divorce, canceling the betrothal, and putting in a word for a girl not yet of marriageable age would all be ways of increasing the number of Nuer women in circulation. Another young man, John Thok, reportedly had the favor and consent of his future wife and his future wife's brother, but he did not have the blessing of his future wife's sister or her husband. To remedy this situation, John moved away from the state where his future wife lived to another state to live close to his future wife's sister, in order to impress upon her and her husband his fine qualities as a future affine by demonstrating that he was a hard worker and a decent person.

TRANSFER OF BRIDEWEALTH CATTLE

Even among Nuer in the United States, the transfer of cattle to recognize marriage endures as an important element in claiming paternity and custody of children. This extends to Nuer marriages that take place in the United States. This finding contrasts sharply with Holtzman's statement that "in the United States there are no bridewealth cattle to be returned in the event of divorce" (2000, 401). In my research, I found the use of cattle to recognize marriage alive and well. One Nuer couple who married in the United States, she a widow and he a divorcé, described receiving a call from Ethiopia letting them know that a celebration had taken place the night before to recognize their marriage. They had been married eighteen months earlier in a church in the United States, but it had taken this long to save and transfer enough money to Africa to pay a significant portion of the bridewealth and funds for the celebration. John Wal, a Gaajak man in his early twenties, gave the following detailed financial account of bridewealth reckoned in a transnational context, where the current rate is $3,900: "If you marry here and the girl's father is here, you will pay money by how much one cow will take in money—twenty-eight big cows, two small cows, and five bulls. One bull is $200. One cow is $100. Two little cows are $50 each. That's the way we marry here. That's not the way they do it here, but we will keep this. In our country, the girl cannot choose. We learn that here the girl chooses. In our country we had a law for the marriage." Another Gaajak man I interviewed while in Ethiopia gave a more general accounting of bridewealth, with a different scale for Africa-based and diaspora-based Nuer. "Rich Nuer," especially those based in the United States, are expected to pay twenty to twenty-five cows ($1,500–$2,000); Nuer in camps are expected to pay ten to fifteen cows ($700–$1,000).

A variation on this theme can be seen when males return to Africa to marry. Many men I interviewed were already betrothed to women in Africa, usually through a family intermediary's efforts, so in some cases travel to Africa was to fulfill immigration requirements. In one case, the young man's mother "recruited" a wife, but the young man knew her family. From his perspective, knowing her family was akin to knowing her. He liquidated most of his possessions to purchase a plane ticket. He said that he did not need to travel to Africa to marry according to what he called Nuer law, but he had to do this for official immigration purposes. In Ethiopia he participated in a Christian ceremony to obtain a marriage certificate and submitted paperwork for his new wife to join him in America. He returned to the United States to work to pay for costs associated with his wife's resettlement here, and she eventually joined him. Upon arrival, she was greeted with a celebration at the airport. After a few months, when the man had saved enough money to pay for a party, he pooled resources with another man in a similar situation and they held a joint marriage celebration with food, dancing, and speeches, with the brides clad in matching pale yellow, western-style suits.

Men are also linked to their families in Africa through virilocal, postmarital residence practices. Some men exploit the ambiguity associated with the African concept of marriage as process rather than an event. One man described his dilemma of having a wife (or prospective wife) who was living with his family in Africa and having met a non-Nuer African woman in the United States with whom he had had a romantic relationship. He confessed to being torn about what to do, as he was betrothed to this young woman who was living with his family in Ethiopia, but since he was not truly married according to U.S. norms, there was a loophole that he was contemplating exploiting, especially in light of stepped-up demands from both his family and his future wife in Africa for financial support.

Some transformation from virilocal to neolocal residency practices may have been underway in refugee camp settings, particularly in Kenya, where young people were more likely to be separated from families that they left behind in Ethiopia or Sudan. However, evidence that virilocal residence was still dominant can be seen in the instances, like the one described above, where Nuer men in America who were betrothed or married speak of their wives living with the men's families in Sudan, Ethiopia, or even Kenya.

Therefore, another reason men seek wives in Africa and marry with cattle is to draw upon elders' authority to reinforce their own control over their U.S.-based household. U.S.-based Nuer grapple with managing the migration-induced shift from virilocal to neolocal residency practices. Economic and spatial realities of urban and suburban residence in the United States have played an important part in this shift, as refugees with limited resources must rely on access to low-cost public housing. Yet, even more than in other housing situations, there are strict controls over the definition of the domestic unit eligible to reside in that dwelling. To be eligible for this housing, Nuer refugees must at least appear to conform to U.S. nuclear family–based definitions of domestic units (Ong 1996, 2003).

Nuer live in a range of kinds of dwellings from single-family homes to public housing complexes. In terms of home ownership, I met only one family, who were Anuak, who had taken out a mortgage to purchase their home. One Nuer man expressed regret that he had not followed the advice of the voluntary agency representative who had resettled him, who had recommended that he and his cohort attempt to pool their resources and purchase the house in which they were living. Most Nuer rent homes on the open market, qualify for state-run public housing, or rent homes from landlords willing to accept state subsidies. The quality of accommodation varied dramatically from state to state and even within states. Unlike the urban public housing towers I encountered when I lived on the edge of Harlem in New York City in graduate school, Nuer in places like St. Paul, Minnesota; Nashville, Tennessee; Des Moines, Iowa; and Omaha, Nebraska, tend to reside in public or subsidized housing blocks of no more than a dozen units. In Omaha, for instance, I vividly recall visiting some Nuer who had just moved there from Tennessee to avail themselves of what they had heard was very inexpensive public housing. The squat building looked okay from the outside, but I was immediately overwhelmed by the potent odor of urine-soaked carpeting on the stairs upon entering the building. It was as if the buildings had been abandoned and used as a public toilet before being turned into ac-commodation. In another of the buildings someone had torn the carpet up and removed it, exposing the bare, worn floorboards. Aside from the stench and disrepair, the corridor was rather tidy; there was no debris on the floors. Entering the apartments from the corridors was a pleasant surprise and re-minded me of coming in off the dusty, hectic streets in African cities like Addis Ababa or Nairobi to find soothing compounds, which led to individual well-maintained dwellings. Typical of many other apartments I visited in various states, this particular apartment had a kitchen, a bathroom, and a very large living room, branching off to three bedrooms out of sight. The liv-ing room was dominated by large, seemingly new, matching sectional sofas, decorated with purple-and-white hand-crocheted antimacassars. There was a television and a rather sophisticated looking stereo that blasted Arabic-language music over the sound of the television. The walls had a picture of Tupac Shakur and several pictures of Jesus and were decorated at regular intervals along the top by crosses made from decorative wall border mate-rial. Perched on a shelf were a couple of sports trophies inscribed with a Sudanese name. The wall-to-wall carpeting, while not nearly as filthy as that in the corridor leading into the apartment, was unclean, and the Nuer family living there had covered it with throw rugs.

Residency practices influence other domains of Nuer life in important ways. Social service providers assert, based on anecdotal evidence, that the incidence of domestic violence among Sudanese refugees is increasing as a result of neolocal residence. A refugee services worker told of one such experience:

> One woman wanted to leave her husband because of domestic vio-lence. The husband's family beat the crap out of her, kicking her in the stomach when she was six months pregnant. This happened virtually on the steps of the ORR [Office of Refugee Resettlement] office. She was rushed to the hospital. There is a significant amount of spouse abuse. At the same time, the women chase the men down the street with butcher knives.

It is argued that this housing arrangement shifts the focus from an alliance between families to a more intense relationship between two individuals who may have been only marginally involved in the choice of the selection of their spouse. Tensions arising from this arrangement are aggravated by such factors as long separations when one spouse is resettled before the other (and the potential incorporation of additional children from a genitor that is not the pater); the young age of the wife at marriage; the absence of kin networks in the United States; and stress associated with incorporation into life in the United States intensified by a context of poverty.

One Nuer man in his early thirties whose wife had divorced him in the United States said that he intended to marry a woman from Sudan. Ideally, she would be twenty-five or twenty-six years old and have at least a few years of formal schooling. He dismissed the available Nuer women in the United States: "They come here, and they claim their rights. They are crazy here. They are kids. They must be [are expected to be] mature, but instead they like nightclubs and clothes." In this way, Africa symbolizes a repository of gender purity where women are not corrupted by what men describe as "the unreasonable levels of freedom for women in America."

In addition to relying on elders to select marriage partners in Africa, U.S.-based Nuer also draw upon elders' knowledge of kinship and lineage matters to ensure that a prospective marriage does not break incest taboos. One couple who was married in the United States wrote letters to elders living in camps in Ethiopia to ask for permission to marry because they risked breaking incest rules. They genuinely wanted official sanction of this marriage, in part because they believed, as Hutchinson (1996) documents in Sudan, that the health and well-being of their progeny depended on it.

And a final apparently noncontentious area where it is possible to see the active elaboration of transnational ties between elders in Africa and U.S.-based Nuer is in the naming of children (see chapter 5). Many families whom I interviewed said that elder kin in Africa had chosen the names for their U.S.-born children.

Ways Women and Men in Diaspora Subvert Authority

Therefore, while there are significant and ongoing threads of continuity between life in Africa and the way things are done in the United States, there is also room for the subversion of authority and the renegotiation of roles. One of the dilemmas the Nuer population faces in enforcing social norms is the relative lack of proximate elders. Gender and generation vie with each other for explanatory power in these situations. In some cases, men appeal to elders' authority for reinforcement and operationalize generational authority structures to influence gender relations. Simon Wal, age nineteen, married Nyariek Deng, age fifteen, in a Kenyan camp. Simon's father, who was living in Ethiopia, paid three of the twenty-five cows their family owed Nyariek's family, who were also living in Ethiopia. The families had reached an understanding that Simon would send his father money to buy the remaining cows after he reached America. Simon, his wife, and a friend were resettled in Des Moines. Two months after arrival, according to Simon, Nyariek said, "I don't want to be married. I want to go to school. I want to divorce you. I don't want to be married. I don't want to be controlled, because to be married is to be controlled." Simon reported that he asked Nyariek to talk the matter over by phone with her parents in Ethiopia, but she refused. He also said, "Nuer people gathered in Des Moines to talk to her, and she refused to cooperate." (In particular, her only family member in the United States, her mother's brother, came to talk with her.) The third level of arbitration this couple sought was the state's department of human services. Simon recounted the following conversation between Nyariek, the department's representative, and himself:

> They asked Nyariek whether she wanted to be with [me]. And then they say to her, who can pay your money [the loan for transport to America]? When you came from Africa, you had money on credit, and that money was documented for the head of the family [Simon]. Do you want to pay part and have Simon pay part? And she said yes. And then they asked where she would live because she was fifteen years old. She said she had an uncle [mother's brother] in California. She would go live with him. So they said they wanted to talk to [her mother's brother] first. And I say to them, we have some culture [a Nuer way of doing things]. When we marry we pay something. My father pays something to her father. What can we do? And they say: NO WAY HERE IN AMERICA!! So, you can inform your parents there, and they can do what they want, but here—NOTHING! They said if Nyariek wants to marry again, we go to the court. If I want to marry some other girl, we go to the court first. Or, when I get a job I can go to the court and do the paperwork. She [the social worker] told me when I get a job to call her. So, I got a job, I called her, she got a lawyer, and I paid $660 to divorce.

Nyariek's story brings to mind what Ong describes as "the feminist fervor of many social workers [that] actually works to weaken or reconstitute the . . . family" (1996, 743). The push of the state and the civil institutions work at times in tandem to create pressure that encourages refugees to adopt normative roles with regard to behavior, particularly gender roles. Pressure is exerted through legal, social service, and other channels to promote assimilation to U.S. values. Annette Busby (1998) captures this dynamic in her study of gender relations among Kurdish refugees in Sweden, where she writes that Swedes made the following remark about the Kurdish immigrants: "the problem is their culture." Minnesota, another site that prides itself on its liberal values and has been home to a sizable Hmong refugee population from Southeast Asia for more than three decades, provides another example of this pervasive dynamic. In autumn 1998, in the wake of a terrible tragedy where a young Hmong mother murdered all six of her young children, a local newspaper editorial arrived at a conclusion similar to Busby's—the problem was Hmong cultural norms regarding "patriarchal control" within the family. In the Nuer situation described above, the woman used the fact that elders were at a distance to her advantage. She appealed to the department of human services to support her efforts to divorce, as she was a minor.

Divorce is a vivid example of how Nuer refugee women wield power and subvert the authority of Nuer males in America and Nuer elders in Africa. The baseline data provided by the work of Evans-Pritchard and Hutchinson (1990) make this a fascinating phenomenon to follow over time. At present, it is only possible to speak to the situation of recently arrived refugees, most of whose marriages reportedly were recognized by the transfer of bride-wealth cattle from the husband's family's kraal to that of the wife's family.

Hutchinson (1996) has documented significant shifts in the transition from a cattle-based to a cash-based economy. It is unclear why Holtzman (2003, 401) did not encounter the issue of the transfer of bridewealth cattle, when it was such a pervasive theme in my research. The transfer of cattle remains an important element in claiming paternity and custody of children. In the five divorce cases I have documented in the United States—where children were involved and where the man's family reportedly had paid cattle—the young children went to live with the father. In the words of one Nuer man in his thirties, "If you have a child in Nuer law, you cannot leave your kid. If you divorce, the kid stays with the man. The women don't like to leave the kids, but that is the law." (See Hutchinson 1990.)

In one disputed case, where the man claimed to have paid cattle and other Nuer reported that he did not pay cattle, the child went to live with the mother. I have not recorded instances where the U.S. court system was involved in decisions about Nuer child custody in the event of divorce. However, given the strong tendency in U.S. court cases for mothers to be awarded child custody, and the challenge that would pose to Nuer practices, it is likely that this will emerge as an area of contention. In the two divorce cases that I have followed where cattle have been paid but no children were yet produced, Nuer informants report that the woman's family has returned cattle to the man's family. (I heard of the case of an Anuak single mother whose children had been taken into protective custody, but she, understandably, was unwilling to meet with me to discuss her experience.)

Six months after his divorce from Nyariek, Simon married Sarah Kuach, a young widow who had been recently resettled in the United States, in the Covenant Church. Other Nuer people had suggested that they meet one another. Simon and Sarah knew each other only from a distance in Sudan and the camps in Ethiopia. The cows that were transferred from Simon's family to Nyariek's family were not returned immediately to Simon's family in Ethiopia. It was only when, several months later, Nyariek, while staying with her mother's brother, became pregnant by another man that the cows were returned. At this point members of the Sudanese community sided in favor of Simon and said that the man who had impregnated Nyariek should send money to her family to buy three cows to return to Simon's family. Simon and his second wife, Sarah, moved to South Dakota, where Simon finished his GED and got a job. Sarah enrolled in ESL classes and, pushed into the labor market by strict rules governing public assistance introduced with welfare reform, began working in a factory. Sarah and Simon alternate shifts so that one of them is always home to care for their three small children (see also the case of Nyamal Chuol in chapter 4).

Divorce, child custody, and bridewealth are all areas of contestation and transformation. Pal Both, a Nuer man in his late twenties, noted changing sensibilities with respect to the economic realities of having children in the United States: "When they divorce, it is hard to say whether the children will go with the man or the woman. In USA you have to feed the children of another man. A woman has a hard time to marry if she has children."

Many factors contribute to divorce and men's concern over the role of women in initiating dissolution of the conjugal union. An obvious factor is the three-to-one ratio of adult males to females resettled in the United States. Divorce and the keen interest men take in this issue can also be linked to changes in accepted practice with respect to adultery. Nuer men reported grave consequences in Sudan for men accused of adultery with another man's wife: "These women are married with cows. In Sudan, this man would be killed!" In contrast, in the United States, Nuer note that the law protects not only the wife from her husband's wrath but also the man who committed adultery. Furthermore, married Nuer men assert that it is the single men who have more resources to "seduce women" because they are not supporting a family.

Peter Buometet, a Gaajok man in his early thirties, whose wife was still in Ethiopia awaiting resettlement through family reunification channels, provided this perspective:

> Marriage is very important. If three girls out of one thousand divorce, it is too much. The reasons for divorce are: no food at home, no cow or money at home, or he's not a good worker. But these are not reasons. In Sudan, the wife can go and grow crops or go to the relatives, so they don't care with the man. People share problems in Sudan. The people gather and challenge these things and the girl will go back home.

The inadvertent transgression of incest taboos (*ruaal*) is reportedly the only condition under which divorce is reportedly acceptable. Mat Wal, a Gaaguang man in his twenties who lived with his wife, summarized:

> It is okay to divorce if it is ruaal, if you didn't know and married a blood relation. We call it when an old man marries a young girl a stolen marriage. If the girl is not a good cook, no, no, no that is not in the Nuer law to divorce. We say the girl is *bach*. She is not a good cook. She does not work well.

Related Tensions in Nuer Gender Relations: "Dancing before the Drum?"

Many of my interviews with Nuer men elicited very strong and often negative views about certain Nuer women. As with the disproportionate attention divorce garners relative to the number of cases of divorce I tracked, this seems out of proportion to my observations of daily life in Nuer families. In light of material presented thus far, it bears noting that discourse surrounding gender relations is indicative of and related to other forms of social tensions associated with the leveling effects of migration. A Gaajok man in his thirties put it this way:

> There is a gap between the "knows" and the "don't knows" in Sudan. They become one group in the U.S. If you give advice, the rural dwellers say they already know. Now, they are in one basket, including the ones who jump from nowhere. Machar and Garang, for example, with PhD's, would also be in the same class in America. In this situation, there are no people to lead or to be led. In this society, women feel like they have reached heaven. In our society, women and children are subordinate.

Therefore, men's anger directed toward women that engage in adulterous liaisons or other transgressions is also related to men's inability to exact compensation from the men involved in these relationships. Similarly, the loss of control over wives also signals current and anticipated tensions between fathers and children. Some Nuer parents are contending with generational tensions already; however, it is expected that this will be a more pressing topic as the children of the relatively young Nuer parents in their twenties are raised in the United States. While I did not encounter this among Nuer I interviewed, I did speak with one Somali mother who sent her troublesome teenage son back to Africa as a way of managing his delinquency and other behavioral problems.

Given the disproportionately high number of adult Nuer women relative to Nuer men, women who choose not to remain with their husband have multiple options in choosing eligible Nuer men. Sudanese women whom men perceive as less committed to their families are frequently called tourists. Men charge that the women in the United States have life much easier than their counterparts in Africa. Simon Deng, a Gaajak man in his late twenties summed up this sentiment: "Women in America are tourist women. They [may seem to] do whatever they like. They may change men, but they [still] do the kitchen work. These women are considered with low prestige—like a prostitute. We presume a high chance of a second divorce. There is not really a second marriage. The woman is just a concubine." Jok Jieng, a Gaajok man in his thirties, put it this way: "Women face criticism because women look at family, and men look at the well-being of the whole community and see the tensions between man and wife. Such a creature is useless because she cannot manage her husband and child. Women in the U.S. have it easy. They don't have to share food, etc. They just please themselves."

These women, according to the men, travel from state to state visiting friends and relatives. From an analytical stance, one could argue that these women are maintaining and creating ties of kinship, friendship, and ethnicity, but this is not how Nuer men see it. According to some of my male informants, these were women who did not have jobs, were not caring for children, and were not pursuing educational opportunities. Indeed, Nuer arrangements for child custody—whereby children for whom bridewealth cattle had been paid remained with the father—facilitated the mobility of these women. The emergence of the pejorative moniker *tourist women* may reveal less about any reality of these women's lives and, in effect, be more a lashing out by men to compensate for their diminished capacity to control women.

In attempting to move beyond the he said–she said roadblock, it is worth exploring the other half of the transnational sandwich equation. In addition to the pull of family in Africa, Nuer families have the responsibility of raising their family in the United States. Nuer are struggling with the intersection of Nuer and American cultural ideals about family size and the economic realities of raising children in America. In light of this, Nyajal Chuol, a Nuer woman in her late twenties, explained that she and her husband planned to limit their family to the son and daughter that they already had. Two children, in her estimation, were expensive enough to raise in America. Women spoke to me about using Depo-Provera injections, condoms, and withdrawal before ejaculation for contraception. Conversely, other Nuer couples expressed a desire for six or more children.

Many Nuer couples assert that a key area of family tensions is related to remittances. Sarah Mahler observes, "while a common household economy is often assumed, spouses frequently send remittances independently and for different purposes" (2006, 8). Now that women are contributing significantly to family income, they are demanding control over the allocation of remittances to support their own kin in Africa, as illustrated in the introductory ethnographic description of the woman whose relative in Ethiopia needed money for medical care. Mahler goes on to point out that "when female migrants send remittances home they improve their social standing in their families" (ibid.). Given tensions in Nuer marriages, as well as prospects for a durable peace in Sudan, women remitting to their own kinship networks can be seen as a specific means of investing in their own future and that of their children, should their marriage dissolve or should they wish to return to Africa.

Nuer women's increased access to education and opportunities to generate income is central to shifts in other dimensions of social life. One Nuer man explained Nuer women's access to educational opportunities in Sudan: "Dinka women have more education than Nuer women because the Nuer take girls out of school to get married. We don't have secondary schools for girls that were close to the house. If girls go away to school, the people think that they make prostitution. So, they don't send them." (For a similar observation, see MacDermot 1972.) Yet, even Nuer women with little or no education before arriving in the United States find themselves capable of earning in a month more than their parents in Sudan, or in a camp in a neighboring country, might earn in an entire year.

This is not lost on the Nuer. Peter Buometet, the Gaajok man introduced earlier whose wife is still in Ethiopia, described how he thinks the system is biased toward women in the United States: "There is bias in the workplace against men toward women. It is easier for women to get a job with higher pay. They don't need the husband, so they divorce. The U.S. government gives children to women. Sudanese women say, Ahhh, there are human rights for women. They start dancing before the drum [that is, they are getting ahead of themselves]." While Peter's observation about gendered access to the workforce may appear to run counter to discrepancies with respect to the larger American workforce, his point may be valid for certain segments of the workforce, such as African Americans (Collins 1990).

Nuer themselves see gender relations as a problem area in need of a solution. Paul Atak, a Madi man from southern Sudan who aspires to hold an MAA leadership role and serve as a liaison between Sudanese people and social service providers, addressed a mixed group of social service providers and Nuer men to highlight gender issues that Sudanese faced as a result of migration:

> There is a cultural element to accessing resources through the women. Married women expect their husbands to bring those things; it is their responsibility. How do we address the issue of the husband spending money on luxury items such as the VCR? Men go to the grocery store and buy all fresh food and don't pay attention to the cost. It's an education issue regarding priorities of putting kids' shoes before the VCR. Husbands will, however, become angry if confronted about these issues. You need friends and relatives to convey the message through storytelling.

However, controversy does not characterize all Nuer marriages. William Jiech, a married Gaajak man in his mid-twenties who lives with his wife and two small children, provides a counterpoint to the notion that all Nuer marriages are disharmonious, illustrating the limitations in a monolithic characterization of gender relations among the Nuer in the diaspora:

> The women are good. The men are crazy. The women organize themselves. They organize the families. If a man marries, he has the right to control the family. If you move, you decide a month ago, but you don't tell her until the day before. And you say, we move. The wife cannot fight with him. I have a power. That is why I do that. It is very bad. We see when we come to this country that this is bad. Every member of the family has rights. We have to share life. It's not good to be a Nuer woman in Nuer law. We cannot leave American law and we cannot

leave our mother law. We take the good parts of both. Nuer law is applied by agreement. People are punished by [do not benefit from] fighting.

While there do appear to be limits to how far Nuer women go in challenging Nuer forms of authority, they do exhibit a great deal of independence in terms of decision making and action, which is consistent with how they lived in Africa but exceeds that which might be expected among a group of recently arrived refugees given their low proficiency in English language and limited education. My research supports Heldenbrand's findings in a Shilluk family case study (1996) involving a mother who availed herself of the services of community domestic violence shelters to move to another state with her children and leave her husband behind. As in the example Ong (1996) presents where a Cambodian woman wields control over her domestic situation by using the women's shelter and the social service agencies against her husband, Nyariek (described earlier) and several other young women who arrived in the United States as minors made use of social services to divorce their husbands. One possibly surprising phenomenon, from a U.S. perspective, is the willingness of women, for a variety of reasons, to migrate in order to leave their husbands and, in the process, their children. The distance to be traveled or a lack of familiarity with a location does not appear to deter women who are contemplating a move. Yet, in contrast to men, women seem less likely to set out to a destination where they have no kin or other ties.

Women appear to pool resources in the form of reciprocal gifts to mark life cycle events, but they do not appear to use a formalized credit scheme to do so. Mary Gach, a mother in her early twenties, spent about $100 on food for people coming to her home to celebrate the first birthday of her daughter, Changkuoth. Consequently, she had no money to buy an American-style birthday cake to share at the ESL class she attended daily. Her friends in the class, she said, chipped in to buy the cake to share in class. She also told me that when her daughter was born, other Nuer "family and friends" came to visit her and the baby. Each visitor typically gave her $20 "to buy soft things for the baby." In addition to her nuclear family, Mary's kin in the United States includes her husband's father's brother's son and his wife and children; and Mary's mother's brother's daughter and her husband and children. Mary's friends include another Nuer couple and their children who live in their apartment complex, Nuer women whom she knew from Sudan or the camp in Ethiopia, and women she had met in her ESL class.

Mary Gach and other women do establish cooperative bonds. To a certain extent, they form reciprocal networks to assist one another with child care.

But there were limitations to these relationships. In one case, two Gaajak women who appeared to be good friends lived in the same apartment building with their respective families. When I was visiting one, the other invariably came to visit. Their children played together. One day, when sitting and chatting with one woman, the other knocked and came in the door carrying a bowl of food and eating. She went immediately to the refrigerator, grabbed a spoon and a jar of Hellmann's mayonnaise and deposited a huge blob on top of her food, continued eating, and soon left. This event prompted me to ask the woman who lived in the apartment whether the women pooled resources and shared cooking. She quickly and definitively said that they do not. Nor did she seem disturbed by her neighbor's behavior. Parties are another matter; there people do share food.

Women and families take turns visiting one household on any given Saturday. People drop in and out of the hosts' home throughout the day. If people are hungry, they ask the woman hosting for food, or they go to the cupboard, get a bowl, which they rinse in the sink, and serve themselves from the pot on the stove. The hosts also have a large stock of soda pop for guests, which they distribute in a ritualistic manner. If supplies run out, the husband will go to the supermarket to buy more. Visitors also go to the refrigerator and fill children's bottles with whole milk or serve themselves a glass.

Only about ten Nuer women whom I met had even low levels of formal schooling before arriving in the United States; most had none. My sample is perhaps biased because many of the opportunities that I had to meet women were through the ESL class, which tended to cater to women with very low literacy and English-language skills.

Nyandit Lual, a particularly dynamic woman in her early twenties, took the recently arrived young wife, Esther Kier, of her male relative into her home to teach her about "things in America." Esther and her husband, Ruey Kui, had been officially married in Ethiopia, but she had been awaiting resettlement. Nyandit taught Esther many basics, such as how to use the gas stove and the appliances in the laundry room of the apartment building; how to substitute ingredients obtained from the Egyptian grocery for familiar recipes; how to use voice mail and call waiting; and what products were available in U.S. stores for her hair. Nyandit also took off days from her work at a dry cleaner's to spend a few days at the home of Nyanpal Kuey, who had just given birth to a set of twins. Nyandit's husband and a Nuer woman who lived in their apartment building cared for their three small children during her absence.

That Nyandit's husband cares for their children in her absence suggests the ways in which fathers are involved in raising their children. Some couples struggle to adapt to their changing environment and U.S. expectations for gender roles. Other couples seem to take the changes in stride, extracting what they find helpful from Nuer culture and incorporating U.S. norms in other ways. This range of experiences and ways of managing change is consistent with what one would expect for an emerging diaspora population.

Nuer women are a very important part of a complete depiction of Nuer refugee experiences in America. Yet Nuer men are numerically dominant, are easier to communicate with for researchers not fluent in Nuer, and generally seem to have more time to talk unencumbered by child care responsibilities and domestic duties. Nonetheless, women's voices need to be heard. Additional research focusing on women's experiences is needed to fully understand the ways in which the process of resettlement is gendered.

7

Conquering Omaha

Secondary Migration in Context

As a visible manifestation of decision making, migration within the country of resettlement, referred to as either internal or secondary migration, provides an important window into the shifting values ordering Nuer society in the United States.[1] It also reveals tensions inherent in the process of incorporating a transhumant pastoral population into U.S. society. Weighing options and resources is a vital component of the processes of refugee adjustment to, and incorporation in, U.S. life, and nowhere is the outcome of this decision-making process more apparent than in choice of residence. Although refugees have very little say in determining the site of primary resettlement, they have virtually unlimited latitude in determining subsequent moves. In their seemingly irrational choices about where to set up households after being placed in the United States, Nuer stymie providers of refugee services. Particularly puzzling to non-Nuer is that when Sudanese refugees migrate, at least in this stage of the incorporation process, their motivation for moving is not necessarily to achieve geographic consolidation. In other words, Nuer are on the move in the United States, but they are just not gravitating to the same city, state, or regional destination.

Outsiders' perception of irrationality, I argue, is tied to discussions regarding the ways in which certain social groups, such as Africans (Mudimbe 1988) and refugees (Malkki 1995), are imagined as well as a tendency to delimit the social field in which migration is analyzed into national and international spheres. Marc Rodriguez (2004) notes that international and internal migration studies have unfolded in relative isolation from one another, with each operating within these distinct fields of expertise rather than across them. This dichotomization divorces the experiences of refugees in the United States from the larger trajectory of international migration, which brought them to the United States. Despite recent strides in theorizing international migration as a social process that "span[s] their home and the host society" (Basch, Glick Schiller, and Szanton Blanc 1994, 4), the links between internal and international migration continue to be discounted.

Aristide Zolberg, for example, asserts that internal migration is a separate and less complex category of migration:

> The fact that states control the movement of persons across their border highlights the distinctive character of international migration as a social process: whereas internal migration constitutes a mere relocation, its international counterpart entails not only relocation, but a temporary or permanent *change of jurisdiction of membership*. Accordingly, while internal migration may be analyzed as an essentially economic phenomenon, international migration is more complex because an irreducibly *political* element also enters into its composition as well. (1990, 5; emphasis in original)

Nuer internal migration is complex and thus poses challenges to Zolberg's model. First, internal and international migration are related, not discrete, processes on the same trajectory. Second, internal migration has complex social characteristics that cannot be reduced to economically driven relocation alone. Third, internal migration, particularly in the wake of welfare reform in the United States in 1996, also signals a change of jurisdiction of membership that affects access to resources. The U.S. Supreme Court ruling in *Saenz v. Roe* on the "right to travel" within the United States highlights the highly politicized nature of migration within nation-states as well as between them.[2]

Asserting Authority

As in the case described in chapter 5, Joshua Lual and Nyaboth Yang, a married Nuer couple in their twenties, and their two young grammar school-aged children were resettled in Tennessee in 1994. Arriving from a refugee camp in Ethiopia, the family had been involved in the Presbyterian Church in both Sudan and in the camps in Ethiopia. Soon after arrival, their resettlement agency put them in contact with Presbyterian clergy at a church in Memphis. There was an outpouring of material and other support from church members, who were outraged and saddened by the plight of Sudanese Christians. The resettlement agency caseworker helped Joshua obtain a job in a shoe factory. Joshua kept the job for three months, and he and his family attended church regularly. One day two church members went to visit the family at their apartment and found it deserted but still filled with the furniture and most of the secondhand clothes, dishes, and toys donated by church members. (Church members did not know what had become of Joshua until they received an e-mail some months later from a Presbyterian pastor in New York who told them that Joshua had tired of his job in the factory that paid too little for the long hours that he worked and offered no future.) In upstate New York that same week, a local Presbyterian Church received a call from a shelter. Joshua, his wife, and their two children had just arrived on a Greyhound bus from Memphis.

Church members mobilized and assisted the young family with housing, clothing, transportation, and a job for Joshua. After that Joshua slipped in and out of different jobs. Nonetheless, a warm relationship developed between the Nuer family and American members of the congregation over the course of the two years they spent in upstate New York. Joshua obtained his GED. Nyaboth attended ESL classes, gave birth, and got a job at Burger King. Nyaboth's seventeen-year-old cousin (mother's brother's daughter), Mary, came by plane from San Diego to live with them, help with the children, and attend school. One day, however, some Nuer members of the church dropped by to visit Joshua and discovered that he had loaded his car and was preparing to depart. There was little room in his car for the possessions he had accumulated, again largely second-hand items from members of the congregation. Joshua, his wife, and their children were moving back to Memphis without fanfare or farewells. Mary was not accompanying them and had arranged to move in with another Nuer family in New York. Joshua's Nuer friends cleared the remaining furniture, dishes, and clothing items from the apartment. His Nuer friends had the task of telling the American church members, who were closest to Joshua and his family, that Joshua and his family had left. The Americans were puzzled and felt betrayed, especially since Joshua had left without saying goodbye.

This case is significant to an understanding of Nuer secondary migration on several levels. As in the experience of many Sudanese refugees, the male head of household made the migration decision for the family. One Nuer woman explained that it was a husband's right to tell the woman, with notice of only a day or two, that they were going to move. She echoed the words of the male Gaajak informant in chapter 6 who advised other men, "If you move, you decide a month ago, but you don't tell her until the day before. And you say, we move. The wife cannot fight with him." However, women also decide to move, as illustrated by previously described cases and as exemplified above by Mary's leaving her husband. Outsiders to Nuer social life would characterize Joshua's move as spontaneous, but an insider's view shows how it is the product of ongoing deliberations about gender relations in the Nuer diaspora and provides one example of men's efforts to reestablish control within families in a diasporic setting. Men whose wives leave them are disparaged by other Nuer for their perceived inability to manage their family. Joshua's decision was, in part, an attempt to exert control over his family, which he felt was threatened by Mary, who had moved from California to New York after leaving her husband. Joshua felt that she and other Sudanese women in New York were a negative and threatening influence on his wife. In particular, he feared that these women might influence Nyaboth to leave him. Goaded by other Nuer men, he moved back to Memphis in an effort to exert control over his wife, preserve his marriage, maintain his family, and assert his authority.

Conquering Omaha

Chuol Pal, a Nuer man in his twenties, was resettled in Virginia in 1995. He and two other Nuer men his age, whom he knew from his village in Sudan and who had been resettled in Washington, D.C., decided to move to South Dakota, where more Nuer lived. Washington had received only a small number of Sudanese refugees, and very few of them were Nuer. Furthermore, the South Dakota jobs at the meatpacking plant reportedly paid much higher wages than jobs in D.C., and they paid particularly well for those who were willing to work overtime. The three young men stayed in South Dakota and worked for several months at the meatpacking plant. One of Chuol's friends lost his thumb while operating a beef-processing machine. After this experience, his friend decided to take the small payment that he had received from the meatpacking company and workers' compensation for the accident and move to Minnesota to enroll in school. Chuol was not planning to leave South Dakota, but he could not afford the rent without his two friends. So he too moved to Minnesota. Friends from school in Ethiopia advised Chuol to apply for public housing. Eight months later, Chuol obtained a comfortable apartment in St. Paul public housing. Chuol spent two years attending GED classes during the day, working at night as a security guard, and waiting for his wife to come from Africa to join him. When Chuol heard that his wife was definitely coming, he went shopping to spruce up the apartment: plastic beads to hang in the doorway and a black-and-gold bedroom suite.

Eventually, when his wife, Nyanchien, arrived, Chuol held a large celebration in a Seventh-Day Adventist church to mark the occasion. Shortly after her arrival, Nyanchien enrolled in a high school that had programs for non-English-speaking students. Chuol and Nyanchien had many Nuer and American friends, and together they had four extended family members in St. Paul. They had affordable housing in a decent neighborhood that was close to a public transportation route. Both were enrolled in school, and

Chuol had part-time employment. Six months after Nyanchien had arrived, she and Chuol boarded a bus and moved to Nebraska.

This case illustrates a number of dispersal dynamics for Nuer in the United States. First, like Joshua, Chuol was resettled before his wife. It also illustrates a dynamic that Louise Lamphere, Alex Stepick, and Guillermo Grenier (1994) document among immigrants in the workplace: newcomers to the United States frequently work in the packing and processing of meat and poultry. Like other African immigrant and refugee groups, Nuer have gravitated toward educational opportunities (See Alitolppa-Niitamo 2000; McSpadden 1999; Woldemikael 1997). Chuol's mobilization of all available connections—birth-village contacts from the Sudan, kin, and friends from school in Ethiopia—to forge a new life in an unfamiliar setting is common among Nuer. Chuol and Nyanchien's case, like that of Joshua and Nyaboth, entailed a move from a state with higher levels of welfare benefits (Minnesota) to a state with lower levels (Nebraska). From the perspective of a refugee service provider, Chuol and Nyanchien's story represents one of the most puzzling cases and thus appears irrational: despite outward appearances of having all the necessary services and support to make the transition to a successful life in the United States, the couple still moved to a new state. Beyond social indicators of "success"—job, school, housing—cultural factors prevail.

What is unclear to outsiders is that Chuol has political aspirations. In his words, "I need a place where there has to be a population. What I do is organize people." He had tried unsuccessfully to launch his own community organization (MAA) in Minnesota, where about five hundred Nuer live. Given the existing organizations and the small and dispersed population, he could not garner sufficient support to launch his own MAA. Omaha, Nebraska, however, did not have a long-established MAA, as it had received only two Sudanese primary resettlements, but it was quickly emerging as a Nuer hub. Hundreds of Nuer from other states had begun to move there in 1997. Some remained, while others returned to the states they had left or moved on to other states.

Nuer gave many reasons for the move to Omaha. The most common reason was very inexpensive public housing. While this was true, the limited number of available units was quickly depleted. Chuol, who was unsure exactly how many Nuer or other Sudanese people lived in Nebraska, hoped to establish himself by relying on patrilineal (father's brother's son, father's brother's son's son) and matrilateral (mother's brother's son) kin, people from his village in Sudan, and friends from school in Ethiopia. He hoped to make Omaha a base that would encourage other Nuer people to move to Nebraska.

This brings to mind William Durham's observation about the strategic deployment of ethnicity: "Ethnicity is both an identity and an instrument; it is at once a statement of cultural membership and a tool or a weapon by which members attempt to negotiate improved standing with a social system" (1989, 38). Accordingly, when I asked Wal Rut, a Gaajok man, why people were leaving states like Minnesota that provided day care programs, health insurance schemes, (relatively) generous welfare benefits, interpreters for social services, and so on to move to Nebraska, where these services were less available (at that time), he quipped that "they were going to conquer Omaha." While this response may seem nonsensical outside a Nuer context, it has an intriguing level of meaning for Nuer men with few educational credentials, who have limited immediate opportunities to advance their social status in U.S. society (see chapter 5). Investment in education appears to be a long-term strategy, while acquiring positions as MAA leaders provides a short-term opportunity.

The mushrooming of the Nuer population in Omaha is intriguing. Yet it is very significant that it is one of many sites where Nuer live. For instance, California, Georgia, Iowa, Maine, Minnesota, Nevada, New York, South Dakota, Tennessee, Texas, Virginia, and Washington are also locations where Nuer live. Significantly, within a particular state, Nuer live in widely dispersed areas. This national distribution does not correlate in any meaningful way with any known social variables, such as lineage or religious affiliation.

Dispersal as an Investment Strategy

Through dispersal, Nuer increase the number of nodes through which they gain access to resources. In Sudan, the Nuer lived in an ecological setting that experienced famine cycles. Distribution over a wide geographic area is one survival strategy. I do not suggest that their social organization in any way impels them to disperse; rather their form of social organization has the capacity to sustain and absorb mobility without losing a sense of group connection, and this is affirmed in the symbolic recognition of arrivals and the devaluation of departures.

In other cases I have documented, this dispersal strategy has become transnationalized. Some families pool resources to secure resettlement opportunities in the United States for one family member as a means of diversifying the family's survival options. This strategy contradicts the American assumption that families seek to live in close proximity and echoes Jonathan

Bascom's findings for Eritrean refugees living in Sudan (1998): when repatriation to Eritrea became a possibility at the end of the war between Eritrea and Ethiopia, families opted to send some members to Eritrea while others remained in Sudan. In this way, families were able to test the waters in a new environment while maintaining a stake where they were.[3]

Nuer refugees represent a much smaller population than other refugee groups in the United States. Despite their small numbers, Nuer still tend to live very widely dispersed throughout the country. While Holtzman (2000, 37) points out that "Nuer express a desire to live close to one another," my ethnographic research shows contrary examples. For instance, one thirty-year-old Nuer man who had chosen to live with his family in a neighborhood with no other Sudanese told me, "It is better to live closer to strangers than friends." An eighteen-year-old Nuer woman elaborated: "Nuer prefer to live with a little distance between them. They like to be close enough to visit, but not too close [so as not] to fight." The case study of Joshua and Nyaboth illustrates how migration can be used to manage one's family when there are perceived negative influences in a particular locale. Another Nuer man in his mid-twenties explained that if someone does something shameful or regrettable, "The best and most respectful thing that person can do is get out of sight and go live elsewhere." One Nuer man in his thirties, who was struggling to balance work and study, said, "It is good to get away from [Nashville]. It is good to get away from the distractions, from the Sudanese. The Sudanese make distractions. They ask you to send money to Africa. They give you misinformation that might make you depressed and unable to study. These are distractions."

Clearly, assumptions about the nature of social groups, particularly "family," as assembled through engagement with the bureaucratic apparatus for refugee resettlement, create certain expectations about refugee groups and residency. Carol Mortland and Judy Ledgerwood, in their analysis of secondary migration among Southeast Asians in the United States (1987), demonstrate how efforts to place Hmong refugees with "family" failed. Hmong still moved and asserted their own choices about living not just close to family but to certain family members. Assumptions about the benefits of family members living in close proximity may reveal outmoded, idealized assumptions about a past agrarian, sedentarized U.S. society. For the pastoral Nuer, as Evans-Pritchard more than half a century ago pointed out, it is characteristic of Nuer villages to be "spread out as freely as the nature of the ground permits" (Evans-Pritchard 1951a). In Evans-Pritchard's description, spatial solidarity is a function of seasonal fluctuation. People live in varying degrees of proximity depending on seasonal need. My research shows that these social relations and their spatial orientations are redeployed in diasporic settings. Through mobility and migration, Nuer develop and maintain social relationships that were important in an African setting and serve as an investment for future eventualities.

The case of Joshua and Nyaboth represents a series of complex negotiations, spanning not only spatial issues, but also social issues touching on gender, generation, kinship, and affinal ties. Generally, outsiders to the community, such as service providers and policy makers, are in a position to witness only the geographic displacement and not the concomitant social processes governing migration patterns. This range of migration experiences is not readily reduced to archetypal models.

Among Nuer refugees, internal and international migration are articulated, rather than discrete, processes. Migration within the United States is a part of a transnational process, crosscutting ties within the United States engaging kin and affines as well as those that extend to family in Africa and throughout the global Nuer diaspora. Social values are renegotiated and redeployed to account for changing circumstances. Social groupings are reconstituted to override the domestic units put together by the refugee resettlement apparatus. In some instances parents living in Africa exert familial control from afar through their designees living in the United States. In other instances, the transnational context of limited familial control offers unprecedented opportunities for independence and self-determination.

Refugee service providers sometimes conclude that the Nuer move because they are nomads. This interpretation is problematic because it misses the critical distinction between describing a form of social organization that has the capacity to absorb and sustain mobility and positing a genetically derived wanderlust, which Stephen Jay Gould (1998) identifies in migration theories earlier in the twentieth century. Nuer values associated with social organization do not impel mobility. Rather the elasticity of social ties functions as an available adaptive mechanism in the face of scarce resources and change. Insofar as migratory practices differentiate Nuer from their host society in the United States, mobility can be viewed as a mechanism defining the boundaries of the social group (Barth 1998). James Scott discusses the ways in which "Nomads and pastoralists . . . hunter-gatherers, Gypsies, vagrants, homeless people, itinerants, runaway slaves, and serfs have always been a thorn in the side of states" (1998, 1). Some would argue that the U.S. ethnoscape is a result of patterns of migration (Appadurai 1991, 191); however, there is a qualitative difference between westward expansion and the recurrent and unpredictable nature of Nuer migration. Furthermore, historians appear to hold a more positive view of the role of migration in shaping

American society than do contemporary social service workers. In public health terms, for example, a common question on surveys is designed to detect individuals and families who move three or more times in a twelve-month period; these cases are deemed at risk for any number of social and biological ills, because it is assumed that those who migrate have fewer and more superficial social ties. Among the Nuer, I would suggest that the contrary is true. It is precisely because of the existence of enduring social ties that Nuer are able to migrate repeatedly within the United States. Mobility serves as a mechanism to maintain social connections for both present purposes and future contingencies.

Arrivals and Departures

Americans' disappointment with how Nuer take their leave and Nuer people's dismay with how Americans greet newcomers are significant cultural differences and merit further elaboration. Symbolic rituals of greeting and displays of hospitality mark Nuer mobility. Hospitality, particularly the signaling of arrival, is an important aspect of Nuer social life. Yet the ritual aspects of Sudanese hospitality differentiates markedly between arrivals and departures. The following anecdote from my field notes illustrates this dynamic. My female Nuer traveling companions and I left Minneapolis and arrived in Des Moines in the wee hours of the morning after driving five miserable hours on the interstate in lashing rain, high winds, and impenetrable fog. Turning back because of the weather was not an option: in the trunk of our car were 160 sheets of *injera* flat bread purchased from an Ethiopian restaurant for $130 that were going to be served at the party celebrating the arrival of two young brides from camps in Ethiopia.

It was 2 a.m., and we had no specific address for our destination. We relied on the memory of one of our passengers to locate the apartment building. A couple of false turns and fifteen minutes later, we found it. I cringed at the thought of arriving at such a late hour, but we were greeted with warm, heartfelt handshakes. Some of the women who had not seen each other for some time hugged. Indeed, the whole public housing complex came alive with Nuer men, women, and children, who greeted us as we sorted out sleeping accommodations. Only a few of the Nuer who greeted us actually lived in those apartments. Others lived elsewhere in Des Moines or were themselves visitors from other states, such as Nebraska, Minnesota, South Dakota, Tennessee, Texas, or California. They had assembled to greet us and other carloads of Nuer who were arriving for the marriage festivities.

People mingled in the parking lot before heading off in clusters, sorted by gender, to various apartments. As out of town guests, we held court in one of the apartments while others came to greet us. Each person knocked before opening the door and paused to remove his or her shoes upon entering and was served a frosty can of soda pop. We chatted for several hours with different groups of people. The infants tended to doze off, but the toddlers and older children never seemed to fade. My female traveling companions, who had slept in the car, stayed up till dawn laughing, talking, discussing, and preparing the food that we would eat the next day.

We stayed two nights in Des Moines. When it came time to depart, no one bid us farewell. One of the women who had traveled with us was going to remain in Des Moines for a few days to take the driver's license examination (which was reputed to be easier to pass there than it was in other states). A young male high school student returned with us in her stead. We had to turn away his friend, who had arrived in Des Moines by bus for the celebration for lack of space in the car. Other than the interaction regarding who would travel with whom, we did not say goodbye to anyone. I was not even able to locate our hosts, who had provided accommodation, to thank them.

This experience of boisterous and spirited arrivals followed by unmarked departures was repeated in my journeys to other states for other events and echoes what MacDermot (1972, 140) describes in his fieldwork with Nuer in Ethiopia. After spending a number of days in a Sudanese household celebrating, chatting, eating together, even sharing a bed, departures were unmarked. Groups of people and individuals would dribble off with no word or gesture signaling departure, just as Joshua and Nyaboth had left New York in the case described above.

One interpretation of the ritual and performance surrounding arrivals is that arrival reaffirms the existence of the group by renewing social ties. And a departure from one location entails an arrival in another. Secondary migration and mobility within the United States can be viewed as deliberate social investment strategies to reaffirm old and generate new social ties.

Secondary Migration Literature and Methods of Measurement

Refugees literally and figuratively often are "placed" in their resettlement state according to the scatter approach, which disperses members of a particular refugee group across the United States. The stated intent of this policy is to reduce the impact of any one refugee group on a particular receiving community as well as to encourage refugee assimilation into U.S.

society. Many refugees tend to migrate from the location in which they were originally resettled for one reason or another (Forbes 1985; Lieb 1996; Mortland and Ledgerwood 1987; Wong 1995). While these migrations may entail moves within states to different cities or counties, the moves that garner the greatest attention are those that traverse state lines. Therefore, as Zolberg (1990, 5) argues regarding a change of jurisdiction of membership, it is not simply the fact that people are mobile but the order of geographic and administrative boundaries that they cross that renders their mobility significant to the state.[4]

Providers of refugee services attempt to curtail postresettlement migration. From the perspective of policy makers and practitioners in refugee resettlement, caseworkers expend considerable time and resources on each resettled refugee. For example, the caseworker secures an individual or institutional sponsor, arranges housing and ESL classes, gives instruction in how to ride the bus and where to shop, enrolls the refugee in the state economic assistance program, and assists with obtaining employment. The expectation is that resettled refugees will make use of these arrangements as they move toward economic self-sufficiency. Indeed, in an outcomes-based evaluation of a refugee resettlement organization, success is defined most often as the resettlement organization's ability to produce refugees who both obtain and retain employment. Refugees who leave the state in which they were originally resettled often cannot be tracked, so even if they obtain employment they cannot strictly be considered successes.

Consequently, secondary migration has been an ongoing concern for those engaged with refugee policy and refugee services. Indeed, in the early 1980s, in response to the secondary migration of Southeast Asian refugees, the U.S. Department of Health and Human Services convened a task force to address the issue. The interest of the federal government in this topic highlights the challenges this practice poses for efforts to effect any state-based control or monitoring of refugees after arrival in the United States. From the perspective of refugees, however, these moves may represent just one more stop on a long trajectory of migration. In fact, arrival in the United States may represent the first time, after perhaps years of involvement in the refugee apparatus, that they are not enmeshed in a rigid web of policy dictates and regulations.

Understandings of secondary migration processes and patterns are further clouded by a tendency to adopt either an excessively macroanalytic or excessively microanalytic approach to the research problem. Researchers attempt to infer the behavior of individuals and groups based on statistical findings from analyses of population data. At the other extreme, a much less systematic approach can be seen in the attempt to generalize refugee flows from anecdotal experience drawn from a small number of cases.

There are two established macroanalytic methods for looking at secondary migration among refugee groups. Susan Forbes (1985) reviewed data on refugees receiving public assistance in particular states. By looking at the first three digits of the social security number, she was able to determine the state of issuance, which she used as a proxy for state of arrival. A limitation of this method is that it can only capture the migration of those refugees who receive public assistance. The second method uses change of immigrant status data from the Office of Refugee Resettlement (see, for example, Wong 1995). ORR readily acknowledges limitations with regard to the reliability of these data due to illegible handwriting and uncertainty about state of residence when filing the form. (For example, a Nuer man could have been resettled in Tennessee and still receive mail at a particular address where his friends or family live. He could move to Georgia but still complete the form in Tennessee when he returns to visit.) A further limitation to both these methods is that they present information on only two snapshots in time rather than length, duration, and texture of the migration process. They present information on the refugee's resettlement location and current location at the time the study was conducted but no information on the points in between. In the case of Joshua and Nyaboth presented earlier, for instance, these methods may never have discerned that the family left Tennessee for two years before returning.

Theoretical models of refugee secondary migration in the United States are derived primarily from the documentation of large numbers of Hmong refugees who migrated to California's Central Valley in the 1980s (Finck 1986; Lieb 1996). This migration was disproportionate to the Central Valley's available jobs and public resources and spawned the assumption that refugees migrate to states with higher levels of welfare benefits.

The welfare magnet effect is a volatile issue in terms of support for refugee resettlement. Immigration to the United States is brokered at the level of the federal government, yet, as noted earlier, incorporation of the immigrants into the economic and social spheres is the responsibility of individual states. Furthermore, refugees are caught in a dilemma: to be a refugee, they are constructed as victims who fled with the clothes on their backs, yet, as Ong suggests, they are incorporated into the United States through a system that weighs "those who can pull themselves up by their bootstraps against those who make claims on the welfare state" (1996, 739).

Sudanese refugees are aware of the self-sufficiency ideal toward which they are expected to strive after arrival in the United States. One of the first paragraphs in the U.S. government orientation booklet for refugees notes that self-reliance is highly regarded in their new host country. Refugees also learn that they are expected to repay the transport loan that brought them to the United States. While they are eligible for receipt of public assistance, they receive direct and indirect cues about the extent to which obtaining public assistance is stigmatized in the United States.

Testing the Welfare Magnet Hypothesis

The welfare magnet argument is widespread in policy studies of refugees in the United States. I studied interstate migration among a sample of predominantly Nuer Sudanese refugees in the United States. In order to test the relevance of the welfare magnet hypothesis for Sudanese refugee migration,[5] I have examined interstate migration in relationship to the level of welfare benefits of origin and destination states.

A brief elaboration on methodology is necessary to understand the following discussion. The data I used to arrive at these findings came from a computerized database of more than seven hundred Sudanese men, women, and children that I maintained between 1996 and 2000 during the initial phase of ethnographic fieldwork. I updated the database regularly. However, any measurement of a process as fluid as secondary migration can only reflect snapshots in time. The database contained, among other variables, information on the state in which the individual or family was originally resettled, history of residency, and the state of current residence. An unforeseen outcome of the development of this census was the accumulation and organization of data that lent itself to a test of the hypothesis that Sudanese refugees who engage in internal migration after resettlement in the United States are drawn to states with higher levels of public assistance benefits. Within the database, I was able to identify 291 adults (age sixteen or older) for whom I had reliable residency data.

My conversations and interviews with Sudanese refugees had led me to believe that decisions surrounding interstate migration were far too complex to be reduced to simple economic calculations related to receipt of public assistance. This complexity is illustrated in the cases already presented. However, the opportunity to subject my data to systematic analysis provides useful macroanalytic insights.

Incidence of Mobility among Sudanese Refugees

Anecdotal evidence from refugee service providers suggests that Sudanese refugees tend to migrate more than other refugee groups. Based on this sample of 291 adults, my findings support that claim. Of this sample, 73 percent (213) have lived in more than one state since arrival in the United States.[6] The duration of residency in their initial resettlement state before undertaking the first move varied from several days to several years. Within the first six years in the United States an individual or family lived in anywhere from one to six different states.

A little more than a quarter (27 percent, or 78 individuals) remained in the state in which they were originally resettled. This does not mean that they have maintained the same residence since arriving in the United States, but if they did move, it was within the same state. These findings represent somewhat higher levels of secondary migration within a particular group than has been reported for previous waves of refugees to the United States, such as the Hmong, Khmer, and Vietnamese (see Mortland and Ledgerwood 1987). The different rates may be attributable to social differences among groups, methodological differences in data collection, the changing social milieu at time of arrival in the United States, or any combination of the three. From a quantitative perspective, a limitation of this analysis is the relatively small size of the sample, which was not randomly generated. This approach has an advantage over established quantitative methods (described above) because it can assess the more pertinent "last known move" rather than simply the move from arrival to current state. For example, if a refugee moved from Texas to Minnesota, where he or she lived for several years, to New York, it is possible to analyze the most recent and more relevant move from Minnesota to New York. Another advantage is that this sample reflected a diverse array of individuals within a particular group encountered through ethnographic fieldwork and was not limited to those accessed from welfare rolls.

The findings do not support the assertion that Sudanese refugee migration can be explained primarily by the pull of states with higher cash assistance benefits. Of the 213 Sudanese adults in the sample, some Sudanese refugees moved to states with a higher level of cash assistance benefits; many more moved to states with the same or lower levels of benefits. (This information is detailed in the appendixes.) This finding was obtained by examining the last known interstate migration among states that offer high, medium, and low levels of cash assistance benefits. Nearly two out of five (38 percent, or

82 people) of the sample did move to states with higher levels of benefits. However, 131 people (62 percent) moved to states with the same or lower levels of benefits. These findings demonstrate how ethnographic data can be analyzed and presented in a format that can be useful to policy makers and planners in making decisions that affect refugees' lives. As for the ways in which Sudanese refugees themselves weigh various resources in making decisions about mobility, clearly it is impossible to discount the pull of more generous cash assistance benefits for some individuals and families. In fact, to deny that refugees move for reasons other than to position themselves to use resources most effectively is to strip them of their role as social actors. I suggest that it is necessary to view the notion of resources as a variable cultural construct. Southern Sudanese refugees are in most cases moving to attain a more favorable situation for themselves or their families. What we really need to understand is what constitutes a more favorable situation and how Nuer weigh various kinds of resources to achieve that.

Discussion of Findings: Routes and Destinations

The findings presented thus far demonstrate that nearly three-quarters of Sudanese refugees in the sample make at least one interstate move and that their mobility cannot be explained primarily by the pull of more generous welfare benefits in a particular state. Mortland and Ledgerwood's review of secondary migration from an anthropological perspective (1987) examined the migration patterns of Southeast Asian refugees in the United States. They concluded that secondary migration could be understood best when factors relating to social organization were taken into account. In the case of the Hmong and Vietnamese refugees they studied, the principle of patron-client relations was an important explanatory variable in understanding patterns of mobility. Similarly, the Sudanese case presented above shows the importance of the connections between mobility and social ties in understanding secondary migration.

Baker and Aina put forth a broader and more viable model for exploring migration within Africa. Migration can be understood by examining "the interaction between definitions of options and alternatives, the perception of these, and the willingness and capacity to make choices and implement them" (1995, 14). This point can be demonstrated quite dramatically by the following two examples. John Jak, a twenty-four-year-old Nuer man who lived in six different states between 1994 and 1998, explained that the main reason for his mobility was courtship: "I am young, single. I might meet a friend. First you have to meet a friend before she can be your wife." Given the three-to-one ratio of Nuer men to Nuer women living in the United States and the scarcity of unmarried Nuer women, his Nuer marriage prospects in the United States would be restricted largely to girls who are not yet of a marriageable age or women who are unhappily married.

In another case involving a series of migrations within the United States, myriad factors fed the decision of when and where to migrate. Matthew Duach was resettled as a "free case" in Kansas City, Missouri. Later, he moved to be closer to patrilateral kin living in Texas. Matthew and a friend, Deng Changkuoth, then left Texas to attend school in Minnesota.

> We saw the [Sudanese] people in Minnesota, and there was misbehavior there. There was drinking, and we don't drink. So, I said, let's go to California. We tried to find a job. Deng found a job there, but I didn't. Then there was this one company that hired me, but they wanted to send me to Alaska to work on a contract. In January, when I came back from Alaska, the [my] family in Africa had been talking with the [my] family in Dallas. The family in Africa wanted the family in Dallas to find out about me. Chuol, my family member in Dallas, said I had to come back to Texas and stay there. I couldn't go away. But, when I came back in January I couldn't find a job at that time of year in Dallas. I got a job immediately in New Orleans, and that's not a long drive to Dallas.

In terms of how Nuer themselves explain patterns of migration, Timothy Deng, a Gaajok man in his thirties, suggested the following reasons, in order of priority, to explain why Nuer refugees might move after resettlement:

> When people first come, they are eager to speak good English and reunite with family members. Once they are here, they move for better jobs or housing. And finally, they are moving to welfare places, especially the married ones. If you go to the welfare state, you can get an education. Why work when there is no chance for education? Especially those who are married, they get assistance. This way they are free for schooling without being homeless.

A key finding among the cases I have examined in my research is that the formula for calculating where it is financially beneficial for a Nuer family to live is complex and defies simple economic approaches to understanding migration. Access to educational opportunities, for example, appears to be a significant force propelling interstate migration among southern Sudanese refugees in the United States. Southern Sudanese have long-term experience of traveling to avail themselves of educational opportunities. Salih notes that in South Kordofan Province in Sudan, "Education has spread; new skills, expectations and needs have developed, needs that cannot be absorbed or satisfied by the village. Migration is recognized as a means of fulfilling these new needs and expectations" (1994, 124).

Similarly, Timothy's explanations are consistent with refugee studies that suggests that mobility is determined by social factors within the group as well as structural factors in U.S. society.[7] Yet what the literature neglects to point out and what this Nuer informant does not articulate is that some Nuer refugees are as likely to move away from a location as they are to move toward another location, as we saw in the case of divorce earlier. Frequently, there is a conflation of the decision to migrate and the choice of a destination (Kosinski and Prothero 1974, 5). Literature on refugee studies emphasizes the attraction of both kin and an ethnic community. Yet it is important to realize how ethnicity and kinship are deployed in strategic ways (Durham 1989, 138). Networks can be seen both as sources of support and sources of tension. There can be tension associated with those oft-cited "ties that bind." This phrase is used most frequently to connote bonds of an enduring quality; yet these same ties can be viewed as restrictive. Both these dynamics are integral to an understanding of Sudanese secondary migration patterns.

Earlier I noted that most of the southern Sudanese refugees in this sample made at least one interstate move. Given the scatter approach to resettlement, which tries to minimize the impact of any one ethnic group in a particular community by settling small numbers in a widely dispersed manner, one could hypothesize that the Sudanese then move to achieve geographic consolidation. Sudanese refugees have been resettled in at least thirty-six states and still maintain populations in fifteen or more (see chapter 3). This demonstrates that geographic consolidation does not appear to be occurring to a substantial degree. Therefore, states simultaneously experience Nuer out-migration and in-migration among secondary migrants.

The ethnographic data shown in table 7.1 illustrate the range of reasons given for interstate migration and the occasionally competing and contradictory nature of discourse surrounding migration within the United States, rendering it challenging to theorize. This chart highlights the problem of attributing migration decisions to a simple dichotomy of push and pull.

Dispersal can be seen as a strategy deployed by Nuer to ensure that resources in one location are not overtaxed, allow multiple nodes to exploit resources, contribute to the good of the individual and the corporate group, and offset crises in one location by maximizing opportunities elsewhere. This strategy is facilitated by Nuer social organization, which offers greater elasticity of social ties and thus permits alliances and kin affiliations to be deployed as needed in the face of irregular and discontinuous contact. Mobility, as manifested in secondary migration, is a mechanism by which these ties are maintained.

Table 7.1. Reasons for Interstate Migration Decisions

State	Reason for Leaving	Reason for Coming
Calif.	"It's hard to find a job in Calif. because of Hispanics."	"Now I can go to school full-time and welfare takes care of the kids."
		Returning to wife and children after summer working in Tenn. to maintain benefits
		Mild climate
D.C.	Poor job opportunities	Politics in Sudan
Iowa	"In Iowa, there is a lot of crime."	"People move to be closer to family."
	"The police called you at any time. There is not a good administration. They give you tickets."	Came to stay with mother's brother after divorce of husband
	Dissatisfaction with Sudanese community organization	Came to visit and take driver's license exam. Enrolled in school and decided to stay.
Minn.	Was enrolled in a job training program, but "it was not moving fast enough in the education."	Relative lives here
		Better educational opportunities
	In trouble with police	Higher age cutoff for opportunities
	Owed church money	
		Good-paying job ($7.14 per hour)
	"It takes too many hours to work to pay rent."	Leaving domestic violence situation in another state. Had relatives here.
	Conflict over finances in Sudanese community organization	
	Child died	
	Housing is expensive.	

continued

N.C.	"There were no jobs in N.C."	
Neb.	"Too much snow"	"I need a place where there has to be a population. What I do is organize people."
	"There is misbehavior there."	
		To find office job (just graduated from job-training program)
		Attractive to young men because of greater levels of freedom: "boys run away and go there to steal cars."
N.Y.		"To be with husband"
		"To be closer to family"
S.Dak.	Couldn't afford rent without roommates	Kids can play outside and be safe.
		Job opportunities Opportunity to be church pastor
Tenn.	"When you do something wrong, you have to go to a distant place to show people you did not do things intentionally" [after impregnating girl in state of previous residence].	"When I came here to Tenn., SCOT [the Sudanese Community of Tennessee] was failing. People were fighting. Now, I am head of the organization."
	"I worked as a custodian, a housekeeper, . . . in a tire company [etc.]. I had two jobs most of the time. It was too hard to go to school and to work."	Jobs
	"There is a lot of crime in Tenn."	
Tex.	"In Tex., I worked for $4.25 per hour in a hotel. It was too hard to support the family. You have to work lots of jobs."	
	"There is too much crime. The Mexicans are corrupt."	

Global Transactions

Sending Money Home

The slogan "Reliability you can trust" emblazoned on a map of Africa greeted me as I waited to meet up with friends outside Western Union in the sprawling, dusty Ethiopian capital, Addis Ababa. Staring at this sign, I was struck by the vital role these ubiquitous money transfer offices play in larger transnational processes. Estimates vary widely, but it is known that they shuffle a substantial portion of the more than \$232 billion sent home by 200 million migrants each year (IDS 2006). Quadrupling in size from fifty thousand agents in 1998 to more than two hundred thousand in 2004, Western Union offices (and other businesses like them) serve as store fronts, or localizing venues, for the daily, lived experience of globalization (Simpson 2004). Therefore, in a world on the move, they offer a unique window into the linkages between refugees in the diaspora and those who remain in Africa and help to illuminate the concept of globalization from below.

The unidirectional north-south flow of cash from southern Sudanese refugees to their compatriots in Africa is situated within more complex, multidirectional transnational processes involving people, goods, and information. This siphoning off of resources inevitably affects not only the social, cultural, and economic integration of southern Sudanese in the United States over time but also the future for Nuer refugees in Ethiopia. Under these circumstances, money transfer offices were not just facilitating the flow of cash; they were catalysts for rapid social change among southern Sudanese in Ethiopia. Moreover, in commentary that engages contemporary debates surrounding the meaning of globalization, what makes this even more compelling is that these processes were occurring among some of the most marginalized, disenfranchised, and purportedly powerless people on earth—refugees who had been pushed out of their country of origin, many of whom did not have a legal right even to reside in Addis Ababa. This finding lends support to the argument that we need to understand globalization in terms that extend beyond the narrow, economically bounded definition of "the growing liberalization of international trade and investment, and the resulting increase in the integration of national economies" (Griswold, in Lewellen 2002) to one that appreciates "the intensification of global inter-connectedness, suggesting a world full of movement and mixture, contact and linkages, and persistent cultural interaction and exchange" (Inda and Rosaldo 2002).

Africa as a whole receives some $8.1 billion (about 5 percent) of the total estimated expatriate workers' remittances to developing countries (Hugo 2006, 7). While receiving some $211 million per year in remittances, or 2.6 percent of its GDP, Ethiopia is one of the poorest countries on the planet; it ranks next to last in per capita health expenditure in Africa, and the average life expectancy is about forty-five years. Ethiopia hosts approximately one hundred thousand Sudanese refugees. And it is within this adverse environment that Sudanese refugees must carve out a daily subsistence and attempt to plan for the future.

Who Are the Senders?

The previous chapters have described the twenty-five thousand Sudanese who have been resettled in the United States as refugees. A minuscule per-centage of those displaced have gained access to official third-country reset-tlement placements. North America and Australia have emerged as key des-tinations for those southern Sudanese who have been resettled as refugees. Sudanese in Canada, Australia, and other places are important to the overall context of Sudanese migration and transnational ties. Here, however, in or-der to provide an in-depth treatment of the subject, I narrow my focus to linkages between southern Sudanese in the United States and in Ethiopia.

Previous chapters also have documented that as a refugee population ar-riving in the United States, most Nuer lacked formal schooling beyond the secondary level and have been integrated into the lowest socioeconomic tiers. Many ardently seek educational opportunities and are striving to carve out a place for themselves in the United States that allows them to meet their U.S. responsibilities while addressing the needs of those Nuer left behind in Africa. This arrangement means that those who are themselves least finan-cially stable and most marginalized in U.S. society are shouldering the hu-manitarian burden for the aftereffects of Africa's longest-running civil war.

International migration scholar Nicholas Van Hear notes that "one of the most important influences refugees and other migrants can have on their countries of origin is through the remittances they send." (2003, 1) In this case, as with many other refugee populations fleeing civil conflicts, the impact is not necessarily limited to country of origin but applies to neigh-boring countries of asylum where refugee populations with diverse national origins reside. Van Hear goes on to describe the variety of methodological reasons that make it impossible to calculate what percentage of the annual $100 billion in migrants' remittances is sent by refugees. These limitations include the patchiness of remittance data, the impossibility of disaggregating refugee remittances from those of other migrants, and the fact that refugees remit to a constellation of countries, not just their country of origin.

On average the unmarried Sudanese men living in the United States I interviewed estimated sending about $5,000 per year to relatives in Ethiopia and Kenya. Due to all the limitations Van Hear identifies, it is hard to assess to what extent these experiences are representative of the larger Sudanese refugee population. However, this amount is consistent with the overall average of migrants' remittances of $2,000 to $5,000 per year (IDS 2006). Within this relative data vacuum, one could hypothesize an upper limit of $15 million per year, if each of the twenty-five thousand Sudanese refugees resettled in the United States were to send $50 each per month (or enough to support one person in Ethiopia). Ethiopia is only one of several countries where Sudanese refugees are seeking asylum; nonetheless this amount rep-resents a still plausible 7.1 percent of the total annual reported remittances to Ethiopia of $211 million.

While it is impossible with available data to calculate precise amounts, it is possible to describe the ways Sudanese refugees remit using both for-mal and informal avenues. Formal money transfer channels like Western Union—or one of its key competitors, MoneyGram—are used heavily. Di-rect bank transfers are a theoretical option (particularly for sums where the sending fee exceeds $50), but I did not interview anyone who exercised this avenue. Informal, but not casual, ways to dispatch funds include sending money with acquaintances making the trip back to Africa and using what are termed *alternative remittance systems* (see Omer n.d.; Ahmed 2006). Until events of September 11, 2001, Somali remittance companies, or *hawala*, pro-vided a regularly used lower-cost alternative to sending money from North America to Ethiopia. Interviews with Sudanese in the United States before 9/11 elicited a description of a process where people went to the home of a Somali immigrant and gave him money and details about the recipient. The Sudanese counterpart in Ethiopia would go to collect the money from the Somali man's "brother" in Ethiopia. This system made transactions slightly cheaper than Western Union, particularly for sending smaller sums. Scrutiny of these Somali remittance companies and new governmental regulations have closed many of them or driven them underground. As a result, even if Sudanese still use hawala, they are no longer eager to disclose this in interviews. The other informal approach is to send funds and goods along with Sudanese who are making the temporary journey back to Africa, often to visit relatives and, in some cases, to negotiate marriage matters.

With each of these modes come advantages and disadvantages. How African customers weigh these options has become big business for remittance companies like Western Union who have their eye on the markets ushered in by the post–Cold War surge in African emigration, as reflected in the fact that more Africans immigrated to the United States during the 1990s than had come during the previous 180 years (Hume 2002). This dramatic increase was a result both of changes in U.S. immigration policy and destabilization and of the resulting power vacuum as regimes toppled in numerous African countries. Therefore, while remittances have long been recognized as a dimension of Latino or Irish migration, to name two of the best-documented examples, little has been written about the experiences of African remittances.

Remittances are vital to understanding globalization from below, and as will be described later, many recipients depend on this cash flow for daily subsistence. Residing illegally in Addis Ababa, many urban southern Sudanese refugees are "unbanked," making it risky to manage large sums of cash. Carrying cash on their person is perilous, as is hiding it in their rented accommodations. In light of these constraints, funds optimally are transferred as needed (usually monthly). While this option offers advantages to the sender, who is most likely operating on a send-as-earned basis, it is decidedly more costly over time. Western Union, for instance, charges about $15 to send $50 from the United States to Ethiopia, the minimum monthly allotment needed to subsist as an urban refugee in Addis. Sending this amount in twelve monthly remittances would cost $180 in sending fees; if the annual total of $600 were sent in one installment, it would cost the sender only $50. This fee structure encourages sending larger amounts less frequently; however, this practice does not always meet the needs of senders or recipients.

One of the alternatives, sending money with people traveling back to Africa on short-term visits has the advantage of eliminating or diminishing transfer fees, but it also presents drawbacks. Certainly the lack of availability of someone trustworthy traveling when you wish to make a payment is a barrier. And traveling with large amounts of cash can present problems for the carrier when arriving in Ethiopia. This approach also affords less privacy than Western Union: whom you are sending money to (and whom not) along with how much and how often become a matter of social scrutiny. The resulting gossip acts as a mechanism of social control, giving recipients some degree of influence on senders' behavior.

Formal and informal modes of remitting pose other challenges. When using Western Union, the recipient usually is required to present identification and to know the answer to a security question. This can be problematic if the recipient is residing in Addis illegally and lacks documentation, does not speak the principal language, Amharic, or is unable to travel to a Western Union agent location. In some cases, a Sudanese who does have documentation (for example, by virtue of being registered as a student, married to an Ethiopian, or legitimately in Addis Ababa on a pass from the refugee camp) serves as a broker. The recipient needs to know that money is awaiting him or her. Practically, this requires contact through a telephone call or one of the ubiquitous internet kiosks. In Addis some Sudanese with long-term Ethiopian connections have access to a telephone or a post office box. They take messages and deliver mail for a small service fee. Access to a free e-mail account through Yahoo! or Hotmail, and use of Western Union can eliminate the need for such a communication broker.

Even when the broker is eliminated, others in the community keep tabs on who is receiving remittances and how often. In my own experience, I found that numerous Sudanese in Ethiopia communicated with me via e-mail to request assistance after my fieldwork there. These requests ceased when I began to send money to one individual to pay for his school fees, suggesting an understanding that my resources were being channeled to a particular individual and rendering me unavailable to others. Sudanese remittance recipients report that there is an understanding that funds marked for educational costs must be used for that purpose, while money for food or rent is viewed as a corporate asset. If the money is being used improperly, for alcohol rather than school fees, for example, this information is communicated quickly back to the sender, who will most likely stop payments or redirect them to someone else in the family who is deemed more responsible.

Even if the recipient is fulfilling his or her end of the agreement by going to school or supporting the family, remittances still can stop abruptly. The flow of remittances is utterly dependent on the well-being and employment of the sender. A number of those without means in Addis had come there at the behest of their sponsor abroad, only to be stranded there when the remittances stopped. In some cases the Sudanese relative in the United States lost his or her job with the recent economic downturn, showing what happened at the conclusion of the period of economic prosperity that Holtzman (2000) describes. In other cases, the sender fell ill. In still others, he got married and now had to worry about dependents in his newly formed nuclear family. This experience can, however, be gendered, and marriage can also usher in opportunities for women to initiate sending remittances. (For a discussion of gender and remittances, see also Mahler 2006.) For some Sudanese, this meant they could not get enough cash to return to the camp. Others preferred the option of remaining in Addis, cadging a meal and a place to sleep off of others who did have a "relative." This option, at least, offered hope in a way that being "warehoused" in the refugee camp did not.

Clearly, if Africans who have been resettled in the United States are using resources to support families in Africa as well as their immediate families here, this has some impact on their integration into a new society. It may mean they are foregoing educational opportunities in lieu of income-generating ones. They could also eschew the entry-level job with upward mobility potential for the one that simply pays more per hour now. If parents are working more hours during shifts when their children are at home in need of care, this raises questions about how this sharing of resources will play out in the next generation (see Levitt and Waters 2002; Portes and Rumbaut 2001).

However, when considering these potential negative impacts on integration, two points must be considered. First, since many southern Sudanese refugees have access only to entry-level jobs in the United States, they may be barred from working the desirable shifts anyway. The second point has to do with positionality. Often it seems that some of the anti-immigration rhetoric arguing that remittances are a threat to social cohesion in the host country does not pause to consider the choice immigrants face: do you invest in your family in the United States at the expense of your mother or other children who are suffering in another country? Or do you diversify and spread your resources more thinly over more people?

The Impact of Remittances

The remittances sent by Sudanese refugees to family and friends in Ethiopia do not just sustain family and friends; they broker possibilities for dramatic social change in the form of reconfigured residential patterns, local economies, and power structures.

SHAPING RESIDENTIAL PATTERNS

More than 35 Western Union offices dot the landscape of Addis Ababa, the third-largest city in Africa, with five million inhabitants; there are 188 locations nationwide. Living in the shadows of these offices are several thousand refugees from Sudan who depend on the remittances accessed through these offices for daily subsistence. To retrieve the resources housed within these kiosklike structures, in a country where a shared taxi ride costs twelve cents per rider and a filling meal less than a dollar, all you need is a control number, the answer to a test question (for example, your grandfather's name), and a "relative" somewhere abroad. America, Canada, Australia, or even Norway will do. If not a relative, you might hope for a "friend," perhaps a schoolmate or someone you knew from your hometown. These "relatives" and friends are those Sudanese who found some way to migrate to another country.

Some Sudanese come to Addis Ababa when they receive instructions via telephone from a Sudanese sponsor living abroad that there is money awaiting them in the capital. Even the rumor that a relative might be thinking of sending money is enough to prompt people to make the journey. The money often is earmarked for educational costs for the individual to complete his (and it is usually a male) secondary or tertiary education at one of the countless private colleges in Ethiopia. These school fees cost about $39 per month, excluding room and board. It might also be earmarked for treatment for those who cannot get adequate health care in the refugee camps in western Ethiopia. Others come to escape "security situations," created by vendettas levied against them or their families, because a relative might have "been involved in killing" as a soldier. Many are simply caught in the cross fire of recent flare-ups between camp refugees and local inhabitants that have driven even most of the international organizations who provide programming and services out of the area. While international agencies, like UNHCR, treat refugees as victims who need support, some local inhabitants view refugees as interlopers who deplete assets such as firewood and who have access to resources like education and a steady food ration that locals may lack.

Others come to Addis as prospectors of sorts, hoping to get information to establish a connection with a long-lost relative or friend abroad. This process is facilitated by the Nuer cultural injunction not to refuse someone who needs a meal or a place to sleep. Food can always be made to stretch a bit further. Even if the bed is full, there is still room on the floor, as I found in one case where a dozen high school–age boys shared a ten-by-ten-foot room with one bed. They took turns as to which six boys got the bed and which six got the blanket on the hard cement floor. In this way, even those without an immediate link to benefactors abroad still benefit by having food and shelter needs met. While one of these boys may have had a relative abroad sending remittances, the other eleven tapped into this resource and kept themselves afloat, if only barely.

A few come to Addis directly from Sudan, as in the case of the woman, her husband, their three children, and the woman's sister whom I met in a dwelling with a dirt floor and a roof of corrugated tin. In this case, the family sold what cows remained in their herd after the latest assault from the devastation of the war in Sudan and over many days made their way on foot across the border to Ethiopia. They bypassed UNHCR camps en route to Addis. The purpose of the journey was to seek treatment for their three-year-old daughter who suffered from stomach pains. By skirting the refugee camps and heading directly to the capital, where they hoped to receive remittances from a relative in the United States, this family's experience speaks to refugees' perception of the inadequacy of the response of the so-called international community in meeting their basic needs. It also highlights the spuriousness of viewing refugees as powerless and fleeing unthinkingly without a plan. Finally, it emphasizes the limitless reach of globalization, where even the most seemingly isolated regions are tied into a larger system along whose lines cash, information, and even people flow relatively unencumbered, even in the midst of a civil war.

The demographic profile of the Sudanese who arrive in Addis is also revealing. Cash flows facilitated by expanded global networks reshape residential patterns. Gender ratios in the Ethiopian refugee camps are reportedly about half male and half female. This ratio of men to women in Addis shifts to three to one, echoing the gender imbalance reported among Sudanese in the United States. Therefore, while equal numbers of males and females may leave Sudan for Ethiopia, many more men continue on to the capital. Reasons for more Sudanese males than females in Addis include access to the cash necessary to make the trip from the camps to Addis, the pursuit of secondary and tertiary education as a predominantly male activity, and the issue of protection and security. I did interview a few women who were in Addis without a husband or immediate male relatives. They lived with other women and their young children in compounds. I met one Ethiopian woman, married to a Nuer man who was living in the United States with one of their children and another wife. The woman instructed me to contact the father when I got home to tell him to take the second child who was living in

Ethiopia or to send monthly support for the child. Personal security was also an issue. I interviewed one man who had lost a tooth when he was beaten the previous night "just for being Sudanese."

In these ways, money transfer offices act as a sort of siren, beckoning those with little hope and an elevated tolerance for risk to Africa's urban slums. Thus, remittances play a distinctive role in fueling rural to urban migration in Africa. This overview of residency practices is intimately linked to a discussion of local economies.

RECONFIGURING LOCAL ECONOMIES

Destruction of the means of livelihood is one of the principal reasons people become refugees. Paradoxically, refugees, or asylum seekers as they are sometimes called, are often denied the right to work in their host countries. In Ethiopia, Sudanese refugees' daily survival is subsidized only if they remain in the refugee camps, where they are provided what most concur are inadequate rations. In refugee parlance, those Sudanese in western Ethiopian camps are being warehoused—left for an extended period in camps with no immediate solution in sight. This was especially perilous in western Ethiopia, where tensions between locals and refugees ran particularly high, resulting in the gunning down of seven Ethiopian government refugee workers in their jeep in December 2003 (Lacey 2004). Those Sudanese I encountered in Addis had rejected the fate of being forgotten by the rest of the world and sought to procure some additional support, usually to pay for further education. Since formal employment is illegal for refugees in Ethiopia, they must work in the informal economy or rely on remittances.

Options for employment in the informal economy were very limited for this population. When asked why they came to Addis, many Sudanese said they had feared for their lives while gathering firewood in the areas surrounding the refugee camp. Hearing this story from so many people, I couldn't fathom the insatiable consumption that would necessitate so much wood, envisioning all of western Ethiopia ablaze. It was only later that I understood that people sought firewood not for their own personal use but as a commodity to sell. Gathering firewood or selling their and their family's meager camp rations were the only two ways people described to make money to pay the bus fare from the camps to Addis. Gathering firewood was considered a hazardous activity, as this was resented by local Anuak inhabitants and often prompted bloodshed. Given the limited options to earn an income, most Sudanese relied on direct or indirect access to remittances.

Optimally, those who live in Addis receive monthly stipends, while those who remain in the camps tend to get what people called one-time payments—an installment of cash to meet a designated need, such as medical care. This infusion of cash is fundamental to the survival of Sudanese in Addis, but it is important to appreciate that these remittances support a way of life more complex than simple subsistence. I encountered no Sudanese in Ethiopia who could be considered prosperous by Ethiopian standards, with the exception of those U.S.- and Australia-based Nuer who were back on temporary visits to see family or to look for a wife. However, inequities do exist among Ethiopia-based Nuer from Sudan, and these remittances influenced power hierarchies.

ALTERING POWER STRUCTURES

The transformation of African societies and ways to gain power within them has dominated African Studies literature since at least the middle of the twentieth century. Colonial infrastructures, wage-labor employment (Schapera 1947), Christian conversion (Comaroff 1985), and formal schooling (Bond 1982; Scudder and Colson 1980) are documented as key catalysts of significant social transformation.

Among the Nuer, one thread of continuity running through their entire documented history is the dominance of cattle in marking social status (Hutchinson 1996). In the past decades, educational attainment has been grafted onto this arrangement. In the current climate of civil war, cattle keeping, while still pursued, is risky and educational credentials do not guarantee access to employment or, as experienced by Nuer in the diaspora, employment commensurate with qualifications (Abusharaf 2002).

Ironically, those in the diaspora may appear, at first glance, to be worse off than their African counterparts. In one family I followed, one brother worked in the United States in low-level positions in factories and meat-processing plants to support not only his U.S.-based nuclear family but also his extended family in Ethiopia, including a brother who was attending law school in Addis. The U.S.-based brother was constantly exhausted from working the night shift and caring for the children when his wife left for her day-shift job. He had deferred his own educational aspirations. The Africa-based brother, on the other hand, dressed in a three-piece suit each day to attend law school at a private college and enjoyed no small measure of social status from this experience. This example raises some important questions about how these two men's lives and relative experiences of being successful will unfold over time. It is, however, important to recognize that superficial markers of status such as clothing, or relative prosperity within a context of poverty, do not speak to overall well-being. Despite appearances, the brother in Africa lived a hand-to-mouth existence. In being utterly dependent on his brother abroad, his experience underscores that within this chaotic and fragmented social order, access to a remitting sponsor abroad has emerged as a marker of status and a promise of human security.

Cash Flows in Context

Remittances serve as a lifeline for many in developing countries (IDS 2006). It is crucial to understand this north-south cash flow within a more complex set of multistranded and multidirectional transnational flows involving people, goods, and information.

While refugee status is conferred at the level of the individual, the experiences of Nuer refugees demonstrate the ways in which the actions of individuals were undertaken on behalf of family (or corporate) groups. In one case, a family pooled all the blankets they had just been given by UNHCR and sold them (see chapter 4); the eldest living son was selected to undertake a perilous journey from the refugee camp in Ethiopia to a camp in Kenya that was known to be offering resettlement slots. Holtzman (2000, 22) describes a similar experience for a Nuer family who sold the tent the UN issued them. From Nuer I interviewed in Ethiopia, I learned that "resettlement forms," which enabled people to apply to have their case considered by UNHCR, were scarce. When forms did become available, they were distributed on a representational family basis throughout the camp. Therefore, even to have access to a form to apply for resettlement, people were indebted to their family for having been the one selected to apply.

Therefore a north-south cash flow, while seemingly characterized by an imbalance between who is giving and who is receiving, needs to be seen within a larger temporal and spatial context. These reciprocal arrangements allow the person who benefited from resettlement in the United States to meet social and familial obligations toward those who remain in Africa. At one time the family invested in the individual; now it is his turn to repay the group. In so doing, however, those in the diaspora who remit money are perhaps obtaining some peace of mind and most assuredly maintaining a stake as a member within a complex web of social ties. One thirty-year-old Nuer man I interviewed in the United States who had spent a year in university in Cairo, after a long day of filling out papers and forms for school, commented, "Refugees are cowards." When I asked him what he meant, he included himself in that category and said that "the real men stayed to fight in Africa; the

ones who left were cowards." His words, according to the African repatriation literature, capture the dilemma faced by those who return home after
wars or upheaval (Akol 1994; Allen and Turton 1996). For him, as for many
other Sudanese, sending money home is an opportunity to assuage some of
the negative feelings they have in grappling with what psychologists might
call survivor's guilt.

In addition to psychological comfort, senders also invest in their futures
by securing rights in marriage through the transfer of bridewealth cattle.
They may also invest in familial cattle herds for those living outside the
camps in western Ethiopia. One man in the United States spoke of trying
to help his camp-based family build a home in a nearby town (for about
$2,000). Many hold out hope for a lasting peace in Sudan. If that material-
izes, a history of remittances will ease the transition back to African society
for those who choose to return.

Those who remain in Africa take advantage of the opportunity to send
items home with those returning to the United States after brief sojourns
abroad and crochet antimacassars and bed covers in fluorescent pinks and
yellows. They also send beaded items, often with a Christian motif, to deco-
rate the walls of people's apartments in the United States to remind them
of home. Reading material, like the Bible, in Sudanese languages is hard to
obtain outside Africa and is also desirable to send.

In addition to goods, those who remain in Africa might perform services
for those in the diaspora, like obtaining a baptismal certificate for immigration purposes. In addition to the bridewealth funds discussed earlier, some
of this money is used to recruit and provide upkeep for the betrothed living
with the groom's family. There are other family obligations, like the care of
the young and the elderly. In one case, a U.S.-based Nuer sent money to en-
able his brother in Africa to marry a second wife. At the time neither brother
was interested in taking a second wife, but they made this arrangement to
honor their father's request. By the U.S. brother supplying the cash and the
Africa-based brother providing the service, they worked together to meet
familial obligations and maintain the family across national borders.

The sending of remittances by southern Sudanese refugees to their compatriots in Ethiopia is a largely undocumented practice that is difficult, if not
impossible, to identify from a macrolevel vantage point. My ethnographic
view of these remittances highlights how vital they are in sustaining life
under very difficult circumstances. More than just sustaining life, however,
the remittances alter social life in unexpected and powerful ways through

shaping residential patterns, local economies, and power structures. Viewed in this way, remittances need to be incorporated into the paradigm of factors precipitating rapid social change in Africa.

These remittance processes provide a dynamic view of globalization on the local level and an alternative take on north-south cash flows to Africa. Instead of aid flowing in through the usual cast of governmental characters to be doled out as they deem fit, I have offered possibilities through which to explore the impact of cash trickling directly into the hands of ordinary people. In so doing, I hope to have contributed to a broadening of how we understand globalization as a complex phenomenon socially mediated from below.[1]

Seasons of Moving

Back home, there is a season of moving. You aren't sad when you leave the permanent home for the temporary home, because you know you will go back. Those who died are going back to the permanent home. Those who died are going to the house of God.

These words, spoken by a Nuer pastor at a memorial service for a Nuer child who died of illness in Nashville, highlight the centrality of migration to the Nuer experience. This study has situated Nuer as a pastoral population with an established history of migrating to optimize resources. Nuer have used migration as a means of survival for their entire documented history. Sudan has felt the effects of civil war for the past five decades—when not embroiled in full-scale war, Sudan has been involved in projects to rebuild its society and institutions. Therefore, neither migration nor the effects of conflict are unknown to Nuer people. What has changed is the scale and magnitude of violence, the instruments of conflict, and the alternatives that individuals and collectivities may pursue. The Nuer have become international refugees negotiating the complex geographical terrain and social apparatus that affords international movement. They are by no means passive but active actors in the making of their own histories. What is different from conflicts of the past is the recognition by the rest of the world with respect to events in Sudan and the impact of war on its population and the role of the Nuer in constructing their own social trajectories. This study has highlighted the perception of Christian religious persecution as one of the variables that renders the Nuer experience notable to the United States in recent years. Yet, as it has also demonstrated, religious tension is one of many threads feeding conflict in contemporary Sudan that needs to be understood within a broad historical framework that incorporates precolonial, colonial, and postcolonial realities.

This ethnography has examined Nuer within a framework of refugee migration. In exploring the tension between Nuer refugees as victims of larger structural events beyond their control, this study has focused on their active roles in negotiating their way through complex and shifting circumstances. The experiences of these refugees lend support to the growing body of work documenting the ways in which strategies for survival do not eclipse all other culturally informed social projects. Examples presented in this study have illustrated the ways in which Nuer people carried on social life and planning for the future in the midst of extreme social change. For Nuer refugees, one site where these activities took place were refugee camps. Therefore, as Malkki (1995) has demonstrated in her work with Hutu refugees in Tanzania, refugee camps are very much integrated into larger systems and serve as sites of active cultural production rather than isolated spheres cut off from the rest of the world, as they are sometimes portrayed. Refugee camps are then nodes in a much larger Nuer social field and become as significant to an understanding of contemporary Nuer as southern Sudan or the United States.

Refugee status, as determined by definitions based in post–World War II Europe, is conferred at the level of the individual. The experiences of Nuer migrants in this study have demonstrated the ways in which actions of individuals were undertaken on behalf of corporate groups. Indeed, it was often only through the pooling of corporate resources that individuals were able to access third-country resettlement opportunities. For example, families chose sons over daughters in selecting which person should receive collective resources. While this may seem entirely consistent with the ethnographic record with respect to what is understood about Nuer social organization, it runs counter to essentialized notions of refugees reacting to circumstances rather than planning for future contingencies. These are practices much more commonly associated with so-called voluntary migration (for example, Mexican migration to the United States, for which see Portes and Rumbaut 1996), than for refugee, or involuntary, migration. In blurring the distinction between these two migrant groups, the case of Nuer refugees problematizes this categorical dichotomization.

These social investments link Nuer in the United States with those remaining in Africa, and Nuer living in the United States are expected to fulfill certain reciprocal obligations. Nuer do so by remaining in close contact through letters and phone calls, sending remittances, completing paperwork to facilitate family members' efforts to come to the United States, and returning to Africa to visit and to marry. Due to recent technological innovations, these processes are facilitated in terms of rapidity in ways never before possible. Moreover, as case studies have illustrated, this technology is accessible even to those living in relatively remote areas and to those who are not literate.

This study has also pointed to some of the tensions that such relationships and obligations can engender. For instance, the needs of family of origin in Africa can compete with the needs of the family of procreation in the United

States. This dynamic can be seen in the decision to take out student loans to attend school in the hope of obtaining a better job in the future; often this decision necessitates reducing or eliminating remittances to Africa for a specified period of time.

Despite a growing body of literature that challenges statutorily defined refugees as a useful unit of analysis, this paradigm in which "immigrants are pulled out of a country and refugees are pushed" prevails. A number of scholars have argued that this dichotomization of refugees and immigrants is problematic; however, descriptions of refugees that challenge this excessively linear characterization and depict refugees as social actors engaged in activities to maximize their own opportunities tread a fine line. Migration discourse is produced in a highly politicized context (Daniel and Knudsen 1996). The end of the Cold War precipitated massive and interrelated population movements (Fritz 2000). In a context of limited resources, the international community engages in a sort of triage (Zolberg, Suhrke, and Aguayo 1989). Therefore, studies depicting refugees more as actors than victims risk having that characterization misinterpreted and used in unintended ways.

Zolberg, Suhrke, and Aguayo (1989) note that seeing refugees primarily as victims may reinforce and legitimate the filtering system by suggesting that it has identified the "authentic" refugees while rejecting the "inauthentic" refugees (see also Smith 2000). The case studies presented earlier illustrate the limitations in such an approach, given shifting borders and the duration and nature of conflict in Sudan. A blow to the legitimacy of the screening process could prompt a rethinking of global efforts to address not only refugee-producing situations but also the broader geostrategic and economic processes that fuel them. Finally, idealized depictions of refugees and their experiences create unreal expectations for their incorporation into third countries. In particular, by not acknowledging refugees' strategies in securing third-country resettlement, we also ignore the significance and enduring nature of refugees' ties to their country of origin and to others in the diaspora. Moreover, there is the presumption that refugees credit the humanitarian agencies involved in resettlement with facilitating their opportunities for a fresh start in a new country; the ethnographic data presented in this study, however, do not support that assumption. In general, the Nuer case studies I have presented highlight the ways in which Nuer saw their own roles in circumventing obstacles presented by bureaucratic structures.

Reconciling the images of refugees as victims of events beyond their control and Nuer forced migrants' descriptions of the risks they took to gain access to third-country resettlement opportunities is a key theme in this study. Within a conceptual framework that relegates them to the lowest ranks of

the dispossessed, these people assert a certain authority over their own experience. The case studies I have described document a cataclysmic shift
in Nuer social life that overshadows previous depictions of change brought
about by migration to Khartoum (Hutchinson 1996) or refugee camps in
Ethiopia. Yet at the same time these stories only hint at the day-to-day hardships of carving out a life in a new country for a population that, to quote a
Nuer informant, "starts out at less than zero."

One of the ways that I tried to thank people for telling me about their lives
and experiences was to take and share photographs of them and their children. Often, people wanted to pose in their best clothing, holding children,
and often with status items, such as cell phones or toys for the children. The
copies of the photographs I gave them were visual documentation of the
possibilities of life in America. Sent by mail or with other Sudanese traveling
back to Africa, these photos were intended as a means to reassure, perhaps
to boast to, and surely to maintain ties with those left behind in Africa. These
photos of well-dressed, prosperous-looking people stand in stark contrast
to the images of African refugee women with sagging, depleted breasts and
half-naked, scrawny, sickly children seen in the news media and the donor
solicitation materials of humanitarian relief organizations (see Malkki 1992).
Yet each set of images gives only a partial view of the complexity of refugee
experiences that vary over time and space. The international humanitarian
refugee apparatus is equipped to address the latter set of images, but not the
first. And, for that reason, refugees who seek assistance are compelled to
find ways to make their life stories fit that expectation. The discussion in this
study about the ways in which Nuer people learn how to access resettlement
opportunities speaks to this process.

Malkki notes: "Being a refugee entailed prescriptions and prohibitions,
duties and moral responsibilities. It was not a mere label or legality; it was a
status and a collective condition with its own moral weight" (1995, 217). This
study has provided a context in which to interpret the experiences of these
Nuer forced migrants that incorporates the historical and cultural specificity
that Malkki (1995) notes is so often lost in the depiction of African refugees.
It has challenged the paradigm, derived from a psychological understanding of forced migration, that the refugee experience produces "refugee behavior" (Stein 1986). The variation in experiences reported here highlights
the difficulty in speaking of a singular refugee experience even within one
ethnic population, such as Nuer people. This study has pointed to some of
the problems associated with the expectations of refugee service providers
about diverse refugee populations in the United States. To expect Hmong,
Bosnian, and Nuer refugees to have similar paths and patterns of incorpo-

ration in the United States ignores not only the ways in which choices and decisions are informed by cultural systems but the importance of race in the sociocultural matrix in which immigrants are incorporated into the United States (Ong 1996). For example, one of the findings of this study is that Nuer tend to engage in a higher degree of interstate migration than what has been reported for other refugee groups who have been resettled in the United States. I do not argue that Nuer people's culture impels them to migrate; however, I note that Nuer social organization and residence practices provide for a greater elasticity of social ties with the capacity to absorb and sustain higher levels of mobility (see also Barnes and Boddy 1994). Indeed, migration within the United States may serve as a deliberate strategy to re-affirm old and generate new social ties that may be deployed in the face of future contingencies. Similar statements may be made about Hmong, who also tend to exhibit great mobility; however, the comparison is generally made at the level of their shared experience as refugees rather than the fact that Nuer and Hmong have similar systems of segmentary kinship organization. (For a description of Hmong segmentary kinship organization in the United States, see Dunnigan 1982.) Again, within the dominant paradigm for understanding refugees, the forced migration experience eclipses other social variables. And, as noted earlier, very little research has been done on African refugee populations in the United States by way of comparison (see Woldemikael 1997; Wong 1995).

Similarly, ties that refugees and other immigrants maintain with those who remain in the sending countries can also function as an investment strategy. This has been documented amply in transnational studies of migration, but this approach has not been pursued as vigorously in studies of refugees. Refugee studies is hindered in its ability to embrace an approach that recognizes the myriad links between refugees living in third countries and those in the sending countries because of assumptions about refugee "flight" and conditions precipitating departure from country of origin. This study has challenged this notion of permanent rupture, upheaval, and uprootedness that is ubiquitous in forced migration studies by documenting return migration for the purpose of marriage and visiting relatives.

What is problematic in conceptualizing Nuer refugee migration as a response to an acute crisis is the reality of prolonged war. Many of the refugees described in this study may have only known a Sudan marked by war. In a growing number of settings, protracted crises are generating segments of populations for whom displacement is the normal state of affairs (see Indra 2000; Malkki 1997). The perception is that conditions are so terrible in Sudan that people flee the country. Therefore, it becomes difficult to conceptualize the conditions that would allow others to remain. When I asked one Nuer man in his early thirties this very question, about how people could remain in Sudan under such difficult conditions, he replied, "The people who are still in Sudan, they think it is the way [that life is]. You cannot find it in your imagination, but it is what they are used to. They live like this always, so it is what they are used to living like."

In addition to reconsidering and expanding the paradigm in which refugee migration is considered, this study, in line with the project framed by Appadurai (1991, 191), also reexamines notions of people, place, and culture as they apply to one of anthropology's most celebrated case study populations. It is only with the most recent editions of introductory anthropology textbooks that we see an updating of the anthropological record with respect to the Nuer. They refer to Sharon Hutchinson's (1996) work documenting contemporary Nuer daily life that involves coping with the effects of war in southern Sudan and migration to the outskirts of Khartoum.

Slowly, dominant anthropological images of the Nuer of the 1930s are being replaced with more contemporary depictions. More dramatic perhaps than the notion of Nuer living in squatter camps in Sudan is the idea of Nuer men driving minivans with children's car seats, Nuer women wearing uniforms making burgers at McDonalds, and Nuer children responding to their parents in English when spoken to in Nuer. These are dramatic yet everyday examples of social transformation among the Nuer.

This is not to suggest that the refugee migrant population that I describe are the first Nuer to urbanize or to migrate out of Africa. There has been a trickle of Nuer who have emigrated for educational or other opportunities. However, the migratory process that I describe is unique because of the ways in which engagement with the refugee apparatus allowed them to bypass the process of migration described by other scholars (see Findley 1992; Portes and Rumbaut 1996) that involves successive steps of migration resulting in greater distances and longer duration. Many of the refugees described in this study moved from cattle camps in southern Sudan, to brief stays in refugee camps, to suburban America. Similarly, many of these migrants lacked the necessary educational background to qualify as immigrants to the United States under other circumstances. The refugee apparatus became key in facilitating these unlikely candidates for migration to the United States.

The situation I describe in Africa and in the lives of Nuer refugees in America continues to metamorphose even as I write this conclusion. Will there be lasting peace in Sudan? And if so, who among the Sudanese refugees will return to Africa? Will it be for short-term temporary visits or long-term repatriation? Will the U.S. Office of Refugee Resettlement open the gates to accept more Sudanese cases or will it restrict even the flow of immediate family members?

The resettlement of the so-called lost boys of Sudan from Kakuma camp in Kenya to U.S. sites where Sudanese populations are already established (England 2000) represents the most recent cohort of Sudanese refugees in America. These lost boys, who are now young men, left Sudan at a very young age, some as young as four or five. They are not unlike the "GDR kids," who left northern Namibia for camps in Angola at a similarly young age and were subsequently sent to the former East Germany (see Owens 1999); it is widely believed that these youth were enticed away from their families by the SPLA, with promises of improved educational and other opportunities. Some have even characterized camps like Kakuma as soldier farms, where boys are raised to be SPLA fighters. If the youth do not aspire to be soldiers, they have few opportunities. The newspaper reports highlight the lack of ties to family in Sudan because of leaving at such a young age (Simmons 1999; England 2000). Before the recent decision to resettle some of these boys, a U.S. refugee administrator recounted how these youth had gotten word that they could participate in the annual U.S. immigration lottery, which many did, illustrating the point made earlier about the ways in which seemingly isolated refugee camps are very much connected to larger information systems (see Schechter 2004).

While Sudanese refugees in Africa may continue to strategize about how best to engage with the refugee apparatus to secure third-country resettlement, others already living in places like the United States speak of an eventual return to Africa. William, a Gaajok man in his late twenties, said, "My plan is to buy a house in Africa. If I buy a house here, I won't pay for it until I die." But William perhaps illustrates one of the central dilemmas for refugees: he did not know where in Africa he would build his house. "In Sudan, there is too much war. Kenya is no good—the laws are not good and they put you in jail. The children cannot cross the road. The roads are for cars not people." William's open-ended response—which does not address when, how, or even where he would return to Africa—underscores the uncertainty of Sudan's future and refugees' place in an enduring resolution of conflict.

Repatriation difficulties are well documented in a range of African settings (see Preston 1994; Akol 1994). It is likely that the response of Nuer refugees in the United States to potential eventual voluntary repatriation opportunities will vary according to a number of social and demographic factors. And for many southern Sudanese, the only path to lasting peace is the establishment of an independent state of South Sudan.

For those who are moved by the appeal to "not eat the education in

America," given the history of educational access for southerners in Sudan, there likely would be numerous opportunities that may exceed prospects in the United States. For others for whom a return to Africa might result in a reduction in status, economic circumstance, or autonomy, remaining in the United States may well be a more appealing alternative. Male Nuer informants have articulated this with respect to Nuer women, asserting that women enjoy too much freedom in the United States relative to their experience in Africa and they would not return to Africa if it meant they had to relinquish their newly found independence.

One U.S. service provider noted that the Sudanese that she worked with had described "a rift between the Nuer and other tribes . . . [because] the Nuer don't have the conviction to return home. Almost all want to turn their heads when we talk about home. It has been infuriating for Dinka, Shilluk, and Azande. They all have the intention to return home." My data do not necessarily support or refute this observation. However, as the conflict in Sudan becomes increasingly politicized among southerners (see Jok and Hutchinson 1999), if Nuer interests are not adequately represented in the peace settlement, it may well affect prospects for return.

This study has explored the tension between Nuer refugees as victims of events beyond their control and their active roles in the process of being resettled from Africa to the United States as refugees at the turn of the twenty-first century. In charting this migration, I have sought to situate Nuer within a longer social and historical framework. Shifting between micro- and macroanalytic frames, this research has used the Nuer as a case study to highlight the politicized nature of refugee resettlement.

I suggest that the Nuer case blurs the distinction between refugees and other kinds of migrants as currently statutorily defined, providing an opportunity to reassess the paradigm that the refugee experience produces refugee behavior by examining differences in the ways that Nuer describe their experiences relative to other refugee populations, such as Cambodians (see Mortland 1987). In doing so, it has also problematized the ways in which refugees are distinguished from other kinds of migrants, including internally displaced persons and immigrants. Highlighting Nuer refugees' roles as social actors has provided a window into the complex and dynamic social worlds of people who are assumed to be functioning within a minimalist survival-based framework. A greater appreciation of the sociocultural factors informing forced migrants' decisions and behavior has significant applied and theoretical implications.

Appendix

The refugees I interviewed were among the first cohorts of Sudanese refugees to be resettled in the United States. Therefore, many of the findings in this study represent baseline information that will be useful in gauging transformation among Nuer in this country as additional family reunification cases and successive waves of Sudanese cohorts are resettled. Table A.1 shows the year of arrival for the 281 individuals I interviewed.

Table A.2 shows not only reported state of residence at the time of the interview but also gender. In addition to the 489 adults documented in the table, I have data on 248 children that are not reported here. At the time of the interview my U.S.-based informants were residing in twenty different states, providing an unusual degree of breadth for an ethnographic study and contributing a wide range of experiences generated in diverse locales across the United States. Table A.3 documents the extreme geographic diversity of refugee arrivals.

In table A.5 the main diagonal represents the fifty-seven people (27 percent of the sample) who made a lateral move from one state to another with the same level of benefits (low to low, medium to medium, or high to high). The cluster of cells below the main diagonal represents the eighty-two people (38 percent) who moved to a state with a higher level of cash assistance benefits (low to medium, low to high, or medium to high). The cluster of cells above the main diagonal represents the seventy-four adults (35 percent) who moved from a state with a higher to a lower level of cash assistance

Table A.1. Adult Sudanese Interview Sample by Year of Arrival

Year of Arrival	Number of Sudanese	Percent of Sample
1992	13	5
1993	20	7
1994	115	41
1995	85	30
1996	30	11
1997	10	4
1998	8	3
Total	281	101

Note: Due to rounding, percentages do not total 100.

Table A.2. Adult Sudanese Interview Sample by Gender and Residence at Time of Interview

State	Male	Female	Total
Ariz.	4	2	6
Calif.	11	1	12
D.C.	7	0	7
Ga.	5	0	5
Ill.	2	0	2
Iowa	47	24	71
Mass.	1	0	1
Md.	1	0	1
Minn.	106	42	148
N.C.	1	0	1
N.Dak.	5	0	5
Neb.	26	16	42
Nev.	4	0	4
N.Y.	2	3	5
S.Dak.	20	4	24
Tenn.	86	28	114
Tex.	26	6	32
Utah	5	1	6
Wash.	2	0	2
Wis.	1	0	1
Total	362	127	489

Table A.3. Adult Sudanese Interview Sample by Gender and State of Arrival

State	Male	Female	Total
Ariz.	3	2	5
Calif.	11	5	16
Colo.	4	2	6
D.C.	8	0	8
Ga.	4	1	5
Ill.	6	0	6
Iowa	32	15	47
Md.	3	0	3
Me.	1	0	1
Minn.	37	48	85
Mo.	2	2	4
N.C.	5	2	7
N.Dak.	1	0	1
Nev.	5	0	5
N.Y.	7	8	15
S.Dak.	30	8	38
Tenn.	33	7	40
Tex.	38	7	45
Utah	6	1	7
Wash.	2	1	3
Total	238	109	347

benefits (high to low, high to medium, or medium to low). The table illustrates, for example, that twenty Sudanese adults moved from a low benefit level state to another low benefit level state.

In table A.6 data from Aid to Families with Dependent Children (AFDC) 1995 are used to categorize states according to benefit levels. The welfare initiative signed into law in August 1996 replaced AFDC with Temporary Assistance to Needy Families (TANF). However, TANF levels are determined until 2002 on the basis of a state's AFDC spending before passage of the law.

Table A.4. Sudanese Refugees in the United States by Reported Year of Birth, 1983–97

Year of birth	Number	Percent of total	Estimated age in 2000
1918–47	46	1	53–82
1948–57	145	3	43–52
1958–67	641	15	33–42
1968–77	1,858	43	23–32
1978–87	728	17	13–22
1988–97	888	21	3–12
Total	4,306		

Source: U.S. Office of Refugee Resettlement; tabulated by author.

Table A.5. Analysis of Last Known Interstate Move for Sudanese Refugees

The main diagonal represents the 57 (27%) people who made a lateral move from a state with a low to low, medium to medium, or high to high level of benefits. The cluster of cells below the main diagonal represents the 82 people (39%) who moved to a state with a higher level of cash assistance benefits (low to medium, low to high, or medium to high). The cluster of cells above the main diagonal represents the 74 adults (35%) who moved from a state with a higher to a lower level of cash assistance benefits (high to low, high to medium, or medium to low). The following chart illustrates, for example, that 20 Sudanese adults moved from a low benefit level state to a low benefit level state.

Destination	State of Origin		
State	Low	Medium	High
Low	20	19	13
Medium	10	19	42
High	29	43	18

Table A.6. Resettlement States by Level of Welfare Benefits

The following table was adapted from Zedlewski and Giannarelli's 1997 Urban Institute table depicting diversity among state welfare programs. Aid to Families with Dependent Children (AFDC) 1995 data are used to categorize states according to benefit levels of high, medium, and low. The welfare initiative signed into law in August 1996 replaces AFDC with Temporary Assistance to Needy Families (TANF). However, TANF levels are determined until 2002 on the basis of that state's AFDC spending prior to passage of the law.

Source: Sheila R. Zedlewski and Linda Giannarelli, *Diversity among State Welfare Programs: Implications for Reform* (Policy Briefs/ANF: Issues and Options for States). Washington, D.C.: Urban Institute, 1997. Available at: <http://www.urban.org/publications/307033.html>

State	Average Monthly Benefit per Family
HIGH	
Alaska	$724
Hawaii	$664
Calif.	$556
N.Y.	$555
Mass.	$540
Vt.	$536
Conn.	$524
Minn.	$520
R.I.	$504
Wash.	$495
Wis.	$441
Mich.	$414
Me.	$389
MEDIUM	
D.C.	$386
Ore.	$384
N.M.	$373
Pa.	$369
N.Dak.	$362
N.J.	$357
Mont.	$351
Utah	$349
Md.	$347
Iowa	$342
Kans.	$335
Wyo.	$333
Neb.	$319
Ill.	$311
Ohio	$310
Colo.	$309
Ariz.	$301
S.Dak.	$301

LOW

Idaho	$287
Okla.	$283
Del.	$282
Fla.	$277
Nev.	$276
Mo.	$258
Va.	$257
Ind.	$250
Ga.	$249
N.H.	$239
W.Va.	$237
N.C.	$222
Ky.	$204
S.C.	$183
Tenn.	$172
Ark.	$168
Tex.	$159
La.	$158
Ala.	$150
Miss.	$120

Notes

Chapter 1

1. The act defines a refugee as "any person who is outside any country of such person's nationality or, in the case of a person having no nationality, is outside any country in which such person habitually resided, and who is unable or unwilling to return to, and is unable or unwilling to avail himself or herself of the protection of, that country on account of race, religion, nationality, membership in a particular social group, or political opinion. (The term *refugee* does not include any person who ordered, incited, assisted, or otherwise participated in the persecution of any person on account of race, religion, nationality, membership in a particular social group, or political opinion)" (quoted in Holman 1996, 13–14).

2. Under the 1969 OAU Convention Governing the Specific Aspects of Refugee Problems in Africa, the term *refugee* encompasses the definition in the 1951 Refugee Convention and, in addition, includes "every person who, owing to external aggression, occupation, foreign domination or events seriously disturbing public order in either part or the whole of his country of origin or nationality, is compelled to leave his place of habitual residence in order to seek refuge in another place outside of his country of origin or nationality" (quoted in Cohen and Deng 1998, 317).

3. An array of scholars has critiqued the ways in which some involuntary migrants are privileged over others in the application of the refugee definition. See, for example, Keely 1993; Bascom 1995; Cohen and Deng 1998; Colson 1999; Indra 1999.

4. For example, Marvin Harris (1985, 177–78, 196) discusses "pet-like treatment of animals"; Claude Lévi-Strauss (1962, 78–82) expounds on men and totems; Lucy Mair (1962), employs the Nuer as an example of a political system; and Henrietta Moore (1994) discusses phrases such as "Nuer believe . . ." in the construction of voice within narratives.

5. Opportunities to observe the full process of incorporation were limited due to high levels of geographic mobility. For instance, in two cases I was able to observe the resettlement of a wife of a man with whom I previously had established a research relationship. In one of those cases, however, the wife left the husband several months after arrival to live in another state. In the second case, both the husband and the wife moved to another state several months after her arrival. A documentary film, *Lost Boys of Sudan* (2003), does a remarkable job following the process of resettlement from camps in Kenya to the United States. See Shandy (2005) for a review of this and another film on Sudanese resettlement (*A Great Wonder: Lost Children of Sudan Resettling in America*).

6. Examples of services provided include assisting to fill out forms to gain access to resources such as public housing, health care, or financial assistance for educa-

tion; transporting people to appointments for health care, jobs, or securing housing and educational opportunities; occasional financial or other material assistance in the way of clothing, car repairs, groceries, and incidentals; making phone calls to secure housing, access social programs such as winter coats for children and English as a Second Language programs; resolving confusion related to registering for the Selective Service or financial aid for school. I also volunteered regularly as a childcare worker at a Sudanese women's ESL class.

7. Affordable housing of any sort, particularly public housing, is a scarce resource in the primary region where this study was based. Residency in these units is governed by strict income limits as well as limits on the number of occupants.

Chapter 2

1. The U.S. Institute of Peace Web site maintains a digital record of the original documents agreed to and the updates and amendments to previous protocols. These are available at http://www.usip.org/library/pa/sudan/cpa01092005/cpa_toc.html.

2. Andrew Natsios notes that "the situation in Darfur remains one of the worst humanitarian crises in the world," and indicates that "since February 2003 nearly 300,000 people have died and more than 2 million [have been] displaced from their homes" (2005, 89).

3. The last official census in Sudan took place in 1956. Southern Sudanese in the United States critique the reliability of this enumeration and suggest that there was a systematic underreporting by the people themselves to avoid head taxes. Conversely, given the current political climate, people are far more likely to attempt to inflate numbers for their own political aims. The current population figure comes from the CIA World Factbook, <http://www.cia.gov/cia/publications/factbook/geos/su.html#People>.

4. Key figures in both the Sudanese government and the rebel resistance movements hold doctorates and have made contributions to the body of literature available about the current conflict. See, for example, Alier 1990; Garang 1992; Beshir 1968.

5. Condominium rule, as a rather unique form of colonial governance in Africa, merits a brief explanation. The creation of Lord Cromer, British consul general in Cairo from 1883 to 1907, the condominium proclaimed dual Anglo-Egyptian sovereignty in Sudan (July 1980, 492). While Egypt was always a junior partner in this arrangement, it was forced to withdraw from Sudan after the 1924 assassination in Cairo of Sir Lee Stack, governor-general of Sudan.

6. Pitya (1996, 255) details southern groups as follows: the Nilotic group (Dinka, Nuer); Luo group (Acholi, Anywak, Boor, Jur, Pa'ri Lokoro, Shatt, Shilluk); Nilo-Hamitic group (Bari, Lotuho, Toposa); southern Sudanic group (Moru, Madi, Avukaya, Mundo, Kaliko, Lugwara, Baka, Bongo); western Sudanic group (Ndogo, Bviri, Bai, Golo, Yulu, Kresh, Feroge, Bandala, and others of western Bahr al-Ghazal and southern Darfur); northern Sudanic group (Didinga, Longarim [Buya], Murle, and

other small groups of the Nuba Mountains); and the Azande and Makaraka, which are more Bantu than Sudanic.

7. Another film, *Sudan*, directed by John Rawlins, was released in 1945 by Universal Pictures. According to the Academy Awards database, Korda's *Khartoum* was on a preliminary list of submissions from the studios, but it was not an official nomination.

8. The commander in chief of the SPLA, John Garang de Mabior (1945–2005), a Dinka from the town of Bor who was born to a Christian family, was the founder and leader of the SPLM/A. He attended high school in Tanzania then earned a B.S. in economics from Grinnell College in Iowa in 1969 and in 1981 a Ph.D. in agricultural economics at Iowa State University.

9. Operation Lifeline-Sudan consists of UNICEF, the World Food Program, and forty other NGOs. A decade after its inception, during the famine of 1996, OLS was under intense criticism for not having averted a repetition of the famine a decade earlier.

10. Other nations on the list at the time included Cuba, Iran, Iraq, Libya, North Korea, and Syria.

11. Machar, a Dok Nuer, was born in Bentiu in 1952, attended Khartoum University and earned a Ph.D. from the University of Bedford, in England, in 1984.

12. Pitya (1996, 94) notes that from 1842 to 1844 a Catholic priest who had left conflict in Ethiopia for Khartoum established a school for the children of diplomats and traders before returning to Ethiopia.

13. The Verona Fathers also are called Combonians, after Father Daniel Comboni, who was known for popularizing "the method of evangelizing Africa by the Africans" (Pitya 1996, 104).

14. Dr. Lambie was assigned the Nuer language (Pitya 1996, 253). A more well known name among missionaries to Nuer areas is Father Pasquale Crazzolara, an Austrian citizen, who started the first Roman Catholic mission among the Nuer in 1925 called Yoynyang (Pitya 1996, 319–20).

Chapter 3

1. This information was obtained from a UNDP Emergencies Unit for Ethiopia report: <http://www.africa.upenn.edu/eue_web/gambel96oct.htm>.

2. Cuba, for example, is a clear case demonstrating the parallels between U.S. foreign policy and interest in extending humanitarian aid to refugees from that country. For a Cuban case study detailing this process, see Coleman 1996. Another example can be seen in the case of the Hmong. It was only in 1997 that the U.S. government officially recognized the role of the CIA in recruiting Hmong soldiers to fight in Laos—more than two decades after Hmong resettlement in the United States began.

3. An interesting corollary to the present study is southern Sudanese entering the United States via other channels. Anthropologist Sharon Hutchinson reported that

she has been following Sudanese dispersion in Canada, the UK, Kenya, and Australia (pers. comm., February 17, 1999). The lack of reported materials on this topic render it beyónd the scope of this study. A Dallas newspaper reported that a Sudanese man had entered the United States via Mexico and later sought asylum (Trejo 1998). Given the rather large Sudanese population in Canada, there appears to be some Sudanese migration into the United States via that border as well.

4. The Immigrant Act of 1990 identifies the following conditions as grounds for exclusion: "Communicable Diseases of Public Health Significance" (infectious tuberculosis, HIV/AIDS, syphilis, other sexually transmitted diseases, and Hansen's disease, more popularly known as leprosy); "Physical and Mental Disorders with Associated Harmful Behaviors"; "Psychoactive Substance Abuse and Dependence"; and "Other Physical or Mental Abnormalities, Disorders or Disabilities" (Minnesota Department of Health 1992).

5. Priority One refugees include those in immediate danger of loss of life (e.g., political prisoners); Priority Two refugees include former employees of the U.S. government for one or more years. Priority Three are persons with a close U.S. family relation. Priority Four are those with close ties to U.S. foundations, voluntary agencies, or companies for one or more years. Priority Five includes relatives who do not fit in Priority Three. Priority Six are those whose admission is in the national interest of the United States because of their nationality.

6. She did not elaborate on the reasons for these varying rates. One possible explanation could be that as more time passed, resources were devoted to processing family reunification cases. Similarly, as Sudanese refugees become established financially and gain citizenship in the United States they can serve as sponsors for other Nuer.

7. The topic of deportation for criminal activity within the United States is a separate matter that I do not address here. One as yet unsubstantiated story that a Nuer informant relayed was the case of a Nuer man that INS had attempted to repatriate but whom the Sudanese government had refused to accept. The man, according to my informant, was actually transported out of the United States and later had to return, whereupon he was once again put in prison. In contrast to the cases described earlier concerning events that took place before arrival, this man had been jailed for attempted robbery in the United States. A UNHCR worker at a conference on other immigration issues recounted another story of a young Sudanese man who was being threatened with deportation for having tried to punch a man who turned out to be a policeman in a bar in South Dakota.

8. Ahmed Deng Bol's "Nuer" name would be Ahmed Deng Bol Riek Wang Diew Tharjiath Pal Biel Jok Deng Buometet. His son's name could be Jal Ahmed Deng Bol Riek Wang Diew Tharjiath Pal Biel Jok Deng Buometet. The child's name is added to the string of ascending agnatic generations of his father.

9. "The congressionally mandated Diversity Immigrant Visa Program is administered on an annual basis by the Department of State and conducted under the terms of Section 203(c) of the Immigration and Nationality Act (INA). Section 131

of the Immigration Act of 1990 (Pub. L. 101-649) amended INA 203 to provide for a new class of immigrants known as 'diversity immigrants' (DV immigrants). The Act makes available 50,000 permanent resident visas annually to persons from countries with low rates of immigration to the United States" (http://travel.state.gov/visa/immigrants/types/types_1318.html).

10. Voluntary agencies received $720 per capita for each refugee placed in 1997 and $850 in 2005. Under 2005 guidelines, half this amount goes directly to the refugee. Service providers report that this is insufficient to cover resettlement costs. This sum is in addition to cash and in-kind services such as public assistance programs. Refugees are supposed to be provided with the following services: prearrival resettlement planning, reception, basic needs support for thirty days, community orientation and health, employment, and other necessary counseling and referral services.

11. According to the UNHCR Resettlement Handbook (1998, USA/4), family reunification cases are categorized according to level of priority. Priority Three cases include spouses, unmarried sons and daughters, and parents of persons lawfully admitted to the United States as refugees. Priority Four cases include married sons and daughters, siblings, grandparents, and grandchildren of refugees. Given the disproportionate number of individuals seeking resettlement in the United States, Priority Four refugees have little chance of being resettled in the United States on the basis of family reunification.

12. In 1998 a Minnesota voluntary agency provided single adults with food stamps for three months and a $250 monthly subsidy for eight months. A couple received $260 per month for the same period. Unaccompanied minors in high school received $203 per month. People may also have qualified for public housing, although lack of available units makes them difficult to obtain.

13. In 1996, for example, nine of the thirteen refugee groups resettled in the United States from around the globe had a larger proportion of males to females (U.S. Dept. of State 1998).

Chapter 4

1. Kop is a starchy staple made from corn flour. Nuer prepare it in U.S. settings, particularly at festive gatherings. The tasty dish, which I have not seen in other African cuisines, resembles small peas made from corn flour and is quite labor intensive. Corn flour is mixed with water and a bit of (sourdough) starter kept in the refrigerator from the previous preparation. Mixing swiftly and deftly with the right hand while using the left hand to agitate the bowl, the preparer gradually forms small uniform balls. Pouring these balls into a hot pan coated with oil allows them to retain their shape when they are later spritzed with water in a fast circular motion periodically throughout the cooking and steaming process. When the balls are cooked fully, one can add a mixture of sautéed onions, spinachlike greens (obtainable at Middle Eastern grocery stores), and meat.

2. It is not possible to verify whether this is true. And, as noted earlier with respect to Malkki's argument for not triangulating data (1995), it is not really a concern in

this context either. What does seem clear from my ethnographic findings, however, is that the group with whom I worked were among the first cohorts to be resettled.

Chapter 5

1. Evans-Pritchard defines *buth* as "agnatic kinship between collateral lineages" and *mar* as "any and every relationship of a kinship kind between persons" (1951b, 6). He defines *cieng* as "a residential group of any size, from a single homestead to a large tribal division" (1951b, 3).

2. It is meaningful that the word for a journey of short duration, *jal*, is chosen over the word for a journey of longer duration, *hoth*. When I queried numerous informants on whether they perceived their resettlement in the United States as hoth or jal, people unanimously replied hoth.

3. *Nya* means daughter of. Most females' names begin with Nya. *Gat* means son of. Some males' names begin with Gat, such as Gatluak or Gatkuoth.

4. In this respect, the Nuer appear to differ from their Somali counterparts who also entered the United States during the 1990s as refugees. The Somali population in the United States, numbering an estimated forty-five thousand, reportedly has a large number of individuals trained as physicians and other professionals.

Chapter 6

1. One woman who is considered Nuer has a Nuer father and an Ethiopian mother.

Chapter 7

An earlier version of chapter 7 appeared in Hopkins and Wellmeier 2001; it is used here with permission.

1. Internal migration can also refer to migration within one's country of origin.

2. The recent U.S. Supreme Court ruling (*Saenz v. Roe*, no. 98-97) on the "right to travel" within the United States highlights the highly politicized nature of migration within nation-states as well as between them.

3. This brings to mind Francis Deng's (1972) depiction of his father's decision to send Francis to be educated in Christian schools, while sending Francis's brother to be educated in Islamic schools. In face of uncertainty about a rapidly changing society, he diversified the family's options for success.

4. States are the most significant administrative units relating to refugees in the United States. Access to educational opportunity, defined by age and other public assistance benefits, varies by state.

5. For a case in support of the welfare magnet argument, see Peterson and Rom 1990.

6. Refugees in this sample arrived in the United States between 1990 and 1998. Analysis of internal migration at this stage does not indicate any relationship between length of time in the United States and likelihood to migrate.

7. Based on the literature (ORR 1995; Forbes 1985; Stein 1986), we would expect refugees to move for one or more of the following reasons: employment opportunities, the pull of an established ethnic community, more generous welfare benefits, better training opportunities, reunification with relatives, and a congenial climate. Four of the six possible explanations for refugee mobility focus on the attraction to external or structural factors, while only two are related to pulls to sociocultural or intragroup factors.

Chapter 8

1. Another version of chapter 8 appears in *Refuge: Canada's Periodical on Refugees* 23, no. 2 (special issue: *Multiple Homes and Parallel Civil Societies: Refugee Diasporas and Transnationalism*); it is used here with permission.

Bibliography

Films

The Four Feathers. Film. Directed by Zoltan Korda. London: London Films Productions, 1939.

The Four Feathers. DVD. Directed by Shekhar Kapur. Hollywood: Paramount Pictures, 2002.

A Great Wonder: Lost Children of Sudan Resettling in America. VHS/DVD. Directed by Kim Shelton. Subtitled in English. Oley, Pa.: Bullfrog Productions, 2003.

Khartoum. Film. Directed by Basil Dearden. United Kingdom: United Artists, 1966.

Lost Boys of Sudan. VHS/DVD. Directed by Megan Mylan and Jon Shenk. Subtitled in English. San Francisco: Actual Films and Principe Productions, 2003.

The Nuer. Film. Directed by Robert Gardner and Hilary Harris. Carlsbad, Calif.: CRM Films, 1970.

Strange Beliefs. VHS. Directed by André Singer. Strangers Abroad: Pioneers of Social Anthropology. Princeton, N.J.: Films for the Humanities, 1990.

Sudan. Film. Directed by John Rawlins. Hollywood: Universal Pictures, 1945.

Books and Periodicals

Abusharaf, Rogaia M.

1994   Sudanese New World Migration: The Social History of Sudanese International Migration to the United States and Canada. PhD dissertation, University of Connecticut.

1997   Sudanese Migration to the New World: Socio-economic Characteristics. *International Migration* 35 (4): 513–36.

2002   *Wanderings: Sudanese Migrants and Exiles in North America.* Ithaca, N.Y.: Cornell University Press.

Ahmed, Ismail I.

2006   New Regulations Restrict Somali Remittances. *ID21 Insights* (Institute of Development Studies, University of Sussex), no. 60 (January 2006): 5.

Akol, Joshua O.

1994   A Crisis of Expectations. In *When Refugees Go Home*, edited by Tim Allen and Hubert Morsink, 78–95. Trenton, N.J.: Africa World Press.

Alier, A.

1990   *Southern Sudan: Too Many Disagreements Dishonoured.* Exeter, England: Ithaca Press.

Alitolppa-Niitamo, Anne.

2000   From the Equator to the Arctic Circle: A Portrait of Somali Integration and Diasporic Consciousness in Finland. In *Rethinking Refuge and Displacement,* ed. Elzbieta M. Gozdziak and Dianna J. Shandy, 43–65. Selected Papers on Refugees and Immigrants, vol. 8. Arlington, Va.: American Anthropological Association.

Allan, J. A.

1996   Sudan Physical and Social Geography. In *Africa South of the Sahara*, 25th ed., 898–932. London: Europa Publications.

Allen, Tim, and David Turton

1996   Introduction to *In Search of Cool Ground: War, Flight, and Homecoming in Northeast Africa*, ed. Allen, 1–22. Trenton, N.J.: Africa World Press.

Anderson, Mary B.

1999   *Do No Harm: How Aid Can Support Peace—Or War.* Boulder: Lynne Rienner.

Appadurai, Arjun

1988a   Introduction: Place and Voice in Anthropological Theory. *Cultural Anthropology* 3 (1): 16–20.

1988b   Putting Hierarchy in Its Place. *Cultural Anthropology* 3 (1): 36–49.

1991   Global Ethnoscapes: Notes and Queries for a Transnational Anthropology. In *Recapturing Anthropology: Working in the Present*, ed. Richard G. Fox, 191–210. Santa Fe: School of American Research Press.

Archibald, Erika F.

1997   *A Sudanese Family.* Minneapolis: Lerner Publications.

Baker, Jonathan, and Tade Akin Aina

1995   Introduction to *The Migration Experience in Africa*, ed. Baker and Aina, 11–28. Sweden: Nordiska Afrikainstitutet.

Barnes, Virginia Lee, and Janice Boddy

1994   *Aman: The Story of a Somali Girl.* New York: Pantheon Books.

Barth, Fredrik

1998   *Ethnic Groups and Boundaries: The Social Organization of Culture Difference.* Prospect Heights, Ill.: Waveland Press.

Basch, Linda, Nina Glick Schiller, and Cristina Szanton Blanc

1994   *Nations Unbound.* Amsterdam: Gordon and Breach.

Bascom, Jonathan

1995   The New Nomads: An Overview of Involuntary Migration in Africa. In *The Migration Experience in Africa*, ed. Jonathan Baker and Tade Akin Aina, 197–221. Sweden: Nordiska Afrikainstitutet.

1998   *Losing Place: Refugees and Rural Transformations in East Africa.* New York: Berghahn Books.

Behar, Ruth

1996   *The Vulnerable Observer: Anthropology That Breaks Your Heart.* Boston: Beacon Press.

Beidelman, T. O.

1966   The Ox and Nuer Sacrifice: Some Freudian Hypotheses about Nuer Symbolism. *Man*, n.s., 1: 453–67.

1968 Some Nuer Notions of Nakedness, Nudity, and Sexuality. *Africa* 38: 113–31.

1971 *The Translation of Culture: Essays to E. E. Evans-Pritchard.* London: Tavistock.

Benson, Janet

1994 The Effects of Packinghouse Work on Southeast Asian Refugee Families. In *Newcomers in the Workplace: Immigrants and the Restructuring of the U.S. Economy,* ed. Louise Lamphere, Alex Stepick, and Guillermo Grenier, 79–99. Philadelphia: Temple University Press.

Beshir, Mohammed Omar

1968 *The Southern Sudan: Background to Conflict.* London: C. Hurst.

Bixler, Mark

2005 *The Lost Boys of Sudan: An American Story of the Refugee Experience.* Athens: University of Georgia Press.

Bob, Clifford

2005 *The Marketing of Rebellion: Insurgents, Media, and International Activism.* Cambridge Studies in Contentious Politics. Cambridge: Cambridge University Press.

Bok, Francis

2003 *Escape from Slavery: The True Story of My Ten Years in Captivity—and My Journey to Freedom in America.* New York: St. Martin's Press.

Bond, George C.

1982 Education and Social Stratification in Northern Zambia: The Case of the Uyombe. *Anthropology and Education* 8 (3): 251–68.

Bond, George Clement, and Angela Gilliam

1994 Introduction to *Social Construction of the Past: Representation as Power,* ed. Bond and Gilliam, 1–22. New York: Routledge.

Burr, J. Millard, and Robert O. Collins

1995 *Requiem for the Sudan: War, Drought, and Disaster Relief on the Nile.* Boulder: Westview.

Burton, John W.

1974 Some Nuer Notions of Purity and Danger. *Anthropos* 69: 517–36.

1981 Ethnicity on the Hoof: On the Economics of Nuer Identity. *Ethnology* 20: 157–62.

1987 *A Nilotic World: The Atuot-Speaking Peoples of the Southern Sudan.* New York: Greenwood.

Busby, Annette

1998 The Problem Is Their Culture: The Integration of Kurdish Refugees in Sweden. Paper presented at the Society for Applied Anthropology, San Juan, Puerto Rico.

Castles, Stephen, and Mark J. Miller

2003 *The Age of Migration.* 3rd ed. New York: Guilford Press.

Clement, Doug

1996 Strangers in a Strange Land. *Minnesota Medicine* 79: 11.

Clifford, James

1997   *Routes: Travel and Translation in the Late Twentieth Century*. Cambridge, Mass.: Harvard University Press.

Cohen, Roberta, and Francis M. Deng

1998   *Masses in Flight: The Global Crisis of Internal Displacement*. Washington, D.C.: Brookings Institution Press.

Coleman, Joseph

1996   Cubans. In *Refugees in America in the 1990s*, ed. David W. Haines, 102–20. Westport, Conn.: Greenwood.

Collins, Patricia Hill.

1990   *Black Feminist Thought: Knowledge, Consciousness, and the Politics of Empowerment*. New York: Routledge.

Colson, Elizabeth

1987   Migrants and Their Hosts. Introduction to *People in Upheaval*, ed. Scott Morgan and Elizabeth Colson, 1–16. Staten Island, N.Y.: Center for Migration Studies.

1999   Gendering Those Uprooted by Development. In *Engendering Forced Migration: Theory and Practice*, ed. Doreen Indra, 23–39. New York: Berghahn Books.

Comaroff, Jean

1985   *Body of Power, Spirit of Resistance: The Culture and History of a South African People*. Chicago: University of Chicago Press.

Coutin, Susan

2005   Being En Route. *American Anthropologist* 107 (2): 195–206.

Crehan, Kate

2002   Silencing Power: Mapping the Social Terrain in Post-Apartheid South Africa. In *Contested Terrains and Constructed Categories*, ed. George Clement Bond and Nigel C. Gibson, 173–93. Boulder: Westview.

Cuny, Frederick, and Barry Stein

1990   Prospects for and Promotion of Spontaneous Return. In *Refugees in International Relations*, ed. Gil Loescher and Laila Monahan, 293–312. New York: Oxford University Press.

D'Alisera, JoAnn

2004   *An Imagined Geography: Sierra Leonean Muslims in America*. Philadelphia: University of Pennsylvania Press.

Daly, M. W., and Ahmad Alawad Sikainga, eds.

1993   *Civil War in the Sudan*. London: British Academic Press.

Daniel, E. Valentine, and John C. Knudsen, eds.

1996   *Mistrusting Refugees*. Berkeley: University of California Press.

David, H. P.

1969   Involuntary International Migration: Adaptation of Refugees. *International Migration Review* 7 (3/4): 67–81.

Deng, Francis M.

1972   *The Dinka of the Sudan.* Prospect Heights, Ill.: Waveland Press.

1993   *Protecting the Dispossessed.* Washington, D.C.: Brookings Institution Press.

2005   African Renaissance: Towards a New Sudan. *Forced Migration Review* 24: 6–8.

Deng, Francis M., and Prosser Gifford, eds.

1987   *The Search for Peace and Unity in the Sudan.* Washington, D.C.: Wilson Center Press.

Deng, Luka Biong

2005   The Comprehensive Peace Agreement: Will It Also Be Dishonoured? *Forced Migration Review* 24: 15–17.

Dettwyler, Katherine A.

1994   *Dancing Skeletons: Life and Death in West Africa.* Prospect Heights, Ill.: Waveland Press.

Diehl, Keila

2002   *Echoes from Dharamsala: Music in the Life of a Tibetan Refugee Community.* Berkeley: University of California Press.

Douglas, Mary

1980   *Edward Evans-Pritchard.* New York: Viking.

Duany, Wal

1992   Neither Palaces nor Prisons: The Constitution of Order among the Nuer. PhD dissertation, Indiana University.

Dunnigan, Timothy

1982   Segmentary Kinship in an Urban Society. *Anthropology Quarterly* 55: 126–34.

Durham, William H.

1989   Conflict, Migration and Ethnicity: A Summary. In *Conflict, Migration and the Expression of Ethnicity*, ed. Nancie L. González and Carolyn S. McCommon, 138–45. Boulder: Westview.

England, Andrew

2000   Lost Boys. *Saint Paul Pioneer Press*, June 16, 5A.

Evans, T. M. S.

1978   Leopard Skins and Paper Tigers: "Choice" and "Social Structure" in the Nuer. *Man*, n.s., 13: 100–115.

Evans-Pritchard, E. E.

1940a   *The Nuer: A Description of the Modes of Livelihood and Political Institutions of a Nilotic People.* Oxford: Clarendon Press.

1940b   The Nuer of the Southern Sudan. In *African Political Systems*, ed. M. Fortes and Evans-Pritchard, 272–96. London: Oxford University Press.

1951a   Kinship and Local Community among the Nuer. In *African Systems of Kinship and Marriage*, ed. A. R. Radcliffe-Brown and D. Forde, 360–91. London: KPI.

1951b   *Kinship and Marriage among the Nuer.* Oxford: Clarendon Press.

1956   *Nuer Religion.* Oxford: Clarendon Press.

Falge, Christiane

1997   The Nuer as Refugees: A Study on Social Adaptation. MA thesis, Addis Ababa University.

Farnham, Dana

n.d.   Who Represents the Sudanese? Unpublished ms., San Diego.

Feyissa, Dereje

2003   Ethnic Groups and Conflict: The Case of Anywass-Nuer Relations. PhD dissertation, Max Planck Institute for Social Anthropology, Martin Luther University, Halle-Wittenberg, Germany.

Finck, John

1986   Secondary Migration to California's Central Valley. In *The Hmong in Transition,* ed. Glenn L. Hendricks, Bruce T. Downing, and Amos S. Deinard, 184–86. Staten Island, N.Y.: Center for Migration Studies.

Findley, Sally E.

1992   Circulation as a Drought-Coping Strategy in Rural Mali. In *Migration, Population Structure, and Redistribution Strategies,* ed. Calvin Goldscheider, 61–89. Boulder: Westview.

Finnegan, William

1999   The Invisible War. *New Yorker,* January 25, 50–73.

Foner, Nancy

2003   Anthropology and the Study of Immigration. In *Immigration Research for a New Century,* ed. Nancy Foner, Rubén Rumbaut, and Steven J. Gold, 49–53. New York: Russell Sage Foundation.

Forbes, Susan S.

1985   Residency Patterns and Secondary Migration of Refugees: A State of the Information Paper. Washington, D.C.: Refugee Policy Group.

Fritz, Mark

2000   *Lost on Earth: Nomads of the New World.* New York: Routledge.

Garang, John

1992   *John Garang Speaks.* Edited by Mansur Khalid. London: Kegan Paul International.

Garner, Steve

2004   *Racism in the Irish Experience.* London: Pluto Press.

Gennep, Arnold van

1960   *The Rites of Passage.* Chicago: University of Chicago Press.

Gilroy, Paul

2000   Hitler Wore Khakis: "Race," Propaganda and Aesthetic Politics. Lecture. April 17, Macalester College, St. Paul, Minn.

Gluckman, Max

1956   *Custom and Conflict in Africa.* New York: Barnes and Noble.

Goody, Jack

1995   *The Expansive Moment: The Rise of Social Anthropology in Britain and Africa,
1918–1970.* New York: Cambridge University Press.

Gough, Kathleen

1971   Nuer Kinship: A Re-examination. In *The Translation of Culture: Essays to E.
E. Evans-Pritchard,* ed. T. O. Beidelman, 79–122. London: Tavistock.

Gould, Stephen Jay

1998   The Internal Brand of the Scarlet W. *Natural History* 107 (2): 22–25, 70–78.

Gozdziak, Elzbieta, and John J. Tuskan Jr.

2000   Operation Provide Refuge: The Challenge of Integrating Behavioral Science
and Indigenous Approaches to Human Suffering. In *Rethinking Refuge and
Displacement,* ed. Elzbieta Gozdziak and Dianna J. Shandy, 194–222. Selected
Papers on Refugees and Immigrants, vol. 8. Arlington, Va.: American Anthropological Association.

Gray-Fisher, Dena M.

1994   *Infogram on the Democratic Republic of the Sudan.* Des Moines: Iowa Department of Human Services, Bureau of Refugee Services.

Greenhouse, Carol J.

2002   Altered States, Altered Lives. Introduction to *Ethnography in Unstable Places:
Everyday Lives in Contexts of Dramatic Political Change,* ed. Carol J. Green-
house, Elizabeth Mertz, and Kay B. Warren, 1–36. Durham: Duke University
Press.

Griffin, Gil

1997a   English Patience, Refugee Children Use a New Language to Tell Stories of
Their Old Home. *San Diego Union Tribune,* April 27, D1.

1997b   Southern Sudanese Fled from War to New Hope amid Difficult Times. *San
Diego Union Tribune,* April 27, D1.

Griswold, Daniel

2000   The Blessings and Challenges of Globalization. *World and I* 15 (9). <http://
web3.infotrac.galegroup.com/itw/infomark>.

Gruel, Peter J.

1971   The Leopard-Skin Chief: An Examination of Political Power among the Nuer.
American Anthropologist 73: 1115–20.

Gupta, Akhil, and James Ferguson, eds.

1997   *Anthropological Locations: Boundaries and Grounds of a Field Science.*
Berkeley: University of California Press.

Haines, David W.

1996   Patterns in Resettlement and Adaptation. In *Refugees in America in the 1990s,*
ed. David W. Haines, 28–62. Westport, Conn.: Greenwood.

Harris, Marvin

1985   *The Sacred Cow and the Abominable Pig: Riddles of Food and Culture.* New
York: Simon and Schuster.

Hathaway, James C.

1997   Is Refugee Status Really Elitist? An Answer to the Ethical Challenge. In *Europe and Refugees: A Challenge?* ed. J. Y. Carlier and D. Vanheule, 79–88. The Hague: Kluwer Law International.

Hayley, Audrey

1968   Symbolic Equations: The Ox and the Cucumber. *Man*, n.s., 3: 262–71.

Heldenbrand, Kathleen

1996   Unwitting Pioneers: Sudanese Refugees in the Midwest. In *Selected Papers on Refugee Issues IV*, ed. A. Rynearson, and J. Phillips, 106–26. Washington, D.C.: American Anthropological Association.

Helton, Arthur C.

2002   *The Price of Indifference: Refugees and Humanitarian Action in the New Century.* Oxford: Oxford University Press.

Heywood, Annemarie

1994   The Cassinga Massacre. In *UNICEF Report on Mission to SWAPO Centers,* April 10–14, 1978.

Hill, Richard L.

1970   *On the Frontiers of Islam: The Sudan under Turco-Egyptian Rule, 1822–1945.* Oxford: Oxford University Press.

Hoagland, Edward

1978   *African Calliope: A Journey to the Sudan.* New York: Random House.

Holman, Philip A.

1996   Refugee Resettlement in the United States. In *Refugees in America in the 1990s*, ed. David W. Haines, 1–27. Westport, Conn.: Greenwood.

Holt, P. M., and M. W. Daly

1988   *A History of the Sudan, from the Coming of Islam to the Present Day.* 4th ed. New York: Longman.

Holtzman, Jon D.

1999   My Commute to Nuerland: Fieldwork among Diasporic Sudanese in Minnesota. Paper presented at the American Anthropological Association, Chicago.

2000   *Nuer Journeys, Nuer Lives: Sudanese Refugees in Minnesota.* Boston: Allyn and Bacon.

2003   Dialing 911 in Nuer: Gender Transformations and Domestic Violence in a Midwestern Sudanese Refugee Community. In *Immigration Research for a New Century*, ed. Nancy Foner, Rubén Rumbaut, and Steven J. Gold, 390–408. New York: Russell Sage Foundation.

Hopkins, MaryCarol

1998   Whose Lives, Whose Work? Struggling along the Subject-Colleague Continuum. In *Power, Ethics, and Human Rights: Anthropological Studies of Refugee Research and Action*, ed. Ruth M. Krulfeld and Jeffery L. MacDonald, 57–72. Lanham, Md.: Rowman and Littlefield.

Hopkins, MaryCarol, and Nancy Wellmeier, eds.

2001 *Negotiating Transnationalism.* Selected Papers on Refugees and Immigrants, vol. 9. Arlington, Va.: American Anthropological Association.

Howell, Paul

1954 *A Manual of Nuer Law.* London: Oxford University Press.

Hugo, Graeme

2006 Sending Money Home to Asia. *ID21 Insights* (Institute of Development Studies, University of Sussex), no. 60 (January): 7.

Human Rights Watch/Africa

1994 *Abuses by All Parties in the War in Southern Sudan.* New York: Human Rights Watch.

1996 *Behind the Red Line: Political Repression in Sudan.* New York: Human Rights Watch.

Hume, Susan

2002 Contemporary African Migration to the United States: Are We Paying Attention? Paper presented at the Association of American Geographers, Los Angeles.

Hutchinson, Sharon

1990 Rising Divorce among the Nuer, 1936–1983. *Man*, n.s., 25: 393–411.

1994 On The Nuer Conquest. *Current Anthropology* 35: 643–51.

1996 *Nuer Dilemmas: Coping with Money, War, and the State.* Berkeley: University of California Press.

1999 "Food Itself Is Fighting With Us": A Comparative Analysis of the Impact of Sudan's Civil War on South Sudanese Civilian Populations Located in the North and the South. Paper presented at the Nordic Africa Institute's conference on Poverty, Violence, and the Politics of Identity in African Arenas, Uppsala, Sweden, October 21–24.

2000 Spiritual Fragments of an Unfinished War. Unpublished ms.

Inda, Jonathan Xavier, and Renato Rosaldo

2002 *The Anthropology of Globalization.* Malden, Mass.: Blackwell Publishing.

Indra, Doreen

1999 Not a "Room of One's Own": Engendering Forced Migration—Knowledge and Practice. In *Engendering Forced Migration: Theory and Practice*, ed. Doreen Indra, 1–22. New York: Berghahn Books.

2000 Not Just Displaced and Poor: How Environmentally Forced Migrants in Rural Bangladesh Recreate Space and Place under Trying Conditions. In *Rethinking Refuge and Displacement*, ed. Elzbieta M. Gozdziak and Dianna J. Shandy, 165–93. Selected Papers on Refugees and Immigrants, vol. 8. Arlington, Va.: American Anthropological Association.

IDS (Institute of Development Studies)

2006 Sending Money Home: Can Remittances Reduce Poverty? *ID21 Insights* (Institute of Development Studies, University of Sussex), no. 60 (January): 1.

Jacobsen, Karen

2005   *The Economic Life of Refugees.* Bloomfield, Conn.: Kumarian Press.

Jal, Gabriel G.

1987   The History of the Jikany Nuer before 1920. Ph.D. dissertation, University of London.

James, Wendy

1990   Introduction to *Kinship and Marriage among the Nuer.* Edited by E. E. Evans-Pritchard, ix–xxii. Oxford: Clarendon Press.

1991   The Sudan Distorted. *African Affairs* 90: 299–304.

Johnson, Douglas H.

1994   *Nuer Prophets: A History of Prophecy from the Upper Nile in the Nineteenth and Twentieth Centuries.* Oxford: Clarendon Press.

1988   The Southern Sudan. *The Minority Rights Group Report,* no. 78. London: Minority Rights Group.

2004   *The Root Causes of Sudan's Civil Wars.* Bloomington: Indiana University Press.

Jok, Jok Madut

2001   *War and Slavery in Sudan.* Philadelphia: University of Pennsylvania Press.

Jok, Jok Madut, and Sharon Hutchinson

1999   Sudan's Prolonged Second Civil War and the Militarization of Nuer and Dinka Ethnic Identities. *African Studies Review* 42 (2): 125–45.

July, Robert

1980   *A History of the African People.* 3rd ed. New York: Scribner's.

Kabera, John B.

1989   Education of Refugees and Their Expectations in Africa: The Case of Returnees with Special Reference to Uganda. *African Studies Review* 32 (1): 31–39.

Kapferer, Bruce

1972   *Strategy and Transaction in an African Factory: African Workers and Indian Management in a Zambian Town.* Manchester: Manchester University Press.

Karadawi, Ahmed

1999   *Refugee Policy in Sudan, 1967–1984.* New York: Berghahn Books.

Keely, Charles B.

1993   Internally Displaced People. In *Hunger 1993: Uprooted People.* Third Annual Report on the State of World Hunger, 38–45. Washington, D.C.: Bread for the World Institute on Hunger and Development.

Keen, David

1992   *Refugees: Rationing the Right to Life—The Crisis in Emergency Relief.* London: Zed Books.

Kelly, Raymond C.

1985   *The Nuer Conquest: The Structure and Development of an Expansionist System.* Ann Arbor: University of Michigan Press.

Koser, Khalid
2003　*New African Diasporas*. London: Routledge.
Kosinski, Leszek A., and R. Mansell Prothero
1974　*People on the Move: Studies on Internal Migration*. London: Methuen.
Koltyk, Jo Ann
1998　*New Pioneers in the Heartland: Hmong Life in Wisconsin*. Boston: Allyn and Bacon.
Krulfeld, Ruth M., and Jeffery L. MacDonald, eds.
1998　*Power, Ethics, and Human Rights: Anthropological Studies of Refugee Research and Action*. Lanham, Md.: Rowman and Littlefield.
Kunz, E. F.
1973　The Refugee in Flight: Kinetic Models and Forms of Displacement. *International Migration Review* 7 (2) (Summer): 125–46.
Lacey, Marc
2004　A River Washes Away Ethiopia's Tensions, for a Moment. *New York Times*, June 15, A14.
Lamphere, Louise, Alex Stepick, and Guillermo Grenier, eds.
1994　*Newcomers in the Workplace: Immigrants and the Restructuring of the U.S. Economy*. Philadelphia: Temple University Press.
Lévi-Strauss, Claude
1962　*Totemism*. Boston: Beacon Press.
Levitt, Peggy, and Mary C. Waters, eds.
2002　*The Changing Face of Home: The Transnational Lives of the Second Generation*. New York: Russell Sage Foundation.
Lewellen, Ted C.
2001　*The Anthropology of Globalization: Cultural Anthropology Enters the 21st Century*. Westport, Conn.: Bergin and Garvey.
Lewis, B. A.
1951　Nuer Spokesmen: A Note on the Institution of Ruic. *Sudan Notes and Records* 32: 77–84.
Lieb, Emily
1996　The Hmong Migration to Fresno: From Laos to California's Central Valley. MA thesis, California State University, Fresno.
Liu, W. T., Mary Ann Lamanna, and Alice K. Murata
1979　*Transition to Nowhere: Vietnamese Refugees in America*. Nashville: Charter House.
Lobban, Richard A., Jr., Robert S. Kramer, and Carolyn Fluehr-Lobban
2002　*Historical Dictionary of the Sudan*. Lanham, Md.: Scarecrow Press.
Loveless, Jeremy
1999　*Displaced Populations in Khartoum: A Study of Social and Economic Conditions*. Report for Save the Children. Denmark: Channel Research.

MacDermot, Brian Hugh

1972   *Cult of the Sacred Spear: The Story of the Nuer Tribe in Ethiopia*. London: R. Hale.

Mahler, Sarah

2006   Gender Matters. *ID21 Insights* (Institute of Development Studies, University of Sussex), no. 60 (January): 8.

Mair, Lucy

1962   *Primitive Government: A Study of Traditional Political Systems in Eastern Africa*. Bloomington: Indiana University Press.

1969   *Anthropology and Social Change*. London School of Economics Monographs on Social Anthropology. London: Athlone Press.

Malkki, Liisa

1992   National Geographic: The Rooting of Peoples and the Territorialization of National Identity among Scholars and Refugees. *Cultural Anthropology* 7 (1): 24–43.

1995   *Purity and Exile: Violence, Memory, and National Cosmology among Hutu Refugees in Tanzania*. Chicago: University of Chicago Press.

1997   News and Culture: Transitory Phenomena and the Fieldwork Tradition. In *Anthropological Locations: Boundaries and Grounds of a Field Science*, ed. Akhil Gupta and James Ferguson, 86–101. Berkeley: University of California Press.

McSpadden, Lucia Ann

1999   Negotiating Masculinity in the Reconstruction of Social Place: Eritrean and Ethiopian Refugees in the United States and Sweden. In *Engendering Forced Migration: Theory and Practice*, ed. Doreen Indra, 242–60. New York: Berghahn Books.

Meredith (Hess), Julia

2000   Tibetan Immigration to the United States: Engagements with Bureaucracy and the Limits of the Nation-State. In *Rethinking Refuge and Displacement*, ed. Elzbieta M. Gozdziak and Dianna J. Shandy, 66–86. Selected Papers on Refugees and Immigrants, vol. 8. Arlington, Va.: American Anthropological Association.

Minear, Larry

2002   *The Humanitarian Enterprise: Dilemmas and Discoveries*. Bloomfield, Conn.: Kumarian Press.

Minnesota Department of Health

1992   *Disease Control Newsletter* 20 (4): 25–32. Minneapolis: Minnesota Department of Health.

Moore, Henrietta L.

1994   *A Passion for Difference: Essays in Anthropology and Gender*. Bloomington: Indiana University Press.

Mortland, Carol A.
1987   Transforming Refugees in Refugee Camps. *Urban Anthropology* 16 (3–4): 375–404.

Mortland, Carol A., and Judy Ledgerwood
1987   Secondary Migration among Southeast Asian Refugees in the United States. *Urban Anthropology* 16 (3–4): 291–326.

Mudimbe, V. Y.
1988   *The Invention of Africa: Gnosis, Philosophy, and the Order of Knowledge.* Bloomington: Indiana University Press.

Natsios, Andrew
2005   Implementing the Comprehensive Peace Agreement in Sudan. *Yale Journal of International Affairs*, Summer/Fall, 89–98.

New York Times
1999   Exiled Former Dictator of Sudan Returns Home. March 23.

Nordstrom, Carolyn
1999   Girls and War Zones: Troubling Questions. In *Engendering Forced Migration: Theory and Practice*, ed. Doreen Indra, 63–82. New York: Berghahn Books.

Omer, Abdusalam
n.d.   A Report on Supporting Systems and Procedures for the Effective Regulation and Monitoring of Somali Remittance Companies (Hawala). Paper prepared for UNDP, Somalia.

Ong, Aihwa
1996   Cultural Citizenship as Subject-Making. *Current Anthropology* 37 (5): 737–51.

2003   *Buddha Is Hiding: Refugees, Citizenship, the New America.* Berkeley: University of California Press.

ORR (Office of Refugee Resettlement)
1995   Report to Congress. Washington, D.C.: United States Department of Health and Human Services.

Owens, Jason
1999   "From here, but German?" The GDR Kids and Namibia's German Speakers. In *Homecoming: The GDR Kids of Namibia*, ed. Constance Kenna, 144–51. Windhoek, Namibia: New Namibia Books.

Peterson, Derek, and Jean Allman
1999   New Directions in the History of Missions in Africa. *Journal of Religious History* 23 (1): 1–7.

Peterson, Paul E., and Mark C. Rom
1990   *Welfare Magnets: A New Case for a National Standard.* Washington, D.C.: Brookings Institution Press.

Petterson, Donald
1999   *Inside Sudan: Political Islam, Conflict, and Catastrophe.* Boulder: Westview.

Piot, Charles
1999   *Remotely Global: Village Modernity in West Africa.* Chicago: University of Chicago Press.
Pirouet, Louise
2001   *Whatever Happened to Asylum in Britain? A Tale of Two Walls.* New York: Berghahn Books.
Pitya, Philip L.
1996   History of Western Christian Evangelism in the Sudan, 1898–1964. Ph.D. dissertation, Boston University.
Portes, Alejandro, and Rubén G. Rumbaut
1996   *Immigrant America: A Portrait.* 2nd ed. Berkeley: University of California Press.
2001   *Legacies: The Story of the Immigrant Second Generation.* New York: Russell Sage Foundation.
Power, David, and Dianna J. Shandy
1998   Sudanese Refugees in a Minnesota Family Practice Clinic. *Family Medicine* 30 (3): 185–89.
Preston, Rosemary
1994   Returning Exiles in Namibia since Independence. In *When Refugees Go Home,* ed. Tim Allen and Hubert Morsink, 260–67. Trenton, N.J.: Africa World Press.
Rex, John, and Robert Moore
1967   *Race, Community, and Conflict.* New York: Oxford University Press.
Rodriguez, Marc S., ed.
2004   *Repositioning North American Migration History: New Directions in Modern Continental Migration, Citizenship, and Community.* Rochester: University of Rochester Press.
Salih, Mohamed
1994   Age, Generation and Migration among the Moro of the Nuba Mountains, Sudan. In *A River of Blessings: Essays in Honor of Paul Baxter,* ed. David Brokensha, 114–28. Syracuse, N.Y.: Maxwell School of Citizenship and Public Affairs.
Sanjek, Roger
1990a   Fire, Loss, and the Sorcerer's Apprentice. In *Fieldnotes: The Makings of Anthropology,* R. Sanjek, 34–46. Ithaca, N.Y.: Cornell University Press.
1990b   Urban Anthropology in the 1980s: A World View. *Annual Review of Anthropology* 19: 151–86.
Saris, Jamie
2004   Foreword to *Differently Irish: A Cultural History Exploring 25 Years of Vietnamese-Irish Identity,* by Mark Maguire. Dublin: Woodfield Press.
Sarkesian, Sam
1973 The Southern Sudan: A Reassessment. *African Studies Review* 16 (1): 1–22.

Schapera, Isaac

1947 *Migrant Labour and Tribal Life: A Study of Conditions in the Bechuanaland Protectorate.* London: Oxford University Press.

1951 Kinship and Marriage among the Tswana. In *African Systems of Kinship and Marriage,* ed. A. R. Radcliffe-Brown and D. Forde, 140–65. London: Oxford University Press.

Schechter, James A.

2004 Governing "Lost Boys": Sudanese Refugees in a UNHCR Camp. Ph.D. thesis, University of Colorado.

Schultheis, Michael J.

1989a A Symposium: Refugees in Africa—The Dynamics of Displacement and Repatriation. *African Studies Review* 1: 1–2.

1989b Refugees in Africa: The Geopolitics of Forced Displacement. *African Studies Review* 1: 3–29.

Scott, James C.

1998 *Seeing Like a State: How Certain Schemes to Improve the Human Condition Have Failed.* New Haven: Yale University Press.

Scroggins, Deborah

2002 *Emma's War.* New York: Pantheon Books.

Scudder, Thayer, and Elisabeth Colson

1980 *Secondary Education and the Formation of an Elite.* New York: Academic Press.

Shandy, Dianna J.

2001 Routes and Destinations: Secondary Migration of Nuer Refugees in the United States. In *Negotiating Transnationalism,* ed. MaryCarol Hopkins and Nancy Wellmeier. Committee on Refugees and Immigrants Selected Papers 8, 9–31. Arlington, Va.: American Anthropological Association.

2002 Nuer Christians in America. *Journal of Refugee Studies* 15 (2) (special issue: Religion and Forced Migration): 213–21.

2003 Transnational Linkages between Refugees in Africa and in the Diaspora. *Forced Migration Review* 16 (3): 7–8.

2005 Updating Images of South Sudan. *American Anthropologist* 107 (4): 689–93.

2006 Global Transactions: Sending Money Home. *Refuge* 22 (3) (special issue: Multiple Homes and Parallel Civil Societies: Refugee Diasporas and Transnationalism), ed. R. Cheran and Wolfram Zunzer.

Shandy, Dianna J., and Katherine Fennelly

2006 A Comparison of the Integration Experiences of Two African Immigrant Populations in a Rural Community. *Social Thought* 25 (1): 23–44.

Simmons, Ann M.

1999 Lost Boys of Sudan Look West. *Los Angeles Times,* February 3, 1.

Simpson, Glenn R.

2004 Easy Money: Expanding in an Age of Terror, Western Union Faces Scrutiny. *Wall Street Journal,* October 20, A1.

Smith, Jennie

2000   If Only We'd Had Picket Fences: The Detainment of Haitian Refugees at the Guantánamo Naval Base, 1991–1993. In *Rethinking Refuge and Displacement,* ed. Elzbieta M. Gozdziak and Dianna J. Shandy, 12–42. Selected Papers on Refugees and Immigrants, vol. 8. Arlington, Va.: American Anthropological Association.

Stein, Barry N.

1981a   The Refugee Experience: Defining the Parameters of a Field of Study. *International Migration Review* 15 (1): 320–30.

1981b   Understanding the Refugee Experience: Foundations of a Better Resettlement System. *Journal of Refugee Resettlement* 1 (4): 62–71.

1986   The Experience of Being a Refugee: Insights from the Research Literature. In *Refugee Mental Health in Resettlement Countries,* ed. C. L. Williams and J. Westermeyer, 5–23. New York: Hemisphere Publishing.

Stock, Robert

1996   *Africa South of the Sahara: A Geographical Interpretation.* New York: Guilford Press.

Stoller, Paul

2002   *Money Has No Smell: The Africanization of New York City.* Chicago: University of Chicago Press.

Terry, Fiona

2002   *Condemned to Repeat? The Paradox of Humanitarian Action.* Ithaca, N.Y.: Cornell University Press.

Trejo, Frank

1998   Sudanese Man Given Asylum: Christian Who Feared Religious, Racial Persecution Can Stay in U.S. *Dallas Morning News,* August 22: electronic mail document. http://www.dallasnews.com.

UNHCR (United Nations High Commission for Refugees)

1998   *Resettlement Handbook.* Geneva: Division of International Protection.

UNMIS (UN Mission in Sudan)

2006   Comprehensive Peace Agreement. http://www.unmis.org/English/cpa.htm.

USCRI (U.S. Committee for Refugees and Immigrants)

2003   *World Refugee Survey.* Washington, D.C.: U.S. Committee for Refugees.

2005   *World Refugee Survey.* Washington, D.C.: U.S. Committee for Refugees.

U.S. Commission on Immigration Reform

1997   *Refugees and Humanitarian Admissions: Appendices.* Washington, D.C.: U.S. Commission on Immigration Reform.

U.S. Department of State, Department of Justice, and Department of Health and Human Services

1998   Report to the Congress: U.S. Refugee Admissions for Fiscal Year 1998. Department of State Publication no. 10559. Washington, D.C.: Bureau of Population, Refugees, and Migration Office of Admissions.

U.S. Department of Health and Human Services, Administration for Children and Families, Office of Refugee Resettlement
1995   Report to Congress, FY 1995.
1998   Unpublished data set.
USIP (U.S. Institute of Peace)
2006   Comprehensive Peace Agreement. http://www.usip.org/library/pa/sudan/cpa01092005/cpa_toc.html.
Van Hear, Nicholas
2003   Refugee Diasporas, Remittances, Development, and Conflict. In *Migration Information Source*, 1. June 1. Washington, D.C.: Migration Policy Institute.
Vincent, Joan
1978   Political Anthropology: Manipulative Strategies. *Annual Review of Anthropology* 7: 175–94.
Welaratna, Usha
1993   *Beyond the Killing Fields: Voices of Nine Cambodian Survivors in America.* Stanford: Stanford University Press.
Woldemikael, Tekle M.
1997   Ethiopians and Eritreans. In *Refugees in America in the 1990s*, ed. David W. Haines, 265–88. Westport, Conn.: Greenwood.
Wong, Madeleine
1995   Emerging Patterns of African Refugee Resettlement in the United States. MA thesis, Florida Atlantic University, Boca Raton.
Ying, Hu
1996   Response to Aihwa Ong. *Current Anthropology* 37 (5): 757–58.
Zolberg, Aristide
1989   The Next Waves: Migration Theory for a Changing World. *International Migration Review* 23: 403–29.
1990   The Refugee Crisis in the Developing World: A Close Look at Africa. In *The Uprooted: Forced Migration as an International Problem in the Post-war Era*, ed. Göran Rystad, 87–133. Lund, Sweden: Lund University Press.
Zolberg, Aristide, Astri Suhrke, and Sergio Aguayo
1989   *Escape from Violence: Conflict and the Refugee Crisis in the Developing World.* New York: Oxford University Press.

Index

Dianna Shandy is assistant professor of anthropology at Macalester College, Saint Paul, Minnesota. She teaches courses on forced migration and humanitarian intervention, anthropology, and African Studies. She is the author (with David W. McCurdy and James P. Spradley) of *The Cultural Experience: Ethnography in Complex Society* (2nd ed., 2005).